Handbook of Urbanization in India

The Oxford India Handbooks are an important new initiative in academic publishing. Each volume offers a comprehensive survey of research in a critical subject area and provides facts, figures, and analyses for a well-grounded perspective. The series intends to provide scholars, students, and policy planners with a well-rounded understanding of wide range of issues in the social sciences.

W0234592

OTHER TITLES IN THE SERIES

HANDBOOK OF WATER RESOURCES IN INDIA
Development, Management, and Strategies
John Briscoe and R. P. S. Malik

HANDBOOK OF AGRICULTURE IN INDIA
Shovan Ray (Editor)

HANDBOOK OF INTERNATIONAL HUMANITARIAN LAW IN SOUTH ASIA
V. S. Mani (Editor)

HANDBOOK OF INDIAN SOCIOLOGY (OIP)
Veena Das (Editor)

MAKING NEWS
Handbook of the Media in Contemporary India (OIP)
Uday Sahay (Editor)

HANDBOOK OF POVERTY IN INDIA
Perspectives, Policies, and Programmes
R. Radhakrishna and Shovan Ray (Editors)

HANDBOOK OF HUMAN RIGHTS AND CRIMINAL JUSTICE IN INDIA
The System and Procedure
South Asia Human Rights Documentation Centre

MANAGING BUSINESS IN THE 21st CENTURY
A Handbook (OIP)
Anindya Sen and P. K. Sett (Editors)

HANDBOOK OF ENERGY AND THE ENVIRONMENT
Bani P. Banerjee

HANDBOOK OF URBANIZATION IN INDIA
K. C. Sivaramakrishnan, Amitabh Kundu, and B. N. Singh

Handbook of Urbanization in India
An Analysis of Trends and Processes

Second Edition

K. C. Sivaramakrishnan
Amitabh Kundu
B. N. Singh

OXFORD
UNIVERSITY PRESS

OXFORD
UNIVERSITY PRESS

Oxford University Press is a department of the University of Oxford.
It furthers the University's objective of excellence in research, scholarship,
and education by publishing worldwide. Oxford is a registered trademark of
Oxford University Press in the UK and in certain other countries

Published in India by
Oxford University Press
22 Workspace, 2nd Floor, 1/22 Asaf Ali Road, New Delhi 110002, India

First published 2005
Second edition, Oxford India Paperback 2007
20th impression 2021
Digitally Printed in 2024

ISBN-13: 978-0-19-569049-1
ISBN-10: 0-19-569049-4

Typeset in Garamaond in 10.5/13.2
by Excellent Laser Typesetters, Pitampura, Delhi 110034
Printed in India by Manipal Technologies Limited,Manipal

Contents

Tables and Maps   vii

Acknowledgements   xi

Abbreviations   xii

Preface to the Second Edition   xiv

I   An Overview of the Study   1

II   Overview of Urbanization:
Issues of Definition and Comparability   5

III   Trends of Urbanization and Migration at Macro Level:
Relationship with Employment Situation   26

IV   Trends and Pattern of Urbanization:
An Interstate Analysis   59

V   Socio-economic Aspects of Urbanization:
A State-level Scenario   84

VI   Socio-economic Aspects of Urbanization:
A District-level Analysis for Four Select States   113

VII   The Policy Perspectives   153

VIII   Migration Update and Current Urban Agenda   160

Statistical Appendices   177

References   184

Index   188

Tables and Maps

2.1   Total Population and Urban Population of India (1991 and 2001)   5

2.2   Number of Statutory Towns and Census Towns (1981, 1991, and 2001)   9

2.3a Number of New Towns, Declassified Towns, and Merged Towns (1971 and 1981)   11

2.3b Number of New Towns, Declassified Towns, and Merged Towns (1991 and 2001)   13

2.4   Number of Towns/Urban Agglomerations, Towns Within and Outside the UAs   15

2.5   Towns Declassified and Adjusted Population (2001)   22

3.1   Number of Towns, Percentage, and Growth Rate of Urban Population in India since 1901   27

3.2   Pattern of Internal Migration in India (1961–91)   29

3.3   Percentage of Migrants in Different NSS Rounds in Rural and Urban India   32

3.4   Disaggregation of Total Incremental Urban Population by Various Components   34

3.5   Class-wise Number of Towns, Percentage, and Growth Rate of Urban Population in India   38

3.6a Growth Rate of Metropolitan Cities   41

3.6b Growth Differentials of Core and Periphery of Metropolitan Cities in India   42

3.6c Growth Tendencies of Mega Cities   43

3.7   Growth of Capital Cities   44

3.8   Annual Exponential Growth Rates for Cities and Towns in Different Size Categories   45

3.9   Percentage of Workers in 15–59 Age Group in Different NSS Rounds by Usual, Weekly, and Daily Status   47

3.10a   Percentage of Unemployed Persons/Person Days to Labour Force/
Labour Days in Rural Areas   48

3.10b   Percentage of Unemployed Persons/Person Days to Labour Force/
Labour Days in Urban Areas   49

3.11   Percentage of Usually Employed Persons (Principal and Subsidiary)
by Type of Employment   50

3.12   Incidence of Subsidiary Employment   51

4.1   Level of Urbanization Across States   60

4.2   Annual Exponential Growth Rate of Urbanization Across States   63

4.3a   Percentage of Population in Different Size Categories to
Total Urban Population (1981 and 1991)   65

4.3b   Percentage of Population in Different Size Categories to
Total Urban Population (2001)   67

4.4a   Annual Exponential Growth Rate of Population in
Common Towns/UAs during 1971–81 and 1981–91   70

4.4b   Annual Exponential Growth Rate of Population in
Common Towns/UAs during 1991–2001   72

4.5a   The Average of Growth Rates (1981–91) of
Towns as per their Size Class Distribution in 1981   74

4.5b   The Average of Growth Rates (1991–2001) of
Towns as per their Size Class Distribution in 1991   76

4.6a   The Coefficients of Variation of Growth Rates (1981–91)
of Towns as per their Size Class Distribution in 1981   78

4.6b   The Coefficients of Variation of Growth Rates (1991–2001)
of Towns as per their Size Class Distribution in 1991   80

5.1   Interdependence among Indicators of Urbanization and
Socio-economic Development at State Level (1981)   87

5.2   Interdependence among Indicators of Urbanization and
Socio-economic Development at State Level (1991)   89

5.3   Interdependence among Indicators of Urbanization and
Socio-economic Development at State Level (2001)   93

5.4a   Frontline Districts of Rice Production and Urbanization   99

5.4b   Frontline Districts of Wheat Production and Urbanization   101

5.4c   Frontline Districts of Groundnut Production and Urbanization   102

5.5   Socio-demographic Characteristics of Slums (2001)   108

5.6   Slum Population in Municipal Corporations of Million-plus Cities   110

5.7   Share of Migration in Urban Growth   111

6.1a   Trends and Pattern of Urbanization Across Districts in Maharashtra (1981)   116

6.1b   Trends and Pattern of Urbanization Across Districts in Maharashtra (1991)   117

6.1c   Trends and Pattern of Urbanization Across Districts in Maharashtra (2001)   119

6.2a   Trends and Pattern of Urbanization Across Districts in Punjab (1981)   122

6.2b   Trends and Pattern of Urbanization Across Districts in Punjab (1991)   122

6.2c   Trends and Pattern of Urbanization Across Districts in Punjab (2001)   123

6.3a   Trends and Pattern of Urbanization Across Districts in Bihar (1981)   127

6.3b   Trends and Pattern of Urbanization Across Districts in Bihar (1991)   128

6.3c   Trends and Pattern of Urbanization Across Districts in
Bihar and Jharkhand (2001)   129

6.4a   Trends and Pattern of Urbanization Across Districts in Rajasthan (1981)   132

6.4b   Trends and Pattern of Urbanization Across Districts in Rajasthan (1991)   133

6.4c   Trends and Pattern of Urbanization Across Districts in Rajasthan (2001)   134

6.5a   Interdependence among Indicators of Urbanization and
Socio-economic Development at District Level in
Maharashtra (1981)   137

6.5b   Interdependence among Indicators of Urbanization and
Socio-economic Development at District Level in
Maharashtra .(1991)   138

6.5c   Interdependence among Indicators of Urbanization and
Socio-economic Development at District Level in
Maharashtra (2001)   139

6.6a   Interdependence among Indicators of Urbanization and
Socio-economic Development at District Level in Punjab (1981)   141

6.6b   Interdependence among Indicators of Urbanization and
Socio-economic Development at District Level in Punjab (1991)   142

6.6c   Interdependence among Indicators of Urbanization and
Socio-economic Development at District Level in Punjab (2001)   143

6.7a   Interdependence among Indicators of Urbanization and
Socio-economic Development at District Level in Bihar (1981)   146

6.7b   Interdependence among Indicators of Urbanization and
Socio-economic Development at District Level in Bihar (1991)   147

6.7c   Interdependence among Indicators of Urbanization and
Socio-economic Development at District Level in Bihar (2001)   148

6.8a   Interdependence among Indicators of Urbanization and
Socio-economic Development at District Level in
Rajasthan (1981)   149

6.8b   Interdependence among Indicators of Urbanization and
        Socio-economic Development at District Level in
        Rajasthan (1991)   150

6.8c   Interdependence among Indicators of Urbanization and
        Socio-economic Development at District Level in
        Rajasthan (2001)   151

7.1   Growth Rates of Selected IDSMT Towns   155

8.1   Volume of Migration Since 1961   160
8.2   Migration Streams 1991–2001   161
8.3   Intrastate Migration Streams for Top 10 States   162
8.4   Migration Break-up for Some States 1991–2001   163
8.5a   Migration Profile of Maharashtra 2001   165
8.5b   Migration Profile of Punjab 2001   166
8.5c   Migration Profile of Delhi 2001   167
8.5d   Migration Profile of Uttar Pradesh 2001   168
8.6   Migration as a Component of Growth in Major Urban Agglomerations
        (1991 and 2001)   169
8.7   Migration as a Component of Growth in Major Urban Agglomerations
        (1991 and 2001)   170
8.8   Reasons for Total Migration into Major Urban Agglomerations
        (1991 and 2001)   172
8.9   Migration flows into six Metropolitan Cities since 1961   173
8.10   Internal Migration in China   173
8.11   List of JNNURM Cities   174

MAPS

4.1   Level of Urbanization—India (2001)   61
6.1   Level of Urbanization—Districts (2001)   114
6.2   Districts above National Average (2001)   115

Acknowledgements

This volume is the outcome of a study conducted by K. C. Sivaramakrishnan, Amitabh Kundu, and B. N. Singh with the assistance of Pratishtha Sengupta, A. Shankar, Sanjay Kumar, and Niranjan Sarangi.

We wish to express our gratitude to the Ford Foundation for its support in undertaking this study. The main objective of the study is to gain a better understanding of India's urbanization. While the 2001 Census and the previous Census reports have provided the principal source of data, these have been supplemented significantly by information available in the economic census, NSS, and other sources.

Amitabh Kundu of Jawaharlal Nehru University, Delhi, undertook the complex task of determining the analytical framework for the report and supervising data collection and analysis. He was assisted by Pratishtha Sengupta ably in this regard. B. N. Singh took on the onerous responsibility of going through the various stages of the report and the different chapters including the revisions as necessary. A. Shankar was valuable in preparing several tables and the maps. Sanjay Kumar and Niranjan Sarangi assisted in the compilation and analysis of the data.

As leader of the study team, K. C. Sivaramakrishnan provided overall guidance for the report and had an active role in its final preparation. Sarala Gopinathan cheerfully accomplished the task of typing the manuscript.

The study team would like to record its grateful thanks to Mark Robinson of the Ford Foundation whose strong interest was responsible for undertaking this study. The many suggestions he made after going through the draft report have considerably enhanced its usefulness.

The team also expresses its appreciation and thanks to J. K. Banthia, Registrar General, R. G. Mitra, Dy. Registrar General, and R. P. Singh, Assistant Registrar General of the Census of India. The team greatly benefited from discussions with these key officials during the various stages of the study. The team also appreciates the cooperation and assistance received from the directors of census operations in various states and in particular, D. Chandramouli of Tamil Nadu for participating in the discussions in this regard.

The study team earnestly hopes this report will enable a better understanding of the complex processes and patterns of urbanization and will be of help to various national and international agencies interested in the subject.

K. C. SIVARAMAKRISHNAN

Abbreviations

CMIE	Centre for Monitoring Indian Economy
CT	Census Town
CV	Coefficient of Variation
DPC	District Planning Committee
FDI	Foreign Direct Investment
FSI	Floor Space Index
HCR	Head Count Ratio
IDSMT	Integrated Development of Small and Medium Towns
JNNURM	Jawaharlal Nehru National Urban Renewal Mission
MPC	Metropolitan Planning Committee
NA	Not Available
NAC	Notified Area Committee
NBO	National Building Organization
NP	Nagar Panchayat
NRI	Non-resident Indian
NSS	National Sample Survey
NSSO	National Sample Survey Organization
P	Panchayats
RU	Rural–Urban
SD	Standard Deviation
SRS	Sample Registration System
TCPO	Town and Country Planning Organization
TN	Tamil Nadu
TAC	Town Area Committee

TP	Town Panchayat
UA	Urban Agglomeration
UN	United Nations
URGD	Urban–Rural Growth Differential
UT	Union Territory
VP	Village Panchayat
WF	Work Force
WPR	Workforce Participation Rates

Preface to the Second Edition

This handbook was first published in 2005 and reprinted in 2006. Since the publication of the first edition, two important developments have taken place that will interest urban professionals and researchers. The first is the release of migration data by the Census of India. For a country of India's size and diversity, migration is a matter of demographic as well as socioeconomic interest. The second major development is the launch of the Jawaharlal Nehru National Urban Renewal Mission (JNNURM) by the Government of India in 2006. While it is certainly too early to pronounce any judgement about the outcome of JNNURM, there is no denying the fact that it has aroused considerable interest about urban issues across the country.

Contrary to popular belief that migration is mostly from rural to urban, the census data of 1991–2001 reveals that rural to rural migration is twice as high as rural to urban migration. Again, the rural–urban migration is within the state and not between states and this was as high as 80 per cent during the period covered by the census. This confirms the view that bulk of the migratory movements are not over long distances. For example, total immigration from outside was less than a quarter of the total migratory movement in the state of Maharashtra.

In India, the volume of migration is much less than that of China. Globalization of the economy, increasing investments in various economic sectors, and significant increase in manufacturing activity will certainly stimulate urban migration. This should be viewed as a positive means of finding employment to a labour force that was restricted by the declining opportunities in agricultural employment. However, the resultant growth in urban population and the rapid expansion and densification of urban settlements would pose significant challenges to urban management, some of which are already visible.

In recognition of these challenges and as a response to the increasing demand for improving urban infrastructure, the Central government has launched the JNNURM—the largest initiative to assist the development of urban infrastructure and enhance the capacity of urban local bodies to shoulder responsibilities entrusted to them by the 74th Constitution Amendment. Of the 63 towns and cities covered under the programme, 7 are mega cities and 35 are million plus cities. All state capitals and important urban centres have been covered that include towns of tourist attraction and religious importance.

The JNNURM has been running for little over one year. Some major problems do persist. The division of the Mission into two Sub-missions—one for urban infrastructure and the other for basic services for urban poor is by itself a challenge to be overcome in formulating city development strategies with thrust on economic growth and efficiency on the one hand and on the other providing sensitive responses to the issues of equity and needs of the urban poor. Eventually the success of the programme will be measured by the extent to which city governments are able to take charge of their own destinies.

A new chapter, VIII has been added to the second edition to enumerate the salient features emerging from the migration data and NUR Mission.

June 2007

K.C. Sivaramakrishnan
Amitabh Kundu
B.N. Singh

I

An Overview of the Study

The scope of the study is to obtain a proper understanding of the extent, patterns, and trends as well as the socio-economic and spatial characteristics of urbanization. The objective is to assess better the nature of the policies and programmes required for urban governance and the development and management of urban areas. The Census 2001 is the principal source of data for the study, supplemented by the Economic Census, National Sample Survey (NSS), and other sources.

The report is organized in seven chapters. While this chapter is introductory, Chapter II looks at definitional issues, the adoption of varying criteria for census towns and statutory towns, the process of declassification of urban places, the creation of statutory towns, and problems of comparability of census data. Chapter III analyses the trends of urbanization and migration and their macro-level relationship with employment. Chapter IV deals with these issues at the state level. Chapter V correlates socio-economic aspects of urbanization at the state level. Chapter VI presents these relationships in further detail at the district level in four states, namely, Punjab, Maharashtra, Bihar, and Rajasthan. Chapter VII contains the conclusions of this report followed by a policy perspective.

The study analyses the trends and pattern of urbanization in India by taking into consideration the regional dimension both at the state and district levels. An attempt has also been made to look into the levels as well as growth of urban population across the states and size class of towns/cities as also districts in case of select states. The period covered is basically from 1971 to 2001, using the population census data to understand the structure of urbanization. However, in building a perspective, a longer time frame has been considered wherever necessary.

The Indian economy, seeking stronger integration with the global system, has shown many interesting features in its structure of urbanization and process of urban growth during the last few decades of the twentieth century. Although the basic structure inherited from the colonial regime has dominated and dictated the processes and growth pattern since independence, planned interventions by the central and state government policies have led to some significant departures from trends witnessed in the past. Interventions have tried to modify or moderate plans. These sought to impose constraints on the pattern of urbanization by market forces and bring about regional balance. Although the success of these policies can at best be described as limited, the country did see a number of growth nuclei and corridors along with the emergence of a number of new towns. Understandably, further opening up of the economy since the early 1990s has had additional impact on the pattern and process of urban growth. As the country aspires for a new development regime in the coming decades, it is important to take stock of the pattern and process of urbanization and its implications for present and future economic growth in the country.

It is relevant to indicate the major issues that Indian urbanization is concerned with. Lopsided urbanization, that is, the concentration of urban population in larger towns and cities, is one of the areas that merits study. However, the level of urbanization varies and for some states like Tamil Nadu, Maharashtra, Gujarat, and Karnataka, it is very significant. Some of the smaller states are half urban or more. The 2001 Census has witnessed further changes in the growth pattern and level of urbanization across the states. The definition of urban centres itself has become an important issue in determining the level and growth of urbanization in several states and eventually the country as a whole. Urban growth in Tamil Nadu, Andhra Pradesh, Gujarat, and Kerala, for example, has been examined in some detail and taken up in the present study to elucidate this issue.

Despite the dominance of the large towns in class I state capitals and million-plus cities, the growth pattern of the smaller towns also reflects some interesting features. How far the tempo of urban growth has shifted from the smaller towns has also been analysed in this study. Various socio-demographic characteristics of urban structure, like level of urbanization, sex ratio, literacy, migration, have been examined to explain the rationale of this process. An assessment of the impact of urban growth on employment, income, poverty, and urban environment will help comprehend the complimentarity among these factors.

The last decade is all the more significant from the point of urbanization as the 74th Constitutional Amendment, 1992, poised to empower the urban local bodies of the country was adopted. This amendment places the responsibility for managing cities and towns principally on institutions of local self-government. However, a proper understanding of the scope, pattern, socio-economic, and spatial characteristics of urbanization are an essential prerequisite for urban governance as well as other programmes for the development and management of urban areas.

DYNAMICS OF URBANIZATION

An understanding of past urban censuses is essential to examine the features of urbanization since 1951. It is believed that the 1951 Census, the first in independent India, were overestimated urban population mainly because uniform criteria were not applied in identifying urban centres. In an effort to bring cross-sectional comparability in the data, the Census of 1961 adopted a two-fold criteria to identify urban centres. This led to identification of two types of urban centres, viz., *statutory towns* as notified by the state governments and *census towns* identified by the census of India, using demographic criteria. Although the definition regarding the urban centres has not changed formally since then, the laxity in its implementation by the states seems to have resulted in serious anomalies and erroneous conclusions with regard to spatio-temporal pattern.

The study thus begins with a critical overview of the definitional issues. It has been observed that the data generated by the Registrar General of India, with support from state directorates of census operations, have serious definitional problems. These problems must be analysed and understood, before the data can be used for building an explanatory framework or a policy perspective. The in-depth analysis of the secondary data for select states confirms the apprehension. Indeed, there are problems of temporal comparability of the trends and pattern of urbanization, particularly in the states of Andhra Pradesh, Gujarat, and Tamil Nadu. Further, in case of Tamil Nadu, too, the urban figures in 1991 could be underestimates, due to non-identification of a number of statutory towns.

URBANIZATION: COMBINATION OF CAUSE AND EFFECT

In presenting the current situation, the study covers many aspects such as large urban agglomerations (UAs), the areas of concentration, scope for the other smaller towns to contribute significantly instead of just being mere numbers, and their overall impact on regional development. The growth tendencies of million-plus cities, capital cities, and district headquarters have been considered apart from the class-wise variation over two decadal time spans (1981–2001). An evaluation of the degree and direction of the association among variables like level of urbanization, per capita income, poverty, slum population, migration, non-agricultural enterprises, and other developmental indicators has been carried out. Determining, whether economic development influences urbanization or vice versa, and if so, at what level, is essential in both understanding and accepting the very nature of urbanization in the country. A probe into the interdependencies between urbanization and available amenities/infrastructural facilities reveals the crucial role of the cities in providing essential services. The problems emerging out of unplanned urban growth, for example, growth of slums and environmental degradation are also examined.

URBANIZATION: ROLE OF GOVERNANCE

While acknowledging these challenges it is the issue of governance that needs to be highlighted. Urban management has, for long, been considered within the confines and context of individual municipalities or cities. The phenomenon of agglomerations in urbanization is one of the most pronounced realities of the present. Urban management instead of being only city based has to be agglomeration based as well. However, the UAs have remained as census rather than administrative entities.

COVERAGE OF THE STUDY

An effort has been made to present and analyse these major issues in the backdrop of the overall scenario of urbanization in the country. The study covers 17 major states of the country for a macro-level observation. To bring out the micro-level perspectives, district-level analysis has been taken up in two developed states, Maharashtra and Punjab, and in two relatively backward states, Rajasthan and Bihar. The study has taken three time frames (1981, 1991, and 2001), that is, two inter-censal periods with the cross-classification of districts, states, and India as a whole. It has taken the data support primarily from the population census, economic census, NSS, and the Centre for Monitoring Indian Economy (CMIE). Besides, publications and reports of the Planning Commission and United Nations (UN) have also been used for the database. Other than percentage share analysis, methods such as standard deviation, co-efficient of variation, and correlation have also been used while examining the statistical validity of observations. While examining the recently published census data of 2001, the adjusted growth rates of the towns/cities/UAs during 1991–2001 have been calculated to make the data comparable with those of 1981–91. It has, in particular, examined the growth rates and level of urbanization of 2001 in case of Andhra Pradesh, Tamil Nadu, and Gujarat. These three states,

as per the recent census, have shown some extraordinary exclusions or inclusions in terms of the number of urban centres. The data from the previous census (1991) for these states have been examined and recalculated keeping in consideration the demographic criteria of declaring a place urban. In the same manner, the large number of urban centres in Kerala in 1991 have been verified in term of their eligibility criterion to be declared as urban.

II

Overview of Urbanization
Issues of Definition and Comparability

INTRODUCTION

No account of Indian urbanization can avoid the oft-repeated statement that only about a third of the country's population is urban. The census of 2001 confirms this simple arithmetical figure of 27.78 per cent as the proportion of India's urban population. It was 25.72 per cent in 1991, 23.73 per cent in 1981, and 20.22 per cent in 1971. Yet this single figure alone cannot and does not convey the urban picture. The urban population in several of the states, big and small like Tamil Nadu (43.86), Maharashtra (42.40), Gujarat (37.35), Karnataka, and Punjab (33.9) is well above the national average. Smaller states like Goa (49.77), Pondicherry (66.57), and the city states or territories such as Delhi (93.00) and Chandigarh (89.78) are predominantly urban (Table 2.1).

TABLE 2.1
Total Population and Urban Population of India (1991 and 2001)

States/UTs*	1991			2001		
	Total population	Urban population	% Urban population	Total population	Urban population	% Urban population
Jammu & Kashmir	7,718,700	1,839,400	23.83	10,069,917	2,505,309	24.88
Himachal Pradesh	5,111,079	444,824	08.70	6,077,248	594,881	09.79
Punjab	20,190,795	6,000,882	29.72	24,289,296	8,245,566	33.95
Chandigarh*	640,725	574,646	89.69	900,914	808,796	89.78
Uttaranchal	–	–	–	8,479,562	2,170,245	25.59
Haryana	16,317,715	4,045,170	24.79	21,082,989	6,114,139	29.00
Delhi	9,370,475	8,427,083	89.93	13,782,976	12,819,761	93.01
Rajasthan	43,880,640	10,040,118	22.88	56,473,122	13,205,444	23.38
Uttar Pradesh	139,031,130	27,653,410	19.89	166,052,859	34,512,629	20.78
Bihar	64,530,554	6,711,785	10.40	82,878,796	8,679,200	10.47
Sikkim	405,505	36,984	09.12	540,493	60,005	11.10

(contd.)

TABLE 2.1 contd.

States/UTs*	1991			2001		
	Total population	Urban population	% Urban population	Total population	Urban population	% Urban population
Arunachal Pradesh	858,392	104,806	12.21	1,091,117	222,688	20.41
Nagaland	1,215,573	210,095	17.28	1,988,636	352,821	17.74
Manipur	1,826,714	505,848	27.69	2,388,634	570,410	23.88
Mizoram	686,217	317,040	46.20	891,058	441,040	49.50
Tripura	2,744,827	418,983	15.26	3,191,168	543,094	17.02
Meghalaya	1,760,626	329,079	18.69	2,306,069	452,612	19.63
Assam	22,294,562	2,470,888	11.08	26,638,407	3,389,413	12.72
West Bengal	67,982,732	18,622,014	27.39	80,221,171	22,486,481	28.03
Jharkhand	21,843,911	4,641,227	21.25	26,909,428	5,986,697	22.25
Orissa	31,512,070	4,232,455	13.43	36,706,920	5,496,318	14.97
Chhattisgarh	17,569,620	3,073,903	17.50	20,795,956	4,175,329	20.08
Madhya Pradesh	48,566,242	12,274,144	25.27	60,385,118	16,102,590	26.67
Gujarat	41,174,343	14,164,301	34.40	50,596,992	18,899,377	37.35
Daman & Diu*	101,439	47,538	46.86	158,059	57,319	36.26
Dadra Nagar Haveli*	138,401	11,270	08.47	220,451	50,456	22.89
Maharashtra	78,748,215	30,496,352	38.73	96,752,247	41,019,734	42.40
Andhra Pradesh	66,354,559	17,812,693	26.84	75,727,541	20,503,597	27.08
Karnataka	44,806,468	13,850,702	30.91	52,733,958	17,919,858	33.98
Goa	1,168,622	479,421	41.02	1,343,998	668,869	49.77
Lakshadweep*	51,681	29,089	56.29	60,595	26,948	44.47
Kerala	29,032,828	7,676,371	26.44	31,838,619	8,267,135	25.97
Tamil Nadu	55,638,318	19,027,033	34.20	62,110,839	27,241,553	43.86
Pondicherry	807,045	516,934	64.05	973,829	648,233	66.57
Andaman and Nicobar Islands*	279,111	74,810	26.80	356,265	116,407	32.67

Sources: Census of India 1991 and 2001, Paper–2, Rural–Urban Distribution.

Absolute numbers is another way to understand India's urban present. Even at less than 28 per cent, the total urban population of 285 million is more than the total population of several countries. It is also a little over 10 per cent of the total urban population in the world. There are 5161 urban centres in the country, a thousand more than the number in 1981. Of the total urban population, 68.67 per cent or about 196 million live in class I towns, each with a population of one lakh or more. There are thirty-five cities or agglomerations each with a population of ten lakh or more. These million-plus cities with a total population of 108 million account for 38 per cent of the country's urban population. Contiguous groups of cities, towns, and urban centres is another major phenomenon. There are 382 of them in the country comprising 1162 urban centres. Some basic facts of India's urbanization are indicated below:

from the census as the basis for data collection and compilation. We may begin with an overview of the definitional issues relating to urban data, provided by the population census in the post-independence period, before attempting a temporal and cross-sectional analysis in the subsequent chapters.

Some Basic Facts of India's Urbanization: 2001	
Total urban population	• *285 million*
	• *Percentage to total population of India (27.78)*
	• *Percentage to world's urban population (10.02)*
	• *Percentage to Asia's urban population (21.10)*
	• *Larger than the total population of small countries like France, Germany*
	• *Larger than the total population of big countries like Brazil, USA*
	• *Larger than the total population of parts of continents like Eastern Africa, Western Asia, Western Europe*
	• *Larger than the total population of the whole continent of Australia*
Total population of 35 million-plus cities	• *107.88 million*
	• *Percentage to total urban population (37.8)*
	• *These 35 cities belong to the large group of 206 million-plus cities of Asia*
Total population of 393 Class I cities including million-plus cities	• 195.95 million
	• Percentage to total urban population (68.67)

By all reckoning, Indian urbanization, in numbers, shape, and sizes is formidable. Yet an analysis and understanding of the pace and levels of urban growth are beset with significant problems of definitions and their application by the census as well as other authorities over the past decades.

Questions about the reliability and comparability of urban data, available from the population census, have been raised time and again. The census is the only means of classifying settlements into rural and urban categories and providing population figures at the settlement level. Other sources that give information on various demographic and socio-economic characteristics use urban–rural frame

DEFINITIONAL PROBLEMS IN THE CENSUS DATA

The Census of 1951, the first census in independent India, is believed to have overestimated urban population due to non-application of uniform criteria by the states in identifying urban centres. It reported a high growth rate (annual exponential) of 3.47 per cent per annum during 1941–51 which was attributed, at least partly, to definitional anomalies, besides massive inmigration in the wake of the partition of the country. An attempt was made in the Population Census of 1961 to standardize the concept of urban centre, and make the data cross-sectionally comparable. Happily, the definition has by and large remained unchanged since then, although there have been variations in its application across states and over time.

The Census of 1961 adopted a two-fold categorization to identify urban centres. Firstly, the settlements that were given urban civic status like corporation, municipality, and cantonment, by the state governments were identified as statutory towns. As urban development is a state subject (and so is the responsibility of assigning the civic status), there is a wide variation in the criteria adopted in assigning civic status across the states. Whichever settlements were assigned such a status by the state governments were included in the urban frame by the census and listed as statutory towns. Keeping these in view, and to make the data on urbanization spatially comparable, the census added a category of non-statutory or census towns. Secondly, three demographic criteria were applied to identify these census towns. These were (a) population size of 5000 or more, (b) density of at least 400 persons per square kilometre, and (c) at least 75 per cent of the male workers to be engaged outside agriculture.

The adoption of such a two-fold categorization of 'statutory' and 'census' towns was expected to rationalize the base of the urban frame. Nonetheless, it created problems of temporal comparability since the rather stringent requirements for identifying the census towns resulted in declassification of a large number of towns identified in 1951, based on a less rigorous definition. The urban growth rate of 2.3 per cent during 1951–61 is therefore considered to be on a lower side, largely due to this definitional problem. Spatial comparability also became different. Most of the 1961 census publications mention only corporation, cantonment, notified area committee, and town committee. The publications relating to the

1971 Census further exclude town committee from the above list (see Premi, Gupta, and Kundu 1977).

GROWTH IN NUMBER OF TOWNS/UAS

The total number of towns (counting all the units comprising UAs individually) in the country has gone up by by 660 in 1991 and by 472 in 2001 (Table 2.2). The corresponding increase in the number of UAs, as well, shows a similar trend, the number increasing by 105 in 1991 and by 1 in 2001. Furthermore, the number of towns within the UAs has gone down from 1302 in 1991 to 1162 in 2001 (Table 2.4). It is evident that the number of new urban centres has declined in 1991 from that of 1981 but has gone up considerably in 2001 (Tables 2.3a and 2.3b).

STATUTORY TOWNS

The number of statutory towns has increased from 2758 in 1981 to 2996 in 1991 and further to 3798 in 2001 (Table 2.2). The figure had gone up by 238 only in 1991 while the increase in 2001 is more than three times that, viz., 802. However, the increase in the total number of towns is only 472 in 2001 over the 1991 figure. This is to be explained by declassification and merger of towns in the inter-censal period.

CENSUS TOWNS

Understandably, the number of census towns that had gone up from 1271 in 1981 to 1693 in 1991 declined to 1363 in 2001. Importantly, this is not the first time in the post-independence censuses that the number of towns has remained constant or gone down. With the application of stringent definition of urban centres adopted in 1961, as noted above, the number of urban centres had declined by

TABLE 2.2

Number of Statutory Towns and Census Towns (1981, 1991, and 2001)

States/UTs	1981			1991			2001		
	Statutory towns	Census towns	Total urban centres	Statutory towns	Census towns	Total urban centres	Statutory towns	Census towns	Total urban centres
Andhra Pradesh	85	167	252	116	148	264	116	94	210
Arunachal Pradesh	–	6	6	–	10	10	–	17	17
Assam	65	15	80	74	19	93	80	45	125
Bihar	151	69	220	127	11	138	125	5	130
Chhattisgarh				65	30	95	75	22	97
Delhi	3	27	30	3	29	32	3	59	62
Goa 9	6	15	13	18	31	14	30	44	
Gujarat	70	185	255	79	185	264	168	74	242
Haryana	77	4	81	84	10	94	84	22	106
Himachal Pradesh	45	2	47	57	1	58	56	1	57
Jammu & Kashmir	57	1	58	72	2	74	72	3	75
Jharkhand				45	88	133	44	108	152
Karnataka	244	37	281	179	127	306	226	44	270
Kerala	48	58	106	66	131	197	60	99	159
Madhya Pradesh	275	52	327	322	48	370	339	55	394
Maharashtra	232	75	307	246	90	336	251	127	378
Manipur	31	1	32	28	3	31	28	5	33
Meghalaya	5	7	12	7	5	12	10	6	16
Mizoram	6	–	6	22	–	22	22	–	22
Nagaland	4	3	7	8	1	9	8	1	9
Orissa	95	13	108	102	22	124	107	31	138
Punjab	132	2	134	112	8	120	139	18	157
Rajasthan	192	9	201	199	23	222	184	38	222

(contd.)

TABLE 2.2: contd.

States/UTs	1981			1991			2001		
	Statutory towns	Census towns	Total urban centres	Statutory towns	Census towns	Total urban centres	Statutory towns	Census towns	Total urban centres
Sikkim	8	–	8	8	–	8	8	1	9
Tamil Nadu	120	314	434	111	358	469	721	111	832
Tripura	10	–	10	12	6	18	13	10	23
Uttar Pradesh	678	26	704	710	43	753	638	66	704
Uttaranchal							74	12	86
West Bengal	105	186	291	116	266	382	123	252	375
Union Territories									
Andaman & Nicobar	1	–	1	1	–	1	1	2	3
Chandigarh	2	2	4	2	3	5	1	–	1
Dadra & Nagar Haveli	–	1	1	–	1	1	–	2	2
Daman & Diu	2	–	2	2	–	2	2	–	2
Lakshadweep	–	3	3	–	4	4	–	3	3
Pondicherry	6	–	6	8	3	11	6	–	6
All India	2758	1271	4029	2996	1693	4689	3798	1363	5161

Notes: (a) The towns including those appearing as constituents of UAs have been considered as separate units.
(b) Estimated no. of urban centres have been considered for Assam and Jammu and Kashmir in 1981 and 1991, respectively.

Source: Census of India 1981, 1991, and 2001, Paper-2, Rural–Urban Distribution.

TABLE 2.3a

Number of New Towns, Declassified Towns, and Merged Towns (1971 and 1981)

States/UTs	1971					1981				
	New towns		Declassified towns		Merged towns	New towns		Declassified towns		Merged towns
	Number	% urban popln	Number	% urban popln	Number	Number	% urban popln	Number	% urban popln	Number
Andhra Pradesh	40	4.83	37	3.59	2	32	2.7	1	0.09	NA
Arunachal Pradesh	4	100	–	–	–	–	–	–	–	–
Assam	20	11.47	–	–	–	NA	NA	NA	NA	–
Bihar		50	11.98	–	–	1	34	5	14	1.3 –
Delhi	–	–	–	–	–	27	9.12	–	–	–
Goa	–	–	–	–	–	4	11.16	–	–	–
Gujarat	49	6.11	11	1.05	3	48	3.9	7	0.41	–
Haryana	4	1.55		–	–	19	9.7	1	0.23	–
Himachal Pradesh	7	7.92	1	0.14	–	11	10.1		–	–
Jammu & Kashmir	7	2.74	5	1.98	–	14	5.94	1	0.14	–
Karnataka	29	4.07	9	1.48	6	47	4.5	11	0.61	–
Kerala	22	22.28	15	5.85	11	50	22	32	10.9	–
Madhya Pradesh	34	3.68	3	0.27	–	81	7.2	1	0.04	–
Maharashtra	28	2.24	–	–	5	33	1.8	13	0.32	–
Manipur	7	29.06	–	–	–	24	33.05	–	–	–
Meghalaya	–	–	–	–	–	6	14.73	–	–	–
Mizoram	–	–	–	–	–	4	23.63	–	–	–
Nagaland	–	–	–	–	–	4	27.81	1	0.16	–
Orissa	21	12.47	2	0.85	–	28	9.1	–	–	–
Punjab	2	0.74	3	0.3	–	29	4.5	–	–	–
Rajasthan	12	2.72	–	–	–	44	7.5	–	–	–

(contd.)

TABLE 2.3a: contd.

States/UTs	1971					1981				
	New towns		Declassified towns		Merged towns	New towns		Declassified towns		Merged towns
	Number	% urban popln	Number	% urban popln	Number	Number	% urban popln	Number	% urban popln	Number
Sikkim	–	–	–	–	–	1	1.86	–	–	–
Tamil Nadu	152	7.07	45	3.18	7	30	1.8	13	0.69	–
Tripura	–	–	–	–	–	4	9.14	–	–	–
Uttar Pradesh	58	3.79	–	–	–	382	.17.7	2	0.03	–
West Bengal	45	4.16	–	–	6	78	5.1	1	0.05	–
Union Territories										
Andaman & Nicobar Islands	–	–	–	–	–	–	–	–	–	–
Chandigarh	–	–	–	–	–	2	3.62	–	–	–
Dadra & Nagar Haveli	–	–	–	–	–	–	–	–	–	–
Daman & Diu	–	–	–	–	–	1	100	–	–	–
Lakshadweep	–	–	–	–	–	3	100	–	–	–
Pondicherry	2	32.43	–	–	1	1	0.56	–	–	–
All India	593	5.25	131	1.05	42	1054	6.81	99	0.61	–

Notes: (a) NA—Not available.

(b) The towns including those appearing as constituent units of UA have been considered as separate units.

Sources: Census of India 1971 and 1981, Paper-2, Rural–Urban Distribution.

TABLE 2.3b

Number of New Towns, Declassified Towns, and Merged Towns (1991 and 2001)

States/UTs	1991 New towns		1991 Declassified towns		1991 Merged towns	2001 New towns		2001 Declassified towns		2001 Merged towns
	Number	% urban popln	Number	% urban popln	Number	Number	% urban popln	Number	% urban popln	Number
Andhra Pradesh	37(32)	5.60	13	0.82	12	35 (35)	2.00	79	7.05	10
Arunachal Pradesh	4(4)	28.54	–	–	–	7 (7)	25.63	–	–	–
Assam	13(4)	3.72	–	–	–	37(31)	7.96	5	–	–
Bihar		57(41)	5.90	2	0.05	4	3(2)	0.36	11	2.37
–										
Chhattisgarh	NA	NA	NA	NA	NA	19(18)	5.24	3	–	14
Delhi	10(10)	1.02	2	0.16	6	35(35)	9.19	2	–	3
Goa	16(16)	25.98	–	–	–	17(16)	20.05	3	–	1
Gujarat	29(28)	2.40	–	–	20	43(23)	3.24	63	1.59	2
Haryana	15(8)	3.80	2	0.62	–	15(14)	3.32	4	0.22	
Himachal Pradesh	11	3.30	–	–	–	2(1)	4.67	1	0.79	1
Jammu & Kashmir	16(1)	NA	NA	NA	NA	1(1)	0.20	–	–	
Jharkhand	NA	NA	NA	NA	NA	33(33)	4.17	14	1.86	
Karnataka	51(45)	3.40	19	1.27	7	45(27)	6.48	39	1.16	42
Kerala	90(78)	27.50	1	0.27	–	18(17)	3.71	41	–	15
Madhya Pradesh	143(45)	7.40	1	0.03	4	39(26)	2.29	9	–	6
Maharashtra	62(48)	3.70	11	0.25	22	79(78)	2.51	23	0.54	14
Manipur	6(2)	7.37	7	4.77	–	4(4)	3.82	2	–	–
Meghalaya	–	–	–	–	–	4(1)	11.86	–	–	–
Mizoram	16	19.56	–	–	–	–	–	–	–	–
Nagaland	2(1)	8.17	–	–	–	–	–	–	–	–
Orissa	17(11)	4.00	1	0.15	–	18(13)	2.82	3	–	1

(contd.)

TABLE 2.3b: contd.

States/UTs	1991 New towns Number	1991 New towns % urban popln	1991 Declassified towns Number	1991 Declassified towns % urban popln	1991 Merged towns Number	2001 New towns Number	2001 New towns % urban popln	2001 Declassified towns Number	2001 Declassified towns % urban popln	2001 Merged towns Number
Punjab	7(6)	0.90	21	2.01	–	41(16)	5.20	3	0.22	1
Rajasthan	26(18)	2.00	2	0.19	3	17(17)	1.02	14	1.40	3
Sikkim	–	–	–	–	–	1(1)	24.44	–	–	–
Tamil Nadu	38(38)	1.90	3	0.06	–	456(59)	21.00	61	1.05	32
Tripura	8(6)	36.87	–	–	–	7(6)	12.08	2	–	–
Uttar Pradesh	62(20)	2.30	5	0.12	8	45(42)	1.36	7	–	4
Uttaranchal	NA	NA	NA	NA	–	9(8)	3.44	5	–	1
West Bengal	111(110)	4.60	3	0.08	17	105(102)	4.75	48	–	64
Union Territories										
Andaman & Nicobar Islands	–	–	–	–	–	2(2)	13.93	–	–	–
Chandigarh	1(1)	1.36	–	–	–	–	–	–	–	4
Dadra & Nagar Haveli	–	–	–	–	–	–	56.61	–	–	–
Daman & Diu	–	–	–	–	–	1(1)	49.83	–	–	–
Lakshadweep	1(1)	19.48	–	–	–	–	–	1	–	–
Pondicherry	5(3)	8.22	–	–	–	–	–	2	–	3
All India	856(579)	4.88	93	0.32	103	1138(636)	5.09	445	–	221

Notes: (a) NA—Not available.
(b) The towns including those appearing as constituent units of UA have been considered as separate units.
(c) Within bracket is shown the number of new census towns.

Sources: Census of India 1991, Paper-2, Rural–Urban Distribution; Census of India 2001.

TABLE 2.4

Number of Towns/Urban Agglomerations, Towns Within and Outside the UAs

States	1981			1991			2001		
	Towns/UAs	Towns within UA	Towns outside UA	Towns/UAs	Towns within UA	Towns outside UA	Towns/UAs	Towns within UA	Towns outside UA
Andhra Pradesh	234(4)	22	230	213(15)	66	198	173(37)	74	136
Arunachal Pradesh	6	–	6	10	–	10	17	–	17
Assam	77(4)	7	73	87(6)	12	81	110(10)	25	100
Bihar	164	179(15)	56	164	211(21)	81	190	120(9)	19
111									
Chhattisgarh	–	–	–	–	–	–	84(12)	25	72
Delhi	6(1)	25	5	7(1)	26	6	4(1)	59	3
Goa	15(2)	2	13	26(3)	8	23	38(3)	9	35
Gujarat	220(30)	65	190	225(46)	85	179	180(39)	91	141
Haryana	77(4)	8	73	90(7)	11	83	97(11)	20	86
Himachal Pradesh	46(1)	2	45	55(2)	5	53	56(1)	2	55
Jammu & Kashmir	56(2)	4	54	72(7)	9	65	69(7)	13	62
Jharkhand	–	–	–	–	–	–	95(11)	68	84
Karnataka	250(7)	38	243	254(22)	74	232	237(24)	57	213
Kerala	85(9)	30	76	109(16)	104	93	98(17)	78	81
Madhya Pradesh	303(49)	73	254	433(60)	92	373	368(42)	68	326
Maharashtra	276(14)	45	262	290(18)	64	272	347(15)	46	332
Manipur	32	–	32	30(1)	2	29	29(1)	5	28
Meghalaya	7(1)	6	6	7(1)	6	6	10(1)	7	9
Mizoram	6	–	6	22	–	22	22	–	22
Nagaland	7	–	7	9	–	9	9	–	9
Orissa	103(8)	13	95	119(9)	14	110	132(10)	16	122
Punjab	134(19)	19	115	120(22)	22	98	157(19)	19	138

(contd.)

TABLE 2.4: contd.

States	1981			1991			2001		
	Towns/UAs	Towns within UA	Towns outside UA	Towns/UAs	Towns within UA	Towns outside UA	Towns/UAs	Towns within UA	Towns outside UA
Rajasthan	195(12)	18	183	215(19)	26	196	216(23)	29	193
Sikkim	8	–	8	8	–	8	9	–	9
Tamil Nadu	245(34)	223	211	260(34)	243	226	668(27)	191	641
Tripura	10	–	10	18	–	18	23	–	23
Uttar Pradesh	659(26)	71	663	702(31)	82	671	670(32)	63	638
Uttaranchal	–	–	–	–	–	–	76(8)	18	68
West Bengal	130(32)	193	98	160(38)	260	122	239(21)	157	218
Union territories									
Andaman & Nicobar Islands	1	–	1	1	–	1	3	–	3
Chandigarh	1(1)	4	–	1(1)	5	–	1	–	1
Dadra & Nagar Haveli	1	–	1	1	–	1	2	–	2
Daman & Diu	2	–	2	2	–	2	2	–	2
Lakshadweep	3	–	3	4	–	4	3	–	3
Pondicherry	4(1)	3	3	7(1)	5	6	4(1)	3	3
All India	3378 (276)	927	3102	3768 (381)	1302	3387	4368 (382)	1162	3986

Notes: (a) NA—Not available.
(b) No. of UA is shown within the bracket where they exist. The total no. of towns/UAs obtained by counting UA as a single unit is shown outside the bracket.
(c) The towns including those appearing as constituent units of UA have been considered as separate units.
(d) No. of towns within and outside UA is shown in separate columns.
(e) Figures for Gujarat and Uttar Pradesh do not include 10 and 3 towns, respectively for 2001.
(f) States shown in italics are the new ones and therefore figures are given only for 2001.

Sources: Census of India 1981 and 1991, Paper–2; Census of India 2001.

225 in 1971. In 2001, however, the number of urban centres has gone up from 1991 basically due to the increase in statutory towns (+802) despite a decline in the number of census towns (–330) in 2001. It would, therefore, be appropriate to ask the question whether the census organization has been more rigorous in applying the demographic criteria in identifying urban centres in 2001. Or alternately, can it be attributed to their not applying the criteria more rigorously. The decline in the number of census towns can generally be attributed to several factors other than stringent application of demographic criteria to the settlements at the threshold of entering the urban segment. It could be due to declassification of old census towns or/and not many large villages acquiring the minimum density or percentage of workforce outside agriculture. This, however, is less likely as the 55th round NSS data show a significant growth of non-agricultural employment in rural areas during the 1990s.

Factors Causing Reduction in the Number of Towns/UAs

The decline in the number of census towns in 2001 could also be due to the directorate of census operations being more rigorous or restrictive in applying the demographic criteria to potential urban centres in various states. This indeed seems to be the case, at least in a few states. There was a feeling that several states are not following the criteria rigorously, as indicated by the emergence of a large number of census towns in 1981 and 1991 with predominantly rural characteristics and with population much below 5000. Discussions were held in the office of the Registrar General as also some of the directorates in the states to debate the issue, and resolve

how the demographic criteria can be applied more rigorously.

There are, however, practical difficulties in applying the criteria rigorously. This is because the information on population, number of workers, and workers outside agriculture, for the census year (necessary for applying the demographic criteria) become available only through the census operation. Urban and rural settlements, however, need to be identified well in advance in order to conduct the census. There is, thus, no option but to identify the census towns on the basis of information available in the office of Registrar General and directorates of census operations much before the census date. Understandably, identification of towns is based on the population and its growth rate, reported in the previous census and a few other factors likely to affect the demographic growth and workforce structure. This implies that discretion exercised by the state directorates or even officials at the district level cannot be totally ruled out, no matter how rigorously we may like to implement the demographic criteria.

A similar explanation may be given for the addition of very few UAs in the Census of 2001. It was a matter of concern that several agglomerations in the 1991 Census did not have a statutory town as a constituent other than the core town. The census office wanted to make the identification of UAs less informal and more stringent in the 2001 Census. A few conditions have, therefore, been included for giving UA status to a group of contiguous cities/towns. These are (a) the core town or at least one of the units in the group must be a statutory town and (b) the total population of all the constituent units, that is, towns and outgrowths of a UA should not be less than 20,000 (as per the 1991

Census). Application of these conditions understandably affected a large number of new UAs.

How important is the impact of these factors in deceleration in urban growth would be anyone's guess. It may nonetheless be pointed out that despite the conscious efforts made to eliminate towns with rural characteristics, there are as many as 636 new census towns identified in 2001. This is larger than the figure of 1991, which was only 579 (Table 2.3b). It is, thus, evident that the main reason for the decline in the number of census towns is not the 'laxity' in identifying new towns, but declassification and merger (of old census towns) with other towns as also their being declared statutory towns. As many as 445 towns have been declassified in 2001 as compared to the figure of 93 only in 1991. Furthermore, as many as 221 towns have been merged with the existing towns as compared to the figure of 103 only in 1991.

DEMOGRAPHIC VS DISCRETIONARY CRITERIA

We examine below the demographic and discretionary criteria with examples of Uttar Pradesh, Kerala, and Tamil Nadu to illustrate the point of adoption of strict criteria by some states as compared to others having adopted a somewhat lenient definition for identification of census towns. This has led to the problem of cross-sectional comparability of the data.

CRITERIA FOR STATUTORY TOWNS

(a) Uttar Pradesh: Uttar Pradesh, for example, reported very few small towns in 1961. This was because the directorate of census operations did not include town area committees (TACs) and notified area committees (NACs)

in the list of statutory towns.[1] Similar problems, due to exclusion of some other 'urban local bodies' at the state level, exist, to greater or lesser extent, in many other states as well.[2] The problem could get only partially rectified in the Census of 1971 wherein fifty-eight of these towns were treated as urban in the state (Table 2.3a). In 1981, however, as many as 382 towns were brought under the urban fold, majority of these having the status of TAC in 1961 and 1971. It may, therefore, be advisable to recompute the urban population in the state of Uttar Pradesh in 1961, 1971 by considering these settlements as towns.

(b) Tamil Nadu: In Tamil Nadu, as many as 399 towns have been added in 2001 to the urban list of the state. This action has been significant in determining the urban growth rate of the state between 1991–2001 and level of urbanization in 1991. Urban growth rate of Tamil Nadu is one of the highest (3.6) among the major states of the country. This growth rate has, in fact, doubled up from 1991. Percentage of urban population among the major states is also highest (43.86). However, the inclusion of a large number of towns by a statutory notification has been entirely a matter of state discretion. Tamil Nadu could have notified these towns in the previous census of 1991 itself, which would have reduced the striking differences of urban growth and level

---

[1] Places having TACs were tested on the three demographic criteria for being declared as urban which resulted in the exclusion of 192 places that have been regarded as urban by the local self-government department of the state.

[2] Rural–Urban Relationship Committee found that in 1961, 'the census classified as many as 4197 places with population varying from 5000 to 20,000 as rural although a number of them had urban local bodies'— Report of the Rural–Urban Relationship Committee, Ministry of Health and Family Planning, Vol. I, Government of India.

of urbanization between 1991 and 2001. It
appears the state government decided on the
inclusion of these towns only because of the
74th Amendment and the state government's
perception that all these settlements should be
regarded as urban.

DEMOGRAPHIC CRITERIA

Kerala: The possibility of the demographic
criteria not being applied uniformly across the
states for identifying the census towns is illus-
trated by Kerala. With its unique settlement
pattern, application of population size and
density would be rather fuzzy in the state as
the settlements exist in a continuum. Declara-
tion of urban centres in such a situation ob-
viously involve exercising discretionary powers
by the state directorate of census. Scholars
have pointed out that this indeed has happened in deciding the number of towns as 73
in 1961. The data provided by the 1991 Census
make this problem conspicuous. The number
of urban centres in the state almost doubled
between 1981 to 1991 with the identification
of 73 additional census towns (Table 2.2). The
high growth rate of urban population during
1981–91 (4.76—the highest among the large
states), as also the relatively low growth rates
during 1997–81 (3.19) and 1991–2001 (0.74) be
seen in the context of non-uniform application
of demographic or discretionary criteria in
different censuses.

There are other problems in applying the
demographic criteria due to lack of clarity
pertaining to the non-agricultural workforce.
While most of the volumes of the 1961 Census
follow the condition of three-fourths of working population to be in non-agriculture, the
provisional population totals suggest this condition being imposed on adult male population only. Another variant of the condition is

'at least three-fourths of male population to
be engaged in non-agricultural activities' (see
Premi 1961).

Another important anomaly in the data is
due to non-uniform application of discretionary powers given to the director of census at
the state level. While the scope of such powers
in 1961 was restricted to places not having
urban local bodies, in the 1971 Census, even
those having these bodies seem to fall under
the discretionary powers (see Premi, Gupta,
and Kundu 1977). It is, however, somewhat
satisfying that the recent census publications
do not reflect this discrepancy.

DEFINITIONAL PROBLEMS AFFECTING
TEMPORAL COMPARABILITY

There are a few states where the definitional
problems seem to have affected the level and
growth rate of urban population during the
1990s more seriously than the others. This
needs an in-depth investigation. In Tamil
Nadu, for example, sixty-one census towns
have got declassified and fifty-nine new census
towns have been added, besides the inclusion
of 399 statutory towns in the urban list of
2001. Andhra Pradesh and Kerala are the two
other states wherein there are apprehensions
of under-enumeration of urban population.
Both report declassification of a large number
of census towns—seventy-nine and thirty-
seven, respectively. In case of Kerala, the 1991
Census had identified as many as seventy-eight
new census towns compared to only seventeen in 2001. In case of Andhra Pradesh, too,
there have been as many as thirty-five new
census towns. In a few other states like Gujarat,
West Bengal, and Karnataka, too, as many as
sixty-three, forty-eight, and thirty-four census
towns, respectively have gone out through
declassification. But they have also gained

through the inclusion of twenty-three, 102, and twenty-seven new census towns in 2001. Maharashtra is yet another state that has lost more than twenty-three census towns but it has gained as many as seventy-eight new census towns. It would, therefore, be difficult to argue that the stringency in the application of demographic criteria has adversely affected the urban growth rates, except in case of Tamil Nadu, Kerala, Gujarat, and Andhra Pradesh.

TAMIL NADU

The case of Tamil Nadu needs a special mention in the context of inclusion of a large number of statutory towns. Until the 1990s, the state government appears to have been rather conservative in granting urban status. The number of statutory towns in fact had come down from 120 in 1981 to 111 in 1991 (Table 2.2). The 2001 Census, however, reports as many as 399 new statutory towns accounting for 80 per cent of such new towns in the country. Prior to the adoption of the 74th Constitution Amendment in 1994, Tamil Nadu had rural town panchayats and urban town panchayats that were not considered as statutory urban bodies. However, after the 73rd and the 74th Constitution Amendments, each state had to decide which settlement would be urban (coming under the purview of Part IX A of the Constitution, that is, nagarpalikas) and which would be rural (or panchayats under Part IX of the Constitution). Tamil Nadu declared 620 town panchayats and fifteen townships to be considered municipal bodies and thus acquired urban status 'statutorily'. However, the net addition to the number of statutory towns in the state works out as 399 only due to merger with other towns and declassification. One can argue that the Tamil Nadu government, to an extent, has tried to compensate for its conservative attitude in earlier years and has awarded the urban civic status quite liberally during the 1990s. This is also reflected in the reduction of the number of census towns in the state from 358 in 1991 to 111 in 2001 (Table 2.2), as many among the erstwhile census towns became statutory towns.

Does this action of the state government make urban data in Tamil Nadu non-comparable with those of the other states? Interestingly, it is possible to argue that the figures pertaining to the levels of urbanization were not previously comparable cross-sectionally due to stringent application of the demographic criteria in Tamil Nadu but these have now become comparable. Nonetheless, the problem is not resolved unless the urban population and growth rates in the state for earlier years are adjusted appropriately.

IDENTIFICATION OF CENSUS TOWNS

In order to find out whether the state directorates were more rigorous in 2001 than before, in identifying the census towns, they were requested to clarify whether they have been extra cautious in identifying urban centres or have used criteria different from previous censuses. The responses indicate that criteria have not changed but in the past, census towns have not been identified very rigorously. The only factor that seems to have made an impact is for determining UAs. The UA is a continuous urban spread consisting of a statutory town and its adjoining urban outgrowths, or two or more physically contiguous towns together, and any adjoining urban outgrowths of such towns. The total population of all the constituents should not be less than 20,000. Indeed, this has resulted in a very small increase in their number as also derecognition of several units as UAs in 2001. But this, per se, is unlikely to affect the number of urban centres or urban population. To probe the issues further, an attempt is made here to see whether the declassified towns of 2001 would satisfy the demographic criteria for being considered census towns, using the data from the Population Census of 1991.

DECLASSIFICATION

Andhra Pradesh: Table 2.5 gives the number of declassified towns of Andhra Pradesh in 2001. It may be noted that as many as forty-six out of seventy-nine declassified towns did not satisfy the workforce criteria. The total population of these forty-six towns adds up to more than 874,000. It may be argued that had the demographic criteria been applied properly, these towns would not have been included in the urban list even in 1991. It would, therefore, be reasonable to deduct this population from the urban population of the state in 1991.

Gujarat: A similar analysis has been done for Gujarat. Table 2.5 presents the population and number of towns that were declassified in 2001. It may be seen that of the sixty-three declassified towns in Gujarat, as many as thirty did not satisfy the workforce criterion for eligibility.

Tamil Nadu: Similarly, in Tamil Nadu thirty-five out of sixty-one declassified towns did not qualify as urban centres by the same criterion in 1991. It would, therefore, be appropriate to exclude these from the list of towns in that year.

It may be noted that Tamil Nadu has another problem of comparability of urban data over time. The state had reported a large number of town and village panchayats as census towns belonging to classes IV–VI categories in 1991. The census did not identify these as

statutory towns, implying that they were included in the urban list because of their fulfilling the demographic criteria. Further analysis of urban settlements belonging to classes IV, V, and VI categories for the year 1991, shows that out of 119 town and village panchayats belonging to the above categories, as many as sixty-eight seem to fulfil the workforce criteria, as more than three-fourth of their main male workforce was in non-agricultural activities whereas the remaining, about half of these centres, did not satisfy the population and density criteria. A large number of town panchayats have been brought into the urban list of 2001 as statutory towns, making application of demographic criteria irrelevant. Further, most of the village panchayats, considered statutory towns in 1991, have also been given town panchayat status, qualifying these as statutory towns. This is evident from the fact that the number of statutory towns has gone up while that of census towns has gone down in 2001, as mentioned before. This is attributable to the fact that Tamil Nadu has simply followed the definition of statutory towns, as stipulated by the Registrar General, in identifying the urban centres in 2001. The problem of temporal comparability, therefore, remains unresolved because these centres should have been considered as statutory towns in 1991 as well.

Kerala: In the context of temporal comparability of urban data, the state of Kerala is often mentioned as having a special problem. It has been argued that as many as ninety centres were identified as new towns in 1991 and these did not satisfy the demographic criteria as applied in 2001. In order to test this hypothesis, we have taken all the new census towns of 1991 and examined their eligibility in terms of the share of male workers outside agriculture. It is observed that of the total of

TABLE 2.5
Towns Declassified and Adjusted Population (2001)

	Andhra Pradesh	Tamil Nadu	Gujarat
No. of towns declassified based on 1991 census	79	61	63
Towns did not fulfil workforce criteria (considering 70% instead of 75%)	46	35	30
Population of these towns showing >30% male workforce	874,765	158,266	307,146
Deducting this population from 1991 urban population			
Actual population of 1991	17,812,693	19,027,033	14,164,301
Adjusted population of 1991	16,937,928	18,868,767	13,857,155
Actual growth rate during 1991–2001	1.4	3.6	2.8
Adjusted growth rate during 1991–2001	1.9	3.67	3.06
Actual level of urbanization, 1991	26.84	34.20	34.40
Adjusted level of urbanization, 1991	25.51	33.91	33.65

Source: Census of India, Paper-2, Rural–Urban Distribution, 1991.

ninety towns only twelve did not have more than 75 per cent of male workforce outside agriculture. Furthermore, these twelve towns have missed the cut-off point by only a small margin. One would, therefore, argue that majority of the census towns brought within the urban fold in the Kerala in 1991 did satisfy the demographic criteria and it would be erroneous to hold that the urban population or urban growth reported by the census of 1991 was overestimated. There is, thus, no need to adjust the growth rate of the state for the 1990s as well.

ADJUSTMENTS IN URBAN POPULATION, LEVEL OF URBANIZATION, AND GROWTH RATES

The following conclusions emerge from the study of specific states with large-scale declassification of census towns and/or increase in the number of statutory towns. The necessary adjustments in the population figures as also the growth rate for the 1990s have also been carried out.

(a) The large declassification of census towns in Andhra Pradesh in 2001 is due to the state not applying the demographic criteria rigorously in 1991. Had the criteria been applied properly, there would have been fewer towns and lower urban population in 1991. Consequently, the towns declassified in 2001, which had reported less than three–fourth of their male workforce outside agriculture, have been excluded from the list of towns in 1991. The revised urban population for the state of Andhra Pradesh thus goes down to 16.93 million from the original figure of 17.81 million as reported in the Census of 1991. Correspondingly, the percentage of urban population gets revised downwards to 25.51 instead of 26.84. The adjusted (annual exponential)

growth rate during 1991–2001 works out to be 1.9 as against the record low figure of 1.37.

(b) The revised population figures in urban centres for Gujarat comes to 13.85 million as against the original estimate of 14.16 million. The percentage of urban population in the state thus works out as 33.65 against that of 34.40, reported in the 1991 census. The growth rate of urban population during 1991–2001 thus gets revised to 3.06 instead of 2.80.

(c) In Tamil Nadu, sixty-one towns have been declassified in 2001 on the basis of 1991 census. Out of these, thirty-five towns could not fulfil the workforce criteria. Had the criteria been applied properly in 1991, these towns would have declassified in 1991 itself. After deducting the population of these thirty-five towns from the 1991 population, the revised figure for the urban population in Tamil Nadu works out as 18.86 million as against 19.02 million, and the level of urbanization is 33.91 per cent instead of 34.20 per cent. Adjusted annual exponential growth rate of urban population for Tamil Nadu would thus be 3.67 as against 3.6 during 1991–2001.

(d) To make data temporally comparable, the new statutory towns have been considered as urban centres in 1991. As per revised calculation, this brought down the growth rate of urban population in the state during 1991–2001 to 1.5 against 3.6 and the level of urbanization goes up to 42.12 per cent instead of 34.20 in 1991.

(e) Although states like West Bengal, Karnataka, and Maharashtra have reported large-scale declassification, they have also had a number of new census towns. The problem due to non-rigorous application of the demographic criteria in 1991 appears to be less serious here. It is, therefore, not necessary to adjust the data on urban population here.

Some Findings

Firstly, we have seen in this chapter that the results of the 2001 Census indicate a more judicious and analytical understanding of census criteria than 1991. The present census has recorded as many as 445 declassified towns which is five times larger than (93 in 1991) the previous census. The three-fold criteria for census towns appear to have been applied more rigorously. The 2001 Census has also identified fifty-seven more new census towns than 1991. Moreover, the number of new towns added in 2001, that is, 1138 (636 census towns and 502 statutory towns), is much larger than the total number (445) of declassified (418) and denotified towns (27) of the census. Even the number of merged towns within the big cities is much larger (103 and 221 in 1991 and 2001, respectively) than the previous census.

Secondly, large city-oriented growth is still evident despite a large number of UAs being declassified in 2001 Census. Recent standards (discussed in the chapter) of UA tend to reduce the number of comparatively smaller UAs than the larger ones. On the other hand, a large number of towns have been merged with the already existing big UAs. In states like Karnataka, out of forty-two merged towns, twenty-seven have been merged with Bangalore UA. In Tamil Nadu, out of thirty-two merged towns, eighteen towns have been clubbed with Salem UA. Though the increase in the total number of UAs is negligible, this does not mean that growth is less centrifugal than before.

Thirdly, stricter application of census criteria does make the assessment of urban growth somewhat complicated. For India as a whole, number of declassifications is considerably less than the additions. However, states like Andhra Pradesh, Gujarat, and Tamil Nadu have recorded a larger number of declassifications than additions. In Maharashtra and West Bengal, the net addition of towns is much larger as compared to number of declassification. Share of population in new towns to the total urban population of these two states is significantly higher than the population share of declassified towns. Another significant observation is that the addition of a huge number of new statutory towns in Tamil Nadu, constituting 5.13 million population out of the total urban growth of 68.17 million of the country during 1991–2001 did have a perceptible effect on the urban growth of India. Urban population of the country without this large number of new statutory towns, in fact, would have registered a growth of 2.55 instead of 2.73 per cent during 1991–2001.

Fourthly, this whole exercise of application of criteria in one census and partial application in earlier ones raises important problems about the comparability of data. The Registrar General and respective state directors of census operations have endeavoured to conduct the 2001 Census in a more authentic manner. Separately, one can argue for a relook at the three-fold demographic criteria of the census. For instance, the stipulation that 75 per cent of the male workforce should be engaged in non-agricultural pursuits may not be sustainable since female workforce participation is equally significant.

Finally, large-scale declassification of census towns has not reduced the overall number of towns in the country. This has gone up by 472 whereas the number of statutory towns has gone up by 802—an observation in the chapter has questioned the validity of declaring a statutory town. Notification of a large number of towns under the category of town panchayats in Tamil Nadu has constituted almost 80 per cent of the number of total new statutory towns of the country. The whole exercise of rigorous application of census criteria gets diluted through such 'discretionary' powers of the state government whereby a number of settlements enter the urban frame in a rather ad hoc manner. Such re-categorization has also been evident in states like Madhya Pradesh and Karnataka. Despite the vastness and variety in India, the chapter brings out the need for some uniformity in economic and demographic criteria to maintain the distinction between a town and a village.

III

Trends of Urbanization and Migration at Macro Level
Relationship with Employment Situation

INTRODUCTION

Economic reforms and liberalization in the 1990s were expected to boost urbanization. The proponents of the reform often argued that linking India with the global economy would lead to massive inflow of capital from outside the country as also rise in indigenous investment. This, in turn, would provide an impetus to the process of urbanization since much of the investment and consequent increase in employment would be either within or around the existing urban centres. Even if industrial units are located in rural areas, in a few years, they would be urbanized.

Critics of globalization, however, pointed out that employment generation in the formal urban economy might not be high due to the capital intensive nature of industrialization. A low rate of industrial and infrastructural investment in public sector—necessary for keeping budgetary deficits low—would, however, slow down agricultural growth. This, coupled with an open trade policy, would destabilize the agrarian economy, causing high unemployment and exodus from rural areas. This would lead to rapid growth in urban population. Thus, the protagonists as also the critics of economic reforms converged on the proposition that urban growth in the post-liberalization phase would be high. The data from the 2001 Census, however, prove them wrong.

The present chapter begins with a review of the trends in urbanization and contrasts the actual growth rates with the various projections. The migration trends, components of urban growth, changing structure of urban hierarchy and differentials in the growth rates of urban centres in different size classes, changes in employment and the effects, if any, of structural reforms and development policies, possible impact of changes in urban management, and projections for the future along with their developmental implications are discussed here.

URBANIZATION TRENDS AT THE MACRO LEVEL

India experienced a very high growth rate of urban population, the highest until then, as per the Census of 1951. The annual compound growth rate was as high as 3.47 per cent per annum (Table 3.1). Scholars have dismissed this high growth rate, attributing it to massive migration from across international borders due to partition of the country as also a rather loose definition of urban centres in the first

TABLE 3.1
Number of Towns, Percentage, and Growth Rate of
Urban Population in India since 1901

Census year	No. of towns/UAs	% of urban population to total population	Annual exponential growth rate of urban population
1901	1827	10.84	–
1911	1815	10.29	0.03
1921	1949	11.18	0.79
1931	2072	11.99	1.75
1941	2250	13.86	2.77
1951	2843	17.29	3.47
1961	2365	17.97	2.34
1971	2590	19.91	3.21
1981	3378	23.34	3.83
1991	3768	25.72	3.09
2001	4368	27.78	2.73

Note: Estimated population has been taken for Assam and Jammu & Kashmir in 1981 and 1991, respectively.

Sources: Census of India 1981 and 1991, Paper-2, Rural–Urban Distribution; Census 2001.

census conducted after independence. The adoption of a rigorous definition of urban place in the 1961 Census, as discussed in the previous chapter, resulted in declassification of as many as 803 towns comprising population of 4.4 million. Understandably, the growth rate came down to 2.34 per cent in 1961. The growth rate picked up a bit, going up to 3.21 per cent during 1961–71 (Table 3.1). The increase was largely owing to increase of population in existing urban centres rather than emergence of new towns.

The growth rate of urban population during the 1970s was 3.83 per cent, which is the highest in the last century. A large part of the increase can be attributed to emergence of new urban centres as the Census of 1981 recorded as many as 1054 new towns. As discussed earlier, the definition of census towns may not have been applied rigorously in a few states, resulting in mushrooming of these so called

'new' towns. This high growth, however, set many of the demographers and urban planners speculating on hyper urbanization, similar to what had happened after the publication of 1951 Census results. Even government committees and international organizations talked of the spectre of over urbanization and predicted massive rural–urban (RU) migration and urban growth. Subsequently, the Census of 1991 recorded a significant decline in urban growth. The growth rate came down to 3.1 per cent, which was much below all official projections. The trend went against not only the popular perception of 'urban explosion' but also the projections made by expert groups set up by various government departments.

The same was the story for the 1990s. A number of government committees, set up during the 1980s and 1990s, besides the India Infrastructure Report and the Ninth Five-Year Plan, had predicted high urban growth.

The Taskforce on Urban Development (Planning Commission 1983) had projected urban population in the country for the year 1991 and 2001 using two alternate variants. The high urban growth rate observed during 1971–81 constituted the basis for the computation, and both the projected figures turned out to be much on the higher side.

The other official agencies in India making projections for urban development in the subsequent years maintained the 'optimism' and in fact went beyond that. The Expert Committee for Population Projections for the Eighth Plan had predicted an annual growth rate to be 4.4 per cent during the 1980s and 4.1 per cent during the 1990s. The Eighth Plan document (Planning Commission 1992) lowered down the estimate of urban population by the turn of the century since the census of 1991 had reported a much lower rate of urbanization in the 1980s than anticipated by the expert committee. The projected growth rate of urban population during the 1990s, however, was maintained at 4.1 per cent. The Approach Paper to the Ninth Plan (Planning Commission 1997) did not mention an exact figure but anticipated 'higher rate of growth of urban population'. The Expert Group on the Commercialization of Infrastructure Projects of India Infrastructure Reports (1996), too, implicitly assumed a rapid pace of urbanization as a consequence of new economic policy.

As more recent data on fertility and mortality became available from the Sample Registration System (SRS) in the 1990s, each projection revised the growth rate downwards in sequence. The 2001 Census records a significant decline in urban growth, the annual rate being 2.73 per cent only (Table 3.1). This will be the lowest growth in the post-independence period, if the rate of the 1950s

is revised upwards to take care of the definitional anomalies, discussed earlier. The Population Census 2001, thus, provides an occasion to have a fresh look at our urban database and re-examine our perspective on urbanization.

MIGRATION TRENDS AND PROJECTIONS

During the colonial period, Indians have been described as a highly immobile population. Low levels of education, traditional value systems and other social factors, lower capacity to deal with the uncertainty linked to migration, and poor transport and communication facilities have often been held responsible for their low rate of migration. Kingsley Davis, in the early 1950s, in his pioneering work *The Population of India and Pakistan* had attributed this immobility to the prevalence of caste system, joint families, practice of early marriage, diversity of language and culture, lack of education, and predominance of agriculture in the economy. He argued that a society, bound by caste and family system and traditional values, often acts as a deterrent to migration.

There are several demographers, however, who would not consider the migration rate as very low, notwithstanding the socio-cultural diversity in the country. This is largely due to a high rate of migration among women. Indeed, females have dominated the migration streams within the country due to the practice of marrying outside the village and the women joining the husband or his family after marriage.[1] Migration even among the men has

---

[1] For every hundred women migrants, the number of male migrants is only 38 in 1991. The corresponding numbers are 28, 45, and 80 for intra-district, inter-district, and interstate migrants, respectively.

been relatively high due to natural calamities such as famines that uprooted thousands from the agrarian system and shifted them to cities, towns, and better-off rural areas, in search of sustenance.

By the Davisian logic, one would argue that improvement in the levels of education, transport and communication facilities, shift of workforce from agriculture to industry and tertiary activities would increase mobility in the post-independence period. Interestingly, however, an analysis of the trend in population mobility in India reveals that, despite

significant improvements in education and communication facilities, diversification of the economy, and modernization of norms and values, population mobility has declined at least since the 1960s.

The pattern of internal migration (excluding the international migrants) during 1961–91—lifetime as well as intercensal—has been presented in Table 3.2 for males and females during the 1960s, 1970s, and 1980s, based on the data from population census. It may be noted that there was a decline in absolute numbers of migration during 1961–71. The

TABLE 3.2
Pattern of Internal Migration in India (1961–91)

	Number of migrants (millions)				Growth rates		
	1961	1971	1981	1991	1961–71	1971–81	1981–91
Total population	439.20	548.20	683.30	846.30	24.80	24.70	23.90
Total migrants							
a. Intercensal	66.00	68.20	81.00	80.90	3.20	18.80	0.00
	(15.00)	(12.40)	(12.20)	(9.70)			
a1. Intercensal interstate	8.70	8.50	10.90	11.10	−2.10	27.40	2.00
	(2.00)	(1.60)	(1.60)	(1.30)			
b. Lifetime	134.60	157.40	195.80	222.60	16.90	24.40	13.70
	(30.60)	(28.70)	(29.40)	(26.50)			
b1. Lifetime interstate	14.50	18.60	24.00	27.30	28.30	28.90	13.70
	(3.30)	(3.40)	(3.60)	(3.30)			
Male population	226.30	284.0	353.30	439.20	25.50	24.40	24.30
Male migrants							
a. Intercensal	25.60	26.80	30.40	26.70	4.70	13.70	−12.30
	(11.30)	(9.40)	(8.90)	(6.10)			
a1. Intercensal interstate	5.10	5.10	5.50	5.20	1.50	7.60	−5.20
	(2.20)	(1.80)	(1.60)	(1.20)			
b. Lifetime	41.50	48.80	57.20	60.00	17.60	17.10	5.00
	(18.30)	(17.20)	(16.60)	(13.80)			
b1. Lifetime interstate	7.80	9.60	11.50	12.20	22.90	19.90	5.80
	(3.40)	(3.40)	(3.30)	(2.80)			
Female population	212.9	264.10	330.00	407.10	24.00	24.90	23.40

(contd.)

TABLE 3.2: contd.

	Number of migrants (millions)				Growth rates		
	1961	1971	1981	1991	1961–71	1971–81	1981–91
Female migrants							
a. Intercensal	40.50 (19.00)	41.40 (15.70)	50.50 (15.70)	54.30 (13.50)	2.30	22.00	7.40
a1. Intercensal interstate	3.70 (1.70)	3.40 (1.30)	5.30 (1.70)	5.90 (1.50)	−7.00	57.40	9.50
b. Lifetime	93.10 (43.70)	108.60 (41.10)	138.60 (43.10)	162.60 (40.30)	16.60	27.70	17.30
b1. Lifetime interstate	6.70 (3.20)	9.00 (3.40)	12.50 (3.90)	15.10 (3.80)	34.50	38.50	20.90
Rural male population	186.10	225.30	268.50	324.40	21.00	19.20	20.80
Rural male migrants							
a. Intercensal	15.40 (8.40)	15.90 (7.10)	16.30 (6.30)	13.40 (4.20)	3.50	2.30	−18.00
a1. Intercensal interstate	1.70 (0.90)	1.80 (0.80)	1.80 (0.70)	1.50 (0.50)	9.10	−3.00	−15.80
b. Lifetime	25.40 (13.90)	29.10 (12.90)	30.00 (11.50)	30.40 (9.40)	14.40	3.10	1.10
b1. Lifetime interstate	2.50 (1.40)	3.00 (1.30)	3.10 (1.20)	3.00 (0.90)	18.90	3.00	−2.30
Urban male population	42.80	58.70	84.90	114.90	37.30	44.50	35.40
Urban male migrants							
a. Intercensal	10.20 (23.80)	10.80 (18.50)	14.10 (16.90)	13.30 (11.70)	6.40	30.50	−5.90
a1. Intercensal interstate	3.40 (7.90)	3.30 (5.60)	3.70 (4.40)	3.70 (3.30)	−2.40	13.20	0.20
b. Lifetime	16.10 (37.50)	19.70 (33.60)	27.10 (32.40)	29.60 (26.00)	22.70	37.70	9.20
b1. Lifetime interstate	5.30 (12.30)	6.60 (11.20)	8.40 (10.00)	9.10 (8.00)	24.80	27.60	8.70

Notes: a. Population figures given in the table (total, male/female and rural/urban) pertain to the whole country and include the estimated figures for Assam and Jammu & Kashmir for 1981 and 1991, the years in which the census could not be conducted in these states.

b. The figures in brackets, however, are percentages to the corresponding total population and not necessarily to those given in the table.

c. Lifetime migrants are those that were enumerated at places other than that of their birth.

d. Intercensal migration figures are based on the concept of place of birth for the year 1961. For 1971, 1981, and 1991 the figures are based on the concept of place of last residence, implying that people residing anywhere other than the place of enumeration are considered migrants.

Sources: D-III table for the year 1961 and D-2 tables of the Population Census 1971, 1981, and 1991.

census publications attributed this to positive measures launched to avoid natural disasters, better distribution system for food and other necessities, and better spread of educational and health facilities. No serious study was conducted to see whether the economic disparities had indeed declined and the distribution of basic amenities had become more balanced during the 1960s. Indeed, this thesis can be seriously questioned when one observes an increase in inequalities in various socio-economic dimensions, partly linked with the first phase of Green Revolution.

The growth rate of migrant population picked up marginally during 1971–81 which is reflected in a slight improvement in the percentage of migrants. But this was due to the growth of women migrants that can be attributed to socio-cultural factors. As far as the males are concerned, the growth rates of migrants were less than that of the population, both in rural as well as urban areas, resulting in continuous decline in percentage figures during 1961–91. Importantly, since a large part of female migration is due to marriage and other social factors, it would make sense to look at the pattern of male migration only in order to focus attention on mobility of labour due to economic reasons.

GROWTH IN LIFETIME MIGRATION

The percentage of lifetime male migrants to the total male population has declined systematically during the entire period covered in the study. The proportions of migrants are noted to be 18.3, 17.2, 16.6, and 13.8 in the years 1961, 1971, 1981, and 1991, respectively. The growth rates of lifetime male migrants have also gone down sharply from 17.6 per cent in the 1960s to 5.0 per cent in the 1980s. Further, the decline is very steep in case of rural areas— from 14.4 per cent to 1.1 per cent only. In

urban areas, the percentage growth rate has gone down from 22.7 to 9.2.

GROWTH IN INTERCENSAL MIGRATION

The growth rates of intercensal migrants were 3.5 and 6.4 per cent in rural and urban areas during the 1960s when the male population increased by 21.0 and 37.3 per cent, respectively. In the 1970s, the decadal growth rate of migration for urban males was 30.5 per cent. This was below the growth rate of urban population in the decade, which was around 44.5 per cent. Importantly, there has been a fall in the growth rate of in-migrants in rural areas during the 1970s. The growth rate of male migrants works out as 2.3 per cent whereas the rural population registered a growth rate of 19.2 per cent. During 1981–91, the population in rural and urban areas grew at the rates of 20.8 and 35.4 per cent, respectively. The corresponding growth rates of migrant population were, however, negative, viz., −18.0 and −5.9 per cent, respectively.

The percentage of male intercensal migrants (rural and urban combined) within the country has thus gone down from 11.3 per cent in 1961 to 9.4 per cent in 1971 and further to 8.9 per cent in 1981. The 1980s witnessed further slowing down of migration as the percentage of male migrants to (male) population was 6.1 in the year 1991. The pattern is somewhat different for females. Female migrants grew at a slower rate than the population during the 1960s. The pattern almost reversed in the 1970s. However, in the 1980s female migration also registered a sharp decline. The percentage of female migrants work out to be 19.0, 15.7, 15.7, and 13.5, respectively for the years 1961, 1971, 1981, and 1991. There is, thus, no doubt that an average Indian has become less mobile and the process is rather sharp in the decade 1981–91. This may be seen clearly in terms of decline in the number and proportion of migrants for shorter durations.[2]

GROWTH IN INTERSTATE MIGRATION

It is interesting to note that the percentage of interstate (intercensal) migrants among males has declined systematically since 1961, both for rural as well as urban areas. The fall is relatively sharp in the 1980s, the percentage figures coming down from 0.7 to 0.5 in rural areas and from 4.4 to 3.3 in urban areas. Importantly, the figures have come down even for females viz., from 1.7 to 1.5, during this period. One would, therefore, infer that present level of movement across the states is much less than what has been observed historically. Other factors remaining constant, one would expect an increase in this figure due to the emergence of several new states during the period. The decline, therefore, is significant and must be interpreted as a process of slowing down of population mobility across the state boundaries. It may be argued that the migrants are increasingly getting absorbed within their own states, possibly due to socio-political factors constraining their mobility.

It may be pointed out that women have historically dominated all types of migration streams. What is more important is that there has been an increasing feminization of all the streams in recent decades. As a result of the decline in the growth rate of male migrants being much more than that of women (and even a decline in their number) in recent years, the female–male ratio has gone up in all the migrants streams.

The decline in the percentage of male migrants is confirmed by the data from the NSS (Table 3.3). The figure has gone down from 7.2 per cent in 1983 to 6.9 per cent in 1999–2000 in rural areas. The two figures are 27.0 and 25.7, respectively for urban males. There seems to be a slight increase in the figures during 1993–9 but that can be attributed to a less rigorous definition of migrants in the 49th round, giving a figure on the higher side for the year 1993–4.[3]

COMPONENTS OF URBAN GROWTH

It is important to look at urban growth by its various components over the years and to examine these in the context of the declining

TABLE 3.3
Percentage of Migrants in Different NSS Rounds in Rural and Urban India

Round (year)	Rural		Urban	
	Male	Female	Male	Female
55 (July 99–June 2000)	6.90	42.60	25.70	41.80
49 (January–June 1993)	6.50	40.10	23.90	38.20
43 (July 87–June 88)	7.40	39.80	26.80	39.60
38 (January–December 1983)	7.20	35.10	27.00	36.60

Source: Various NSS reports.

[2] The data further indicate that the percentage of migrants with less than one year or 1–4 year duration has declined substantially during 1981–91.

[3] All normally resident members of the households, residing at any other place for over six months, have generally been identified as migrants by NSS.

mobility of Indian population, as discussed above. The contribution of RU migration in urbanization can be analysed using a simple identity, decomposing the total increase in urban population into several components. The four components identified here are (i) natural increase, (ii) new independent towns less declassified towns, (iii) new towns merging with old towns/UAs and jurisdictional changes, and (iv) net RU migration. The migration component is shown below:

residual component, which conceptually is the addition to the population of common towns due to extension of municipal limits, merging of old towns or inclusion of new towns in the old UAs, as mentioned already. This has been estimated in this indirect manner since it is very difficult to ascertain the population in the new towns, rural areas and outgrowths that have been made parts of a UA during a decade. The fourth component is the net of rural urban migration during

---

- Total increase = Natural increase + new (net) independent towns + merging and jurisdictional changes + net RU migration

Dividing both sides by the total urban population in the base year we obtain:

- Urban growth rate = Natural growth rate + rate of increase due to new independent towns + rate of increase due to merging and boundary changes + migration rate

---

Table 3.4 disaggregates the total increment to urban population into the four components, discussed here. The first component, natural increase, has been estimated by using SRS data of birth rate and death rate for the urban population. The second component, population in new towns less that of declassified towns, is obtained by subtracting the increase in the population of common towns from the total increase in urban population. Importantly, the new towns that emerge as parts of UAs (existing in the base year) would be included in the common towns. This second component would, thus, give the population of only those new towns that are not part of the UA.[4] The third is the

the decade, as obtained from the population census.

Table 3.4 also gives the percentage shares of the four components for the four decades— from the 1960s to the 1990s—besides the absolute increments. One may note the significant shift in the shares during 1971–81, due to increase in the number of new towns. This has been attributed to non-application of stringent criteria for census towns in 1981, as mentioned already. It would, therefore, be useful to look at the temporal shifts by treating the decade of the 1970s as an outlier.

Understandably, the natural increase which is about 60 per cent (children born to the urban population as also to the intercensal

---

[4] The urban population in the base year (U0) may be shown as the sum total of population of common towns (C0) and of those declassified in the terminal year (D0). Similarly, the urban population in the terminal year can be shown as the total of the population of the common towns (C1) and the new towns (N1).

We thus have $U1-U0 = (C1-C0) + N1 -D0$. This implies that subtraction of the increment in population of common towns from the total increase in urban population would give the net increase in urban population due to addition/deletion of towns in the terminal year.

TABLE 3.4
Disaggregation of Total Incremental Urban Population by Various Components

	Population (million)				Percentage distribution			
	1961–71	1971–81	1981–91	1991–2001	1961–71	1971–81	1981–91	1991–2001
Total increase	30.18	49.90	57.70	67.70	100.00	100.00	100.00	100.00
Natural increase on base year population and on migrants	19.50	25.60	35.40	40.20	64.60	51.30	61.30	59.40
Population of new towns less declassified towns	4.16	7.40	5.40	4.20	13.80	14.80	9.40	6.20
Increase due to expansion in urban area/agglomeration	0.87	7.10	4.40	(a) 4.40 (b) 6.60 (c) 8.80	2.90	14.20	7.60	(a) 6.50 (b) 9.70 (c) 13.00
Net RU migration	5.65	9.80	12.50	(a) 18.60 (b) 16.40 (c) 14.20	18.70	19.60	21.70	(a) 27.40 (b) 24.20 (c) 21.00

Note: Computed based on the methodology discussed in the text.
(a) Higher Estimate (b) Middle Estimate (c) Lower Estimate.

Source: Census of India 1971, Paper-II-A, General Population Tables, 1971; Rural–Urban Distribution 1981, 1991.

migrants, less the number of deaths) constitutes the largest component in the total increase. The share of new towns outside the agglomerations has gone down—from 13.8 per cent to 6.2 per cent during 1961–2001. This suggests that the process of urbanization has got spatially concentrated. This has resulted in an increase in the contribution of the third component viz., expansion in urban boundary and merging of towns to about 13 per cent. More importantly, the share of migration (the fourth component) shows a secular increase over the period of 1961–91[5] from 18.7 to 21.7 per cent.

Detailed data from the 2001 Census are not yet available to permit disaggregation of the total increase in urban population into these components. The natural increase, due to the base of year urban population, is the only component that can be estimated using SRS data on birth and death rates. The natural increase among the intercensal migrants can also be estimated using the trend in the proportion (natural increase among intercensal migrants to total increase) observed during the 1980s and 1990s which has gone up from 0.022 to 0.033. It would be reasonable to take this proportion as 0.04 or natural increase among intercensal migrants to be 2.7 million, which assumes growing importance of migration in urbanization, as observed in the past decades. Combining the two, we obtain the total natural increase as 40.5 million during the 1990s. This works out as 59.4 per cent of the total increase in urban population which is slightly less than what was noted in 1991.

[5] As per the study by the Office of the Registrar General, New Delhi, East West Centre, Honolulu, and Bureau of the Census, Washington (1993), the contribution of RU migration in the incremental urban population has declined significantly from the 1970s to the 1980s.

The increase in population due to net addition of independent towns can be obtained by subtracting the increase in the number of common towns from the total increase in urban population. The population figures for the 3415 towns that existed in 1991 as well as 2001 are 211 million and 274 million, respectively. By deducting the increase of 63 million from the total increase of 67.7 million, we obtain the increase due to independent new towns as 4.7 million (Table 3.4). This does not include the population of the new towns that appear as part of the UAs in 2001 as their populations are included in the population of common urban centres.

It is possible to hold that the figure of five million for the independent towns is an over-estimation. This is because the identification of UAs has been done adopting more rigorous criteria in 2001. Consequently, several new towns that would have been part of a UA as per 1991 criteria now appear as independent towns. Given a process of agglomerated urban development in the 1990s, the share of the towns appearing as constituents of UA to the total new towns should be higher in 2001. We may, however, take a conservative estimate by taking the proportion to remain unchanged over time. The number of independent towns can thus be revised downwards to 426 from 487, as noted in the 2001 Census. Correspondingly, the population due to the net addition of new towns can be reduced from 4.85 million to 4.24 million on a pro rata basis. We would argue that this estimate is still on a higher side.

The data on migration as also population of the rural areas merged with UAs are likely to be available only after another two or three years and hence there is no other option for the present than to estimate the figures based on certain assumptions. One may like to work out the number of new towns merged with UAs, using the figure of the new towns coming under UAs as a proxy. This would, however, be erroneous, as the number has gone down from 294 in 1991 to 205 in 2001 primarily due to application of stricter criteria, as noted already. Had the same definition been applied in 1991, we would have had fewer new towns appearing as part of UAs in that year.

Given the concentrated pattern of urban growth, one would expect the number of new towns appearing as a part of the agglomeration to be larger than what was observed in 1991. The actual figures as stated above are showing otherwise. The inference regarding the concentrated urban growth can therefore be defended by referring to the fact that the 2001 census reports a larger number of towns merging with the existing towns than in 1991, the respective figures being 221 and 103. Taking this phenomenon of merger of urban centres as an indication of a process of expansion around the large urban centres, one may argue that the increase in urban population due to this factor (the third component) in 2001 would be twice that in 1991. Alternately, one may take the increase to be 50 per cent only. The third alternative would be to assume the figure to remain the same as in 1991. Based on the three alternate assumptions, figures for the third component have been obtained, as shown in Table 3.4. Migration (the fourth component) has then been derived as a residual category and thereby we have three figures, each corresponding to the estimate for the third component of urban growth.

The share of the areal expansion component varies between 6.5 per cent and 13.0 per cent. Correspondingly, the migration component varies between 21.0 and 27.4 per cent. The share of migration jumping up from 21.7 per cent to 27.4 per cent during the 1990s seems unlikely as this would imply a steep rise in the RU migration. This becomes all the more doubtful if one observes that the RU migration during 1981–91 had increased by only 27 per cent (the high growth rate during the 1970s may be ignored since the 1981 census was an outlier). Using this growth rate, one would place the figure for migration at 15.8 million which works out to be 23.3 per cent only. This is closer to the middle-level estimate (estimate b) given in Table 3.4. The projected urban growth due to areal expansion, too, would be closer to the middle of the three estimates. Now, if one accepts the estimate (b) for net RU migration, one would argue that the growth of population in the periphery of UAs would go up by 50 per cent in 2001 compared to the previous census. This would imply that the urban structure in the country would get more skewed and top heavy over time.

The total increase in population during 1991–2001 is 67.7 million as compared to 57.7 million during 1981–91. The population growth attributable to (i) natural increase, (ii) new towns less declassified towns, (iii) increase due to expansion in urban area/agglomeration, and (iv) net RU migration along with the percentage distribution of these components is presented in Table 3.4. The figures given in the table show a fall in percentage terms, the contribution of natural increase from 61.3 to 59.4 even though the population has increased from 35.4 million to 40.2 million in absolute terms. The table indicates a significant reduction in the contribution of population of new towns, from 9.4 per cent to 6.2 per cent, due to expansion of urban area from 7.6 per cent to 9.7 per cent (middle estimate) and in net RU migration from 21.7 per cent to 24.2 per cent (middle estimate).

URBANIZATION PATTERN ACROSS SIZE CLASSES OF URBAN CENTRES

It has been mentioned that the process of urbanization in India is primarily large-city oriented. This is manifested at the national level as well as in a number of states, the share of class I cities being much above that of the others. Importantly, the share has been going up systematically through all the decades in the last century. The present section analyses the changing structure of urban population across size class of settlements over the past ten census decades, putting a sharp focus on the period since independence. The growing top heaviness has been examined in the context of movement of towns across the six census categories as also emergence of new urban centres. Explanation of the changing settlement structure has also been sought in terms of differential demographic growth for towns in different size categories.

It may be observed in Table 3.5 that the class I cities dominate India's urban scene in terms of their share of urban population. This share, though very high, was still comparable with that of other lower-order size categories at the beginning of this century. In 1901, the share of class I cities was 26.00 per cent whereas the class IV and V towns had 20.83 and 20.14 per cent of the urban population, respectively. The share of class I towns has gradually increased. The gaps between the shares have increased significantly during 1931–41, a decade before the independence and partition of the country. At the time of independence, however, a large number of displaced population were absorbed in class I cities. This led to an increase in the share of class I cities by about seven percentage points during 1941–51, similar to what was observed during the preceding decade. The increase was maintained at this level in the following two decades as well. Since the 1970s, however, the increment in the share of these cities has been about 3 percentage points, which has been maintained in the 1990s as well. The percentage of urban population living in class I cities has gone up from 64.89 per cent to 68.67 per cent only. The share of class IV and V towns, has been declining over the entire period. The combined share of these two categories of towns has gone down from 41 per cent to 9.2 per cent during 1901–2001. Importantly, the percentages of urban population in medium towns viz., class II and class III, have remained by and large stable over the entire century. Their shares have hovered around 11 and 13 per cent, respectively.

The massive increase in the share of class I cities has often been attributed to faster growth of the large cities, without taking into consideration the increase in the number of these cities. Indeed, the basic reason for the increasing dominance of these cities is a graduation of lower-order towns into class I category. In 1901 for example, there were only twenty-four towns in class I category. This figure went up to 393 in 2001. This can be attributed to the natural growth of population and RU migration in the towns below the cut-off point of one hundred thousand populations, enabling these to go over the point.

The general impression that larger urban centres in the country grow at a higher rate has persisted not just among planners and administrators but also among statisticians and demographers working in this area. The population census computes the growth rates of towns in a size class by considering the population belonging to that size class in the initial as well as terminal years, without taking note of the generally upward movement of the urban centres. As a consequence, the growth

TABLE 3.5

Class-wise Number of Towns, Percentage, and Growth Rate of Urban Population in India

Census year	Number of towns						Percentage of urban population						Annual exponential growth rate					
	Class I	Class II	Class III	Class IV	Class V	Class VI	Class I	Class II	Class III	Class IV	Class V	Class VI	Class I	Class II	Class III	Class IV	Class V	Class VI
1901	24	43	130	391	744	479	26.00	11.29	15.64	20.83	20.14	6.10	–	–	–	–	–	–
1911	23	40	135	364	707	485	27.48	10.51	16.40	19.73	19.31	6.57	0.54	–0.73	0.46	–0.55	–0.43	0.72
1921	29	45	145	370	734	571	29.70	10.39	15.92	18.29	18.67	7.03	1.57	0.68	0.50	0.03	0.46	1.47
1931	35	56	183	434	800	509	31.20	11.65	16.80	18.00	17.14	5.21	2.24	2.89	2.28	1.59	0.89	–1.25
1941	49	74	242	498	920	407	38.23	11.42	16.35	15.78	15.08	3.14	4.81	2.59	2.51	1.47	1.50	–2.26
1951	76	91	327	608	1124	569	44.63	9.96	15.72	13.63	12.97	3.09	5.02	2.10	3.07	2.01	1.97	3.31
1961	102	129	437	719	711	172	51.42	11.23	16.94	12.77	6.87	0.77	3.72	3.50	3.05	1.65	–4.05	–11.62
1971	148	173	558	827	623	147	57.24	10.92	16.01	10.94	4.45	0.44	4.29	2.93	2.65	1.67	–1.14	–2.32
1981	218	270	743	1059	758	253	60.32	11.63	14.30	9.47	3.66	0.62	4.34	4.43	2.69	2.43	1.64	5.05
1991	300	345	947	1167	740	197	64.89	10.96	13.33	7.89	2.62	0.31	3.84	2.38	2.26	1.02	–0.13	–2.45
2001	393	401	1151	1344	888	191	68.67	9.67	12.23	6.84	2.36	0.23	3.42	1.76	2.15	1.64	1.93	0.80

Notes: a. Size class-wise figures exclude Assam in 1981 and Jammu & Kashmir in 1991.
b. All classes exclude six towns in 1941, four each in 1931 and 1921, and two each in 1911 and 1901 of Goa which could not be assigned to any size class as their population for these years is not available. Total number of towns therefore would not match with the figures of Table 3.1.

Sources: Paper-2, Rural–Urban Distribution, 1981 and 1991; Census 2001.

rate of class I cities work out as very high since this size category would, over time, gain in the number of cities. Understandably, the size categories that lose in number of towns would generally show a low growth rate. Indeed, the class V and class VI categories often show a negative growth rate not because their towns are experiencing depopulation but because many of them move into the higher size categories.

In view of the problems of comparability, scholars have proposed that the base year classification of urban centres should be maintained both for base as well as terminal years for computing the growth rates. This would imply that the population of only those towns that belong to a category in the base year should be added up in the terminal year as well. This would make the number of towns at both the time points the same for each category, in computing the growth rates. Happily, the census itself has given population of common towns in 1991 in Appendix 10 of provisional population totals that are extremely useful in comparing the growth rates across size classes. It may, however, be noted that since the base year categories constitute the basis for classification of towns, all the new towns get excluded from this calculation. Furthermore, even the towns declassified in the terminal year get excluded. This might be responsible for an upward bias in the growth estimates in class V and VI categories as these would claim most of the declassified towns.

It has been argued that the Indian urban structure reflects no distortion and stable morphology as the population growth is more or less uniform across the size classes. It is evident from Table 3.5 that this is not the case. The urban centres in class I categories show distinctly higher growth rates in 1971 than compared to the lower-order towns

(except the class VI towns). Indeed, the class VI towns do not fall in line as they exhibit higher growth rate. One must hasten to add that the class VI towns constitute a special category as many of these are industrial townships, pilgrimage centres or settlements through establishment of a public sector industry in greenfield locations.

The pattern is identical in 1991 although there is a general deceleration in urban growth in all size categories. Nonetheless, one can note the class I cities having an edge over class II, III, IV, and class V towns in terms of the growth rate during 1981–91. Recalculation of the growth rates has been attempted based on the data from census 2001 in an identical manner. It is noted that there are 3415 towns that are common in the Census of 1991 and 2001, after excluding the new towns and the towns declassified in the latter census. The class VI towns have once again registered a higher growth rate during the 1990s compared to even the class I cities, the reasons for which have already been discussed. Among the other size class of urban centres, class I cities maintained a distinctly higher growth rate. One would, therefore, stipulate that the urban structure is becoming more and more skewed due to the higher demographic growth in larger cities, in addition to the other factors discussed here.

These adjusted growth rates (annual exponential growth rate) for class I (common) towns during the 1970s and 1980s are 3.46 and 2.96, respectively. The recent census has indicated a marginal decrease in the growth rate of class I towns to 2.76 per cent, computed on the basis of 291 common class I towns during 1991–2001. Small towns (IV–VI together) though indicate 3.07 and 2.57 per cent growth during 1981 and 1991. This has gone down to 2.22 during 1991–2001. One may, thus, argue that the decline in the growth rate of smaller towns is higher compared to the class I cities. Higher demographic growth in the class I cities is partially due to natural growth and inmigration. It may also be noted that a large number of satellite towns have emerged in the vicinity of these cities. These have become part of the city agglomeration over time. There are also outgrowths that have been treated as parts of the agglomeration by the census. Further, there have been expansions in the municipal boundaries of the class I cities, contributing to urban growth. All these factors have been responsible for the higher growth rate of class I cities.

Metro cities or cities having population of a million or more, corroborate further the thesis of concentrated urban development (Tables 3.6a and 3.6b). Between 1981–91, million-plus cities have, on an average, grown at the rate of 3.25 per cent, which is higher than the growth rate of common towns at 2.83 per cent, during this period. However, during 1991–2001, the growth rate has gone down across all size categories including that of the metro cities. The latter has come down to 2.88 but the growth rate of common towns has declined more sharply to 2.6 per cent. It is, thus, evident that the demographic growth in metro cities is higher than that in common towns or class I cities. The spatial concentration of urban growth can be seen not only in terms of an increase in the share of urban population in class I cities but also in the million-plus cities. The latter claimed about 26.41 per cent of urban population in 1981. This has increased to 32.54 in 1991 and further to 37.81 in 2001.

GROWTH OF MILLION PLUS CITIES/AGGLOMERATIONS

Most of the million-plus cities are multi municipal agglomerations. Such agglomerations comprise a large city in the core with smaller urban areas in the periphery. We have examined the growth of million-plus cities in terms of the core (main city) vis-à-vis the periphery (urban areas around the main city in periphery). In the growth of million-plus cities in the country for two consecutive decades of 1981–91 and 1991–2001, four important features should be noted that is, declining core–growing periphery, growing core–declining periphery, growing core–growing periphery, and declining core–declining periphery. These are presented in Table 3.6c. Jaipur, Faridabad, and Ludhiana do not have an agglomeration. These core cities without any UA have indicated a negative or negligible growth over these two time points. The growth and distribution of population within these large urban areas is not uniform.

An observation of intra-urban agglomeration of large metropolises, however, indicates that within the agglomeration of the large metro cities for example, Greater Mumbai, Kolkata, Delhi, and Chennai have recorded a higher growth in their peripheries than in the cores. Huge population, lack of infrastructure and amenities, cost of living, and stringent land laws, may have decelerated the capacity of the core areas of these cities to absorb the marginal increase of population, which, as a matter of fact, find a place in and around the core city, indicating a faster growth of the UAs. This tendency in urbanization basically indicates an agglomerated trend. Bangalore, however, shows a reverse trend that is, the core of the city is growing faster than the periphery.

Even cities like Jamshedpur and Asansol, now attaining the status of metro cities, have shown fast-growing UA peripheries in 2001. This is significant from the point of regional development. The role of such regional cities will become more meaningful in

TABLE 3.6a
Growth Rate of Metropolitan Cities

Metropolitan cities/UAs	Population			Exponential growth rate	
	1981	1991	2001	1981–91	1991–2001
Greater Mumbai	8,243,405	12,596,243	16,368,084	4.22	2.62
Kolkata	9,194,018	11,021,918	13,216,546	1.72	1.82
Delhi	5,729,283	8,419,084	12,791,458	3.80	4.18
Chennai	4,289,347	5,421,985	6,424,624	2.23	1.70
Bangalore	2,921,751	4,130,288	5,686,844	3.36	3.20
Hyderabad	2,545,836	4,344,437	5,533,640	5.20	2.42
Ahmedabad	2,548,057	3,312,216	4,519,278	2.58	3.11
Pune	1,686,109	2,493,987	3,755,525	3.88	4.09
Surat	–	1,518,950	2,811,466	–	6.16
Kanpur	1,639,064	2,029,889	2,690,486	2.53	2.82
Jaipur	1,015,160	1,518,235	2,324,319	4.00	4.26
Lucknow	1,007,604	1,669,204	2,266,933	4.88	3.06
Nagpur	1,302,066	1,664,006	2,122,965	2.44	2.44
Patna	–	1,099,647	1,707,429	–	4.40
Indore	–	1,109,056	1,639,044	–	3.91
Vadodara	–	1,126,824	1,492,398	–	2.81
Bhopal	–	1,062,771	1,454,830	–	3.14
Coimbatore	–	1,100,746	1,446,034	–	2.73
Ludhiana	–	1,042,740	1,395,053	–	2.91
Kochi	–	1,140,605	1,355,406	–	1.73
Vishakhapatnam	–	1,057,118	1,329,472	–	2.29
Agra	–	–	1,321,410	–	
Varanasi	–	1,030,863	1,211,749	–	1.62
Madurai	–	1,085,914	1,194,665	–	0.95
Meerut	–	–	1,167,399	–	–
Nashik	–	–	1,152,048	–	–
Jabalpur	–	–	1,117,200	–	–
Jamshedpur	–	–	1,101,804	–	–
Asansol	–	–	1,090,171	–	–
Dhanbad	–	–	1,064,357	–	–
Faridabad	–	–	1,054,981	–	–
Allahabad	–	–	1,049,579	–	–
Amritsar	–	–	1,011,327	–	–
Vijayawada	–	–	1,011,152	–	–
Rajkot	–	–	1,002,160	–	

Sources: Paper-2, Rural–Urban Distribution, 1981, 1991, and Census 2001.

TABLE 3.6b
Growth Differentials of Core and Periphery of Metropolitan Cities in India

Metropolitan cities	1981–91		1991–2001	
	Core	Periphery	Core	Periphery
A Declining core; growing periphery				
Ahmedabad	2.11	2.58	2.00	3.11
Asansol	3.64	2.23	0.96	3.56
Coimbatore	1.48	1.79	1.23	2.73
Delhi	3.59	3.80	3.09	4.18
B Growing core; declining periphery				
Bangalore	0.71	3.36	4.79	3.20
C Growing core; growing periphery				
Agra	2.51	2.38	3.46	3.32
Amritsar	1.76	1.76	3.19	3.56
Dhanbad	2.33	1.73	2.71	2.67
Indore	2.75	2.90	3.80	3.91
Jabalpur	1.89	1.60	2.48	2.29
Jamshedpur	0.50	1.98	2.13	2.84
Kanpur	2.30	2.53	3.01	2.81
Patna	1.66	1.80	4.06	4.40
Pune	2.64	3.88	4.83	4.09
Rajkot	2.29	3.86	5.47	4.26
Surat	4.84	4.97	4.85	6.16
D Declining core; declining periphery				
Allahabad	2.52	2.62	2.22	2.18
Bhopal	4.60	4.60	2.99	3.14
Chennai	1.59	2.23	0.93	1.70
Greater Mumbai	1.86	4.22	1.82	2.62
Hyderabad	3.31	5.20	1.58	2.42
Kochi	1.27	3.24	0.24	1.73
Kolkata	0.64	1.72	0.40	1.82
Lucknow	5.35	4.88	3.12	3.06
Madurai	1.36	1.80	0.19	0.95
Meerut	5.19	4.48	3.54	3.18
Nagpur	2.87	2.44	2.33	2.44
Nashik	5.91	4.93	4.94	4.62
Vadodara	3.39	3.65	2.36	2.81
Varanasi	2.60	2.57	1.70	1.62
Vijaywada	2.85	3.21	1.62	1.86
Vishakhapatnam	2.85	5.60	2.55	2.30

Sources: Census of India 1981 and 1991, Paper-2, Rural–Urban Distribution; Census of India 2001.

TABLE 3.6c
Growth Tendencies of Mega Cities

Metropolitan cities	1981–91		1991–2001	
	Core	Periphery	Core	Periphery
Greater Mumbai	1.86	4.22	1.82	2.62
Kolkata	0.64	1.72	0.4	1.82
Delhi	3.59	3.8	3.09	4.18
Chennai	1.59	2.23	0.93	1.7
Bangalore	0.71	3.36	4.79	3.2
Hyderabad	3.31	5.2	1.58	2.42

Sources: Census of India 1981 and 1991, Paper-2, Rural–Urban Distribution; Census of India 2001.

terms of urban–rural integration from the point of view of planning and governance.

A trend of corridor development is also obvious from the pattern of growth of such cities. Proximity of cities such as, Amritsar–Jalandhar–Ludhiana, Vadodara–Ahmedabad–Surat, Kolkata–Dhanbad–Jamshedpur, indicate a spatial concentration of population along these urban corridors. Such type of spatial development is also emerging in other parts of the country as revealed by a recent study by the Centre for Policy Research, New Delhi 'Future of Urbanization—Spread and Shape in Select States'. Implications of these corridors in the urbanization scenario of the country merit a comprehensive study specially from the point of socio-demographic and economic commonalties of the regions.

The analysis of the study based on the urbanization pattern and projections for the next twenty years is indicative of the fact that bulk of the urban population will be living in metropolitan regions. Agglomerations covering several municipal jurisdictions will emerge as a distinct feature of India's urbanization. Agricultural mandi towns, new industrial centres, and service activities located in the metropolitan regions are being located in the

peripheries of metropolitan cities as poly-nodal centres. Most of these agglomerations will grow along transport corridors, but the pattern of growth will not be continuous. These corridors have been attracting a substantial volume of economic activities, such as industry and regional infrastructure. The spatial manifestation of investments and economic change is discernible through continuous or discontinuous sprawl with poly-nodal centres along the corridors. The peripheral areas of large cities along the corridors have been growing and absorbing migrant population in areas lacking basic services. Such developments are exerting considerable pressure on land and other natural resources.

It is important to examine whether the state capitals in the country have been growing differently from the class I cities or the common towns during t he past two decades (Tables 3.7 and 3.8). It is seen that the demographic growth in the capitals of the major states and the national capital is almost at par with that of the million-plus cities. During 1981–91 and 1991–2001, these cities taken together, registered growth rates of 3.36 per cent and 2.79 per cent, respectively. The respective shares of urban population living in the capital cities

TABLE 3.7
Growth of Capital Cities

State	City	1991 census	1981	1991	2001	Exponential growth rate	
						1981–91	1991–2001
Andhra Pradesh	Hyderabad	4,280,261	2,545,836	4,344,437	5,533,640	5.20	2.42
Assam	Guwahati	577,591	NA	577,591	814,575	NA	3.44
Bihar	Patna	1,098,572	916,102	1,098,572	1,707,429	1.82	4.41
Delhi	Delhi	8,375,188	5,729,283	8,419,084	12,791,458	3.80	4.18
Gujarat	Gandhinagar	121,746	62,249	121,746	195,891	6.71	4.76
Haryana	Chandigarh	574,646	421,256	574,646	808,796	3.11	3.42
Himachal Pradesh	Shimla	109,860	70,479	109,860	144,578	4.44	2.75
Karnataka	Bangalore	4,086,548	2,921,751	4,130,288	5,686,844	3.36	3.20
Kerala	Thiruva'thapuram	825,682	519,766	825,682	889,191	4.63	0.74
Madhya Pradesh	Bhopal	1,063,662	672,329	1,063,662	1,454,830	4.59	3.13
Maharashtra	Mumbai	12,571,720	8,243,405	12,596,243	16,368,084	4.22	2.62
Orissa	Bhubaneshwar	411,542	219,419	411,542	657,477	6.29	4.68
Rajasthan	Jaipur	1,514,425	1,015,160	1,518,235	2,324,319	4.00	4.26
Tamil Nadu	Chennai	5,361,468	4,289,347	5,421,985	6,424,624	2.23	1.70
Uttar Pradesh	Lucknow	1,642,134	1,007,604	1,669,204	2,266,933	4.88	3.06
West Bengal	Kolkata	10,916,272	9,194,018	11,021,918	13,216,546	1.72	1.82
Total population		52,953,726	37,828,004	53,904,695	71,285,215	3.36	2.79

Note: The growth rates for towns and cities in different size categories have been computed by considering these by their size class distribution in the base year. Furthermore, the population figures for the base year have been obtained from the census volumes of the terminal year, since the former often get revised due to merging of towns and boundary changes during the decade. Guwahati has been excluded for the period 1981–2001. The city, however, has been included for growth calculations for 1991–2001.

Source: Census of India 1981 and 1991, Paper-2, Rural–Urban Distribution; Census of India 2001.

TABLE 3.8

Annual Exponential Growth Rates for Cities and Towns in Different Size Categories

City	1981–91	1991–2001
Metro cities	3.25	2.88
Class I cities	2.96	2.76
State capitals	3.36	2.79
Smaller towns (Class IV, V, and VI)	2.57	2.22
Common towns	2.83	2.59

Notes: The growth rates for towns and cities in different size categories have been computed by considering these by their size class distribution in the base year. Furthermore, the population figures for the base year have been obtained from the census volumes of the terminal year, since the former often get revised due to merging of towns and boundary changes during the decade. In case of the state capitals, Guwahati has been excluded for the period 1981–91 and its base year population was not available. The city, however, has been included for growth calculations for 1991–2001.

Source: Census of India 1981 and 1991, Paper-2; Census of India 2001.

are 24.8, 25.7, and 25.9 per cent in these three census years. This further confirms the proposition of unbalanced urban growth across size categories. It may nonetheless be mentioned that the growth rates in as many as ten capital cities have declined substantially in the 1990s compared to the previous decade. It is to be considered whether this is because of structural adjustment, expenditure control, and fall in the infrastructural investments by the Central and state governments, adversely affecting the growth of the capital cities.

URBANIZATION IN THE CONTEXT OF CHANGING SCENARIO OF EMPLOYMENT

The sharp decline in the growth rate of urban population during the 1980s and 1990s calls for an explanation. An attempt was made in the preceding chapter to see if this decline could be attributed to definitional factors. It was pointed out that the conceptual problems in different censuses and the discrepancies in application were quite serious and it was advisable to make adjustments in the urban

population figures for 1981, 1991, and 2001 before computing growth rates or making interstate comparisons. However, it was also seen that the definitional problems were unlikely to alter the main trends at the macro level. There is thus no reason to deny that the urban growth rate has decelerated significantly in the past two decades.

It is important to analyse the slow rate of urbanization in terms of macroeconomic changes in the economy. One can argue that the process of industrial growth during the 1990s has been capital intensive and consequently the demand for labour in urban areas has been low, dampening the RU migration flow. To assess the validity of this hypothesis, it will be useful to begin by examining the changes in the levels and structure of employment in recent years and deduce their possible impact on urbanization.

Workforce participation rates (WPR) by usual (principal plus subsidiary) status, defined as the percentage of male and female workers to total population, show fluctuations of around 44 per cent in rural India during 1973–4 and 1993–4 based on the quinquennial data

from the National Sample Survey Organization (NSSO) (Kundu 2001). The rate had gone
up by about one percentage point from 1987–8
to 1993–4. The same was the case in urban
areas as well. The developments in the late
1990s, however, appear very disturbing. The
WPR have declined in rural and urban areas—
both for males and females—by usual, weekly,
and daily employment status. The decline
may be noted as significant in the (15–59)
age group as well, computed after excluding
the children and elderly people (Table 3.9).
Importantly, such all-round decline in WPR
for all categories has not been observed in
any previous year based on the NSS data,
not even in 1987–8, the year when employment was seriously affected by drought. The
decline in WPR indicates that the growth
rate of employment (by usual status) has
been less than that of population during the
late 1990s compared to the previous decade
and a half. Understandably, the former would
be much below that of the 1980s or early
1990s when the population growth rate was
higher.

Interestingly, by weekly and daily status,
WPR had gone up for women and men, for
the total as also 15–59 age group both in rural
and urban areas during 1983–93 (Table 3.9).
The employment scenario since the mid-1990s,
however, has changed drastically.[6] The quinquennial data for 1999–2000 reveal a declining
trend as WPR work out less than those in
1993–4. The WPR by weekly and usual status
for the adult age groups have also gone down

which gives disturbing signals with regard to
recent developments in the labour market.

It is important to note that despite a reasonably high growth in value added in industrial
production in the 1990s, employment in the
organized sector has not grown rapidly. Private sector units within the organized sector
where growth in output has been significant,
have high capital intensity and a low potential
for employment generation. The public sector
units, on the other hand, have also registered
a low growth in workforce. The sluggish
growth in employment in urban areas can also
be attributed to location of large units outside
the municipal limits, because of land, environment, and other restrictions. Furthermore, the
capacity of unorganized activities to absorb
future migrants seems to be drying up over the
years (Kundu and Basu 1995), as reflected in
the data on unorganized sector made available
by the NSS through its enterprise surveys. As
a consequence of all these, the reasonably high
industrial growth in the late 1990s could
not generate much employment. Urban industrial growth, as a result, has failed to attract a
large number of migrants into cities and towns
that could significantly boost the process of
urbanization.

The percentage of unemployed persons (person days) to the total labour force (labour
days) had gone down until 1993–4 (Kundu
1997). This happened by all the three concepts
of employment, canvassed by NSS in both
rural and urban areas (Tables 3.10a and 3.10b).
The decline, nonetheless, is relatively high
by weekly and daily status as compared to the
usual status. This gave an indication of an
increase in part-time and short-duration work.
A large number of households were sending
more of their members to seek or create
employment for themselves as a part of their
survival strategy. The data from the 55th round,

---

[6] The WPR for males (all ages) as well as females
show fluctuations with a slight declining trend during
the period 1994–8 both by usual and weekly status.
The fall in case of women is significantly higher. This
could be indicative of a process of slowing down of
growth of non-agricultural and informal sector jobs in
the late 1990s.

TABLE 3.9

Percentage of Workers in 15–59 Age Group in Different NSS Rounds by Usual, Weekly, and Daily Status

Year round	Rural male		Rural female		Urban male		Urban female	
	Principal	Principal & subsidiary	Principal	Principal & subsidiary	Principal	Principal & subsidiary	Principal	Principal & subsidiary
1977–8 (32nd)	90.20	92.00	40.70	54.20	79.60	81.00	19.30	24.60
1983 (38th)	88.40	90.40	40.10	54.50	79.50	81.00	18.70	23.40
1987–8 (43rd)	86.20	88.70	39.80	51.60	77.90	79.30	18.30	23.50
1993–4 (50th)	86.50	88.40	36.70	51.60	78.80	79.70	18.40	23.40
1999–2000 (55th)	85.50	86.70	33.40	48.20	77.90	78.50	17.60	20.90
	Weekly status	Daily status	Weekly status	Weekly status	Daily status	Daily status	Weekly status	Daily status
1977–8	87.10	81.50	37.70	31.40	78.60	75.70	19.60	17.10
1983	85.40	80.20	36.40	31.60	78.30	75.20	18.40	16.50
1987–8	84.00	83.50	35.30	33.20	77.30	75.10	18.50	17.00
1993–4	85.10	80.90	42.00	34.30	78.20	76.00	20.90	18.10
1999–2000	83.40	78.10	40.80	32.90	77.10	74.40	19.10	16.70

Source: NSSO 1988, 1990, and 1996.

TABLE 3.10a

Percentage of Unemployed Persons/Person Days to Labour Force/Labour Days in Rural Areas

Year round		Male			Female		
		Usual pri+subs status	Weekly status	Daily status	Usual pri+subs status	Weekly status	Daily status
1977–8	(32nd Round)	1.30	3.60	7.10	2.00	4.10	9.20
January–December 83	(38th Round)	1.40	3.70	7.50	0.70	4.30	9.00
1987–8	(43rd Round)	1.80	4.20	4.60	2.40	4.40	9.00
1989–90	(45th Round)	1.30	2.60	–	0.60	2.10	–
1990–1	(46th Round)	1.10	2.20	–	0.30	2.10	–
July–December 91	(47th Round)	1.60	2.20	–	0.70	1.20	–
January–December 92	(48th Round)	1.20	2.20	–	0.60	1.20	–
1993–4	(50th Round)	1.40	3.10	5.60	0.90	2.90	5.60
1994–5	(51st Round)	1.00	1.80	NA	0.40	1.20	NA
1995–6	(52nd Round)	1.30	1.80	NA	0.70	0.90	NA
1997	(53rd Round)	1.20	2.00	NA	0.70	1.80	NA
1998	(54th Round)	2.10	2.90	NA	1.50	2.70	NA
1999–2000	(55th Round)	1.70	3.90	7.20	1.00	3.70	7.00

Source: NSSO 1988, 1990, and 1996.

TABLE 3.10b

Percentage of Unemployed Persons/Person Days to Labour Force/Labour Days in Urban Areas

Year round		Male			Female		
		Usual pri+subs status	Weekly status	Daily status	Usual pri+subs status	Weekly status	Daily status
1977–8	(32nd Round)	5.40	7.10	9.40	12.40	10.90	14.50
January–December 83	(38th Round)	5.10	6.70	9.20	4.90	7.50	11.00
1987–8	(43rd Round)	5.20	6.60	8.80	6.20	9.20	12.00
1989–90	(45th Round)	3.90	4.50	–	2.70	4.00	–
1990–1	(46th Round)	4.50	5.10	–	4.70	5.30	–
July–December 91	(47th Round)	4.10	4.80	–	4.30	5.60	–
January–December 92	(48th Round)	4.30	4.60	–	5.80	6.20	–
1993–4	(50th Round)	4.10	5.20	6.70	6.20	8.40	10.40
1994–5	(51st Round)	3.40	3.90	NA	3.40	4.00	NA
1995–6	(52nd Round)	3.80	4.10	NA	3.10	3.50	NA
1997	(53rd Round)	3.90	4.30	NA	4.40	5.80	NA
1998	(54th Round)	5.10	5.40	NA	6.80	7.80	NA
1999–2000	(55th Round)	4.50	5.60	7.30	5.70	7.30	9.40

Source: NSSO 1998, 1996, and 1994.

however, tell a different story. The unemployment rates in the year 1999–2000 by all the three—usual, weekly and daily status—are higher than in 1993–4. The only exception to this is the category of urban women. It is obvious, the employment situation has worsened significantly in the late 1990s, the change being slightly higher in rural than in urban areas.

Another important dimension of change in the labour market in recent years is the process of casualization. The percentage of casual male workers was noted to have gone up from the quinquennial data, both in rural and urban areas during 1977–93. A similar increase but of a smaller magnitude, has been observed in

the case of females (Table 3.11). Interestingly, the figures have gone up in rural areas after 1993–4 as well for both males and females. The growth of casual employment, however, works out as much less during 1993–9 than the preceding five-year period. In urban areas, the share has actually gone down. The decline is very sharp by about 5 percentage points in case of females. Further, the share of subsidiary (usual status) employment in the population has also fallen sharply during 1993–9 in all the categories, the decline in percentage figures being higher than that of the principal workers. This trend can be observed even when the 15-plus age group is considered (Table 3.12). The growth rate in casual and subsidiary

TABLE 3.11
Percentage of Usually Employed Persons (Principal and Subsidiary) by Type of Employment

Years	Self-employed	Regular employees	Casual labour	Self-employed	Regular employees	Casual labour
	Rural male			Rural female		
1977–8	62.80	10.60	26.60	62.10	2.80	35.10
1983	60.50	10.30	29.20	61.90	2.80	35.30
1987–8	58.60	10.00	31.40	60.80	3.70	35.50
1993–4	57.90	8.30	33.80	58.50	2.80	38.70
1994–5	60.40	6.80	32.80	57.00	2.20	40.80
1995–6	59.00	7.70	33.30	56.40	2.40	41.20
1997	59.40	7.30	33.30	57.00	2.10	40.90
1998	55.30	7.00	37.70	53.40	2.50	44.20
1999–2000	55.00	8.80	36.20	57.30	3.10	39.60
	Urban Male			Urban Female		
1977–8	40.40	46.40	13.20	49.50	24.90	25.60
1983	40.90	43.70	15.40	45.80	25.80	28.40
1987–8	41.70	43.70	14.60	47.10	27.50	25.40
1993–4	41.70	42.10	16.20	45.40	28.60	26.00
1994–5	40.40	43.10	16.50	42.60	30.10	27.30
1995–6	41.00	42.50	16.50	40.00	33.20	26.80
1997	40.00	41.50	18.50	39.70	31.30	29.00
1998	42.50	39.50	18.10	38.40	32.70	28.80
1999–2000	41.50	41.70	16.80	45.30	33.30	21.40

Source: NSSO 1988 and 1996.

TABLE 3.12
Incidence of Subsidiary Employment

Percentage of subsidiary workers to total population

	Rural		Urban	
	Male	Female	Male	Female
1993–4	1.50	9.40	0.80	3.40
1999–2000	0.90	6.80	0.50	2.20

Percentage of subsidiary workers to total population in 15+age group

	Rural		Urban	
	Male	Female	Male	Female
1993–4	1.30	13.90	0.70	4.70
1999–2000	0.90	10.20	0.50	3.00

Source: NSSO 1993–4 and 1999–2000.

employment has, thus, gone down during 1993–9 much more than the principal or regular employment and also than that of the preceding six-year period. Though casual employment is usually in low productive jobs it helped in the decline of poverty. This has been stalled in recent years with consequent implications for urban poverty.

The low growth of employment in the whole decade of the 1990s is also borne out by the data from economic census. The growth rate of own account enterprises during 1980–90 was 3.7 per annum in urban India, which came down to 2.5 per annum during 1990–8. The decline in the growth rate of establishments was phenomenal—going down from 4.8 per cent to 1.8 per cent. Correspondingly, the growth rate of employment declined from 2.8 to 1.1 per cent.

While employment rate as a whole has come down, employment in the casual category has declined more than that in the principal and subsidiary sectors. Changes taking place in the economy may have increased resources in a few pockets but they have not really catered to a large section of population in terms of job opportunities and other economic benefits.

Employment and urbanization usually have a positive correlation but in recent years employment has not grown as expected which in turn has not promoted urbanization.

IMPACT OF STRUCTURAL REFORM AND RELATED STRATEGIES ON URBANIZATION AND MIGRATION

It may be pointed out that the decline in the growth of employment in rural areas is distinctly below that in urban areas. The increase in unemployment is, on the other hand, somewhat sharper. Further, the growth of regular salaried workers in rural areas is much lower than that in urban areas. The growth of non-farm employment is also lower in rural areas. The process of casualization also seems to be unabated for the rural workforce as compared to the urban segment. All these tend to suggest that the urban employment market has fared relatively better. Other things remaining the same, this should encourage RU migration. However, there has been a decline in the share of manufacturing employment partly due to subcontracting and partly due to the increasing fragmentation of the urban labour market. A large part of manufacturing work is currently being done within households, resulting in many of these workers getting classified under the tertiary sector. The earnings of the manufacturing workers, as a consequence, have declined over the years. In recent years, the incentive to move to urban centres in the hope of manufacturing employment has thus gone down.

The volume of migration is determined not by the overall differences between rural and urban averages but what prevails at the margin. There are indications that the gap between the real wages of casual workers in urban and rural areas has gone down in the 1990s. In the 1970s and early 1980s, rural poverty was higher than urban poverty by at least six percentage points. Currently, due to differential price rise in food grains, poverty line in urban areas works out as much higher than that in rural areas. The gap between urban and rural poverty is narrowing down over the years. Despite the employment situation being, on an average, better in urban areas, this could be yet another reason why RU migration and consequent urban growth have declined during the 1990s.

As pointed out earlier, industrial units in the 1990s have come up mostly in the rural settlements or small towns around a few big cities. This is primarily because of easy availability of land, access to unorganized labour market, and less stringent implementation of environmental regulations in these settlements. The poor have been able to find shelter in these 'degenerated peripheries' and find jobs in the industries located therein or commute to the central city for work (Kundu 1989). The entrepreneurs, engineers, and executives, associated with modern industries and business, however, reside within the city and are able to travel to the periphery because of increasing private transport and facilities such as expressways and flyovers in the city. This segmented structure of city growth, emerging in different variants in different regions, has brought the rural migrants largely to the peripheries of a few large cities.

Given the dynamics of urban industrial development, as discussed above, the small and medium towns located farther from the 'emerging global centres of growth', particularly those in backward regions, have not received much private sector investment. The Census of 1991 reveals that the towns having less than 50,000 population, not only have a small proportion of workers engaged in manufacturing, but also fewer households covered through basic services like drinking water, toilets, and electricity. The picture would be similar in the year 2001. With governmental investment in infrastructure and basic amenities becoming less and less over the years, the disparity across urban centres might even go up. The small and medium towns have not been able to finance capital expenditure through internal resources or borrowings from the capital market, which would lead to any significant improvement in the level of amenities. The fiscal discipline, sought to be imposed by the government and credit rating agencies on urban local bodies, has made it impossible for them to undertake infrastructural expenditure of any kind. The deficiency in basic amenities has been a serious hurdle in their attracting private investment from within or outside the country. It is only a few large cities with strong economic bases which have been able to raise resources through bonds and other instruments of credit.

The rate of urbanization could have been higher, if the process of RU transformation was expedited through sectoral diversification viz., increase in secondary and tertiary activities in large villages, helping the latter acquire urban status. There are about 3000 villages having population above 10,000 in the country and their inclusion within the urban fold would have immediately increased the percentage of urban population by five percentage points. It has been pointed out that, for acquiring urban status, it is necessary for a settlement to have 75 per cent of the male workers engaged outside the primary sector, besides satisfying other demographic criteria such as population size and density. Unfortunately, the share of non-agricultural employment in these 3000-odd large villages was less than 40 per cent in 1991. It is, therefore, understandable that only a lesser number of villages have become urban places by the year

2001. This is specially so because the process of sectoral diversification, that is, a shift of workers from agriculture to non-agriculture, has not been very high in the 1990s.

POSSIBLE EFFECTS OF RECENT CHANGES IN URBAN MANAGEMENT

The recent changes in the system of urban governance and planning may have also impacted adversely on urban growth. During the 1950s and 1960s, physical planning controls on location of economic activities and urban land use imposed through master plans and other measures, had put various restrictions on the industrial growth of large Indian cities. These restrictions were also expected to slow down RU migration. At present, however, a strong lobby is emerging, particularly in large cities, pleading for disbanding of all zoning restrictions, building laws, and bye-laws, and making the cities relatively independent of state and Central-level controls. It is argued that decisions regarding location of industries, or change in land use would be taken expeditiously at the local level and thus give impetus to urban growth.

It may be pointed out that planning controls and bye-laws have had little impact in restricting urban growth in the past. In the present environment of relaxation of these controls and decentralization of development planning responsibilities, large cities which have a relatively high tax and non-tax revenue potential have a clear advantage. As a result, these cities have been able to attract industrial investment and much of the incremental urban population.

Importantly, it is also seen that as part of decentralized urban management, envisaged in the 74th Amendment, it is possible for city management to provide differential levels of amenities, based on the willingness of the users to pay, in different parts of a city. This, in a way, can reinforce the disparity in the availability of civic amenities and the process of dividing the cities into rich and poor segments. This process, operationalized through the market and also backed up by governmental programmes can affect inflow of population into these cities adversely. Elitist preference for low density and clean micro-environment has led to strong action against illegal encroachments and evictions, and only selective new construction in core areas and high-income colonies. Low levels of basic amenities, unhygienic living conditions, and deteriorating law and order situation, have also been a strong disincentive for further in-migration into low-income areas. A switch over from planning to free market, therefore, may not give any impetus to urban growth, except in case of a handful of large cities attracting investment.

The impact of certain other aspects of the new system of urban governance on large cities needs to be assessed carefully. Local governments in many of these cities are currently facing two serious problems in attracting foreign and Indian business. One is that of scarcity of land within the central city and/or other suitable locations and the second is lack of capital. In a number of cities seeking to attract national and multinational companies, the floor space index (FSI) in the central areas of the city is increased so that multistoreyed structures can come up, providing space for business houses, commercial activities, and high-income residential units. The strategy of permitting vertical growth in areas with high land values would simultaneously enable the local bodies to generate resources for infrastructural development by selling the extra FSI.

Attempts have, thus, been made in 'select global centres of the future' to provide land at preferred sites to upcoming activities through the market. Apart from simplifying planning and administrative procedures, this has also been done by pushing out 'low valued' activities from these sites. The low-income and slum colonies are the obvious candidates for relocation to city peripheries. The shift has often been carried out directly through eviction of slum dwellers, hawkers, and pavement dwellers. Sometimes, it has been done indirectly and discreetly through slum improvement schemes, 'rehabilitating' them out in the peripheries. Such relocations have taken place in most of the metropolises, irrespective of the political complexion of the government in the state or the city. Some of the government schemes do have a provision for giving the evicted slum dwellers plots or flats in the building being constructed at the original site. It is, nonetheless, erroneous to believe that such allottees would be able to hold on to them for a long time, given their acute need for finance, growing land values, and relaxation in the legal and administrative environment.[7]

Undoubtedly, such measures would, in the long run, push the poor out to the fringes or outside the municipal boundaries of the cities. Privatization of land and civic services, in general, is likely to push up their prices, particularly in large cities. That would invariably slow down in-migration of the poor. It is observed that the migrants in Class I cities

[7] A major concern in the scheme for rehabilitation of slum and hutment dwellers, currently being implemented in Brihan Mumbai, for example, is to prevent future encroachment of land in the central areas. The Study Group (1995) set up for this purpose observes that 'encroachment of any land need to be firmly and quickly removed. For this purpose action needs to be taken as the first signs of unauthorized construction surface. Machinery needs to be established and strengthened ward-wise with police force which should be well equipped.'

in the early 1980s were economically and occupationally better-off than the non-migrants (Premi 1984). In-migration of poor in urban centres is likely to be even lower in the future decades as access to basic amenities would become even less due to a reduction in public expenditure (particularly capital expenditure) on urban development and social sectors.

Given this macro scenario, slowing down in the rate of urbanization, concentration of growth in relatively developed states, and rapid growth in and around a few global centres could be the likely outcome. With governmental investment in infrastructure and basic amenities becoming less and less over the years, the disparity within the urban economy has increased substantially. The data from the Census of 2001 indeed bear out this result. Only a few large cities have experienced modest to high urban growth. A part of the growth can also be seen in their peripheries. The towns, away from the metropolitan regions, that have experienced rapid economic and demographic growth are very few in number. Given this dynamics of urban industrial development, the small and medium towns, located away from the 'emerging global centres of growth', particularly those in backward regions, have not received much private investment. They rarely have the capacity to finance development projects through internal resources or borrowings from the capital market.

PROJECTIONS FOR FUTURE

The growth rates of urban population realized during the 1980s and 1990s are much lower than those projected, except for the UN documents published in the late 1990s. What are the critical factors responsible for the lower growth rate and how can these be incorporated in the model for making future projections? It is indeed true that the deceleration in urban growth during the 1990s is due to a decline in the natural growth rate but most of the projection exercises for India incorporate this factor. The real problem is, therefore, with regard to the assumptions on migration. Most of the projections have erred on a higher side in this regard. Even the UN projections based on exponential function incorporating urban–rural growth differential (URGD) for future years are on a higher side. The underlying assumption that the URGD will pick up and approximate to the global norms (estimated by applying regression equation to URGD of 113 countries having more than two million inhabitants in 1995) in thirty years does not correspond to the factual position.

The urban population was projected to grow at 3.2 per cent per annum during 2000–10 in the 1995 UN Report. In the following decades, it was expected to come down systematically, the figure being only 2.8 per cent during 2020–5. The revised documents of UN, however, give substantially different figures. The growth rates now given are 2.85[8] during 2000–5, declining to 2.52 during 2020–5. Regarding the level of urbanization, the report of 1995 had projected 28.8 per cent in 1991. By the year 2020, 41.3 per cent of the Indian population is expected to be residing in urban areas.[9] According to revised estimates, the percentage of urban population is expected to go up from 28.4 in 2000 to 42.5 in 2025. The least optimistic projection

of the UN relating to urban growth, places the figure at slightly above 2.8 per cent only during the first decade in the present century.

Using the scheme presented here, the annual rate of migration as a percentage of urban population can be estimated for different growth rates of urban population. If the anticipated growth rate of 2.8 per cent is to be achieved, RU migration must be 1.5 per cent per year contributing about 55 per cent of the incremental urban population during the period 2001–10. The crucial question is whether there is direct or indirect evidence that migration would step up in future years and sustain the projected increase in RU migration or in urban population. The analysis of the data on migration during the past few decades does not encourage us to take a positive view on this. The projected rate is much above what may be considered feasible, based on the historical data. The intercensal migrants constitute only 12.6 per cent in 1991. Among the total intercensal migrants, those with less than one-year duration constitute about 11 per cent. Applying this ratio, the annual migration rate would work out as 1.4 per cent. The increase in the rate of immigration is unlikely to compensate for the decline in natural growth to maintaining an overall urban growth rate of even 2.8 per cent, as projected by the UN.

The growth rate of total population is expected to be just above one per cent, as per the UN projections. Assuming that the natural growth rate in urban areas would be slightly below that in rural areas, the former can be taken to be 0.9 per cent. This does not seem to be an optimistic assumption as the natural growth rate in urban areas during the 1990s works out as 1.6, about 0.5 percentage points less than in rural areas. The reclassification factor (the total of second and fourth components) has not contributed more than 17

[8] The UN Report for the year 2001 places the figure at 2.81 only.
[9] The parameters of the model (used for the projection exercise in the UN study), make the increase in the percentage of urban population in the initial years to be low, going up subsequently (but coming down ultimately, at a high level of urbanization).

per cent in the recent past. Given the spatially concentrated nature of urbanization and economic development, one would expect a decline in its share. We have, however, assumed a figure of 15 per cent which is higher than what has been estimated for 2001.

It is important to observe that URGD in India has gone up steadily from the 1950s to the 1970s. While applying the exponential function for projection, the taskforce set up by the Planning Commission had observed that making projection for future URGD would be hazardous for any country like India. Therefore, it did not want to project the percentage of urban population using an increasing or even constant URGD for future years. In fact, in the second variant of the model, it used declining URGD, an assumption that was borne out by facts during the 1980s and 1990s. The figures have gone down from 1981–91 to 1991–2001. It is to be noted that despite taking the view that URGD would decline in future years, the projected urban figures were higher than what materialized in 2001.

It is thus evident that the projection of per cent urban population based on UN methodology on the assumption that URGD would converge with the global norm would be unrealistic. The data for the past few censuses question the validity of the UN assumption. Interestingly, the URGD taken as the average of the observed figures during the last thirty years gives much lower figures of urban population which appear very reasonable. Using the average figures, Dyson and Visaria (2004) have projected the percentage of urban population to be only 35.6 in 2025, which is much below the UN estimates. In fact, their projected figure for 2051 is only 44.3 per cent which is marginally higher than the figure of 42.5 per cent given by UN for the year 2025.

Given the declining mobility of population, including in-migration into urban areas, as inferred from the census and NSS data, even the figure of 44 per cent appears to be on the higher side. It would be safer to place the figure at around 40 per cent, unless of course there is a drastic change in the definition of urban centres.

MAJOR FINDINGS

First, this chapter attempts to analyse the trends in urbanization and migration. Urbanization, as stated earlier, has indicated a significant deceleration in its growth rates in recent decades. Except during the period 1971–81, urban growth as a whole has registered a steady decline in the country. The rate has gone down to 2.73 per cent in the present census (1991–2001) as compared to 3.1 per cent during 1981–91. Further, there also exist dramatic variations in urbanization across the states. The spatio-temporal variation has, therefore, affected the comparability of urban data significantly. Moreover, it tampers with urban growth and the level of urbanization in the concerned states and in the country as well. Data adjustment following such definitional dichotomy has, therefore, been one of the priorities of this study. Despite these differences, it has been argued that at the macro level urban growth has slowed down in the country.

Second, the trends and tempo of various streams of migration have been analysed. Data for lifetime, intercensal (decadal) migration has indicated a decline. Besides this temporal trend, internal migration (interstate) has also not increased. Both the male and female streams are showing a negative growth. A majority of the female migration in the country is due to marriage. In order to highlight the economic factors in migration, male migration has been taken up in particular which has presented a disturbing picture. The share of male intercensal migrants (rural and urban combined) has gone down from 11.3 per cent in 1961 to 9.4 per cent in 1971 and to 8.9 per cent in 1981 and further slowed down to 6.1 per cent in 1991. This distinct decline in male migration is also captured by the data from the NSS. The figure has gone down from 7.2 per cent in 1983 to 6.9 per cent in 1987. Though the figures have improved slightly in 1993–4, that can be attributed to a less rigorous definition of migrants in this round, giving a figure on the higher side.

Third, to have an overall view of urban growth in the country, the components of urban growth for four consecutive decades that is, from 1961–71 to 1991–2001 have been presented. Migration data for 2001 have not been published till now and therefore a hypothetical estimate for this variable has been adopted to show how these components have behaved over the years. Natural increase, having the lion's share, has maintained a more or less uniform percentage (about 60 per cent) during the different time spans. Similarly, RU migration has also performed in a uniform manner, claiming about one-fifth of the total urban growth. Share of new towns without the declassified towns has contributed 13.8 per cent in 1961–71 and decreased to 9.4 per cent in 1981–91. The residual share is accounted for by the areal expansion of UAs which has increased over this long time span. An element of spatial concentration in the process of urbanization can be noticed from the shares of these variables. Share of new towns outside the UA has decreased which indicates that lesser number of villages are achieving hierarchical upgradation to acquire an urban status. Increase in areal

expansion of UAs and an increase in the number of merged towns (from 103 in 1991 it has more than doubled to 221 in 2001) has confirmed this lopsidedness in urbanization.

Fourth, urban growth across the size categories presents some interesting features. Class I towns/cities have grown at a faster rate than other categories. Importantly, the share of urban population in the class I towns/cities is markedly higher than that in the other smaller categories. Consequently, the dominance of class I towns/cities has been maintained as compared to the smaller towns. Indeed, the class I towns/cities have had an edge over the other categories since 1941. Million-plus cities being the larger ones among the class I cities register a higher growth rate than the overall growth of all the class I cities. To be precise, the class I cities during 1981–91 have, on an average, recorded 2.96 per cent growth. Million-plus cities during the same period have grown at the rate of 3.25 per cent. In the next decade the growth rates for class I and million-plus cities are 2.76 and 2.88 per cent, respectively.

Fifth, the chapter has also tried to deal with the implications of structural reform and associated development strategy. So far the economic reforms have unfortunately not been able to bring about the desired changes in urbanization and migration in the country. The chapter has sought to provide an explanation about the extent to which the decline in urbanization and migration is attributable to the recent macroeconomic changes in the country. The capital intensive nature of industry during the 1990s has attracted less labour force and slowed down the tempo in RU migration. One can also notice that WPR has gone down in the late 1990s and the unemployment rate in the year 1999–2000 is higher than the 1993–4. Data from NSS confirm these disturbing trends. Decline in unemployment by daily and weekly status suggests corresponding rate in that more short-term or casual type of work is being generated in the aftermath of recent economic changes. Work opportunities are, therefore lower in the organized sector where growth in output is significantly high.

Urban poverty was much lower by six percentile points in the 1970s and early 1980s. Differential price rise in food grains in urban and rural areas has made this gap narrower. Larger towns having the potential to attract private participation in some of the basic services bring in more intra-city disparity as to who can and cannot pay for basic and reliable urban services. Small towns on the other hand, already having lesser number of households and lesser coverage of basic amenities as captured in 1991 census data, cannot attract private investments. This economic and social disparity has affected the growth of urbanization and migration.

In the end, the chapter has commented on the future projections of urban population. Projections by Indian as well as UN studies appear to have overestimated the future level of urbanization. Given the trend of immobility of population and the nature of economic changes that this country has been exposed to, this chapter has projected a 40 per cent level of urbanization for the country as a whole by the middle of the twenty-first century.

IV

Trends and Pattern of Urbanization
An Interstate Analysis

INTRODUCTION

The level and rate of growth of urban population at the macro level in recent decades have been analysed in the previous chapter. For understanding the dynamics of urban development in a large country like India, it is important to examine the changes in the levels and pace of urbanization across the states. The present chapter attempts to do that based on the data from population census from 1951 to 2001 with special emphasis on the developments in the post-liberalization phase. It analyses the regional pattern of urbanization, focusing on the 1990s and examines how it makes a sharp departure from the past pattern. Besides, the chapter also examines the size class variation of urban centres over the period.

The regional variations in the distribution of urban population are significant. A large proportion of urban population is concentrated in the six most urbanized states, namely, Maharashtra, Gujarat, Tamil Nadu, Karnataka, Punjab, and West Bengal, accounting for about half of the country's urban population. Looking at the 2001 Census figures of individual states separately, Goa emerges as the most urbanized state in the country with 49.77 per cent of its population within the urban frame, besides the union capital territory of Delhi and other union territories. However,

among the major states, Tamil Nadu has claimed to be the most urbanized state comprising 43.86 per cent urban population, followed by Maharashtra (42.40 per cent), Gujarat (37.35 per cent), Karnataka (33.98 per cent), Punjab (33.95 per cent), and West Bengal (28.03 per cent). Of the three hill states of north India, the newly created state of Uttaranchal is the most urbanized with an urban population of 25.59 per cent, whereas Himachal Pradesh is the least urbanized with 9.79 per cent urban population. Among the north-eastern states of the country, Mizoram is the most urbanized state reporting an urban population of 49.50 per cent, while Assam is the least urbanized with 12.72 per cent only (Table 4.1 and Map 4.1). It needs to be mentioned that all these figures, particularly the levels of urbanization, will have to be understood and accepted subject to the definitional and data issues discussed in the earlier chapter.

THE CHANGING PATTERN OF URBANIZATION IN THE POST-INDEPENDENCE PERIOD

PATTERN OF LEVEL OF URBANIZATION ACROSS STATES

The levels of urbanization in most of the economically developed states were high in the

TABLE 4.1
Level of Urbanization Across States

States	1971	1981	1991	2001
Andhra Pradesh	19.31	23.25	26.84	27.08
Arunachal Pradesh	3.70	6.32	12.21	20.41
Assam	–	9.88	11.08	12.72
Bihar	10.00	12.46	13.17	10.47
Chhattisgarh	–	–	–	20.08
Delhi	89.70	92.84	89.93	93.01
Goa	26.44*	32.46*	41.02	49.77
Gujarat	28.08	31.08	34.40	37.35
Haryana	17.66	21.96	24.79	29.00
Himachal Pradesh	6.99	7.72	8.70	9.79
Jammu & Kashmir	–	21.05	23.83	24.88
Jharkhand	–	–	–	22.25
Karnataka	24.31	28.91	30.91	33.98
Kerala	16.24	18.78	26.44	25.97
Madhya Pradesh	16.29	20.31	23.21	26.67
Maharashtra	31.17	35.03	38.73	42.40
Manipur	13.19	26.44	27.69	23.88
Meghalaya	14.55	18.03	18.69	19.63
Mizoram	11.36	25.17	46.20	49.50
Nagaland	9.95	15.54	17.28	17.74
Orissa	8.41	11.82	13.43	14.97
Punjab	23.73	27.72	29.72	33.95
Rajasthan	17.63	20.93	22.88	23.38
Sikkim	9.37	16.23	9.12	11.10
Tamil Nadu	30.26	32.98	34.20	43.86
Tripura	10.43	10.98	15.26	17.02
Uttar Pradesh	14.02	18.01	19.89	20.78
Uttaranchal	–	–	–	25.59
West Bengal	24.75	26.49	27.39	28.03
Union Territories				
Andaman & Nicobar Islands	22.77	26.36	26.80	32.67
Chandigarh	90.55	93.60	89.69	89.78
Dadra & Nagar Haveli	–	6.67	8.47	22.89
Daman & Diu	–	–	46.86	36.26
Lakshadweep	–	46.31	56.29	44.47
Pondicherry	42.04	52.32	64.05	66.57
All India	20.22	23.73	25.72	27.78

Notes: The figures for Goa in 1971 and 1981 (*) correspond to Goa, Daman, and Diu. Data on Assam (1981) and Jammu and Kashmir (1991) are based on their projected population as census was not held in Assam (1981) and Jammu and Kashmir (1991).

Sources: Census of India 1981, 1991, Paper-2; Census of India 2001.

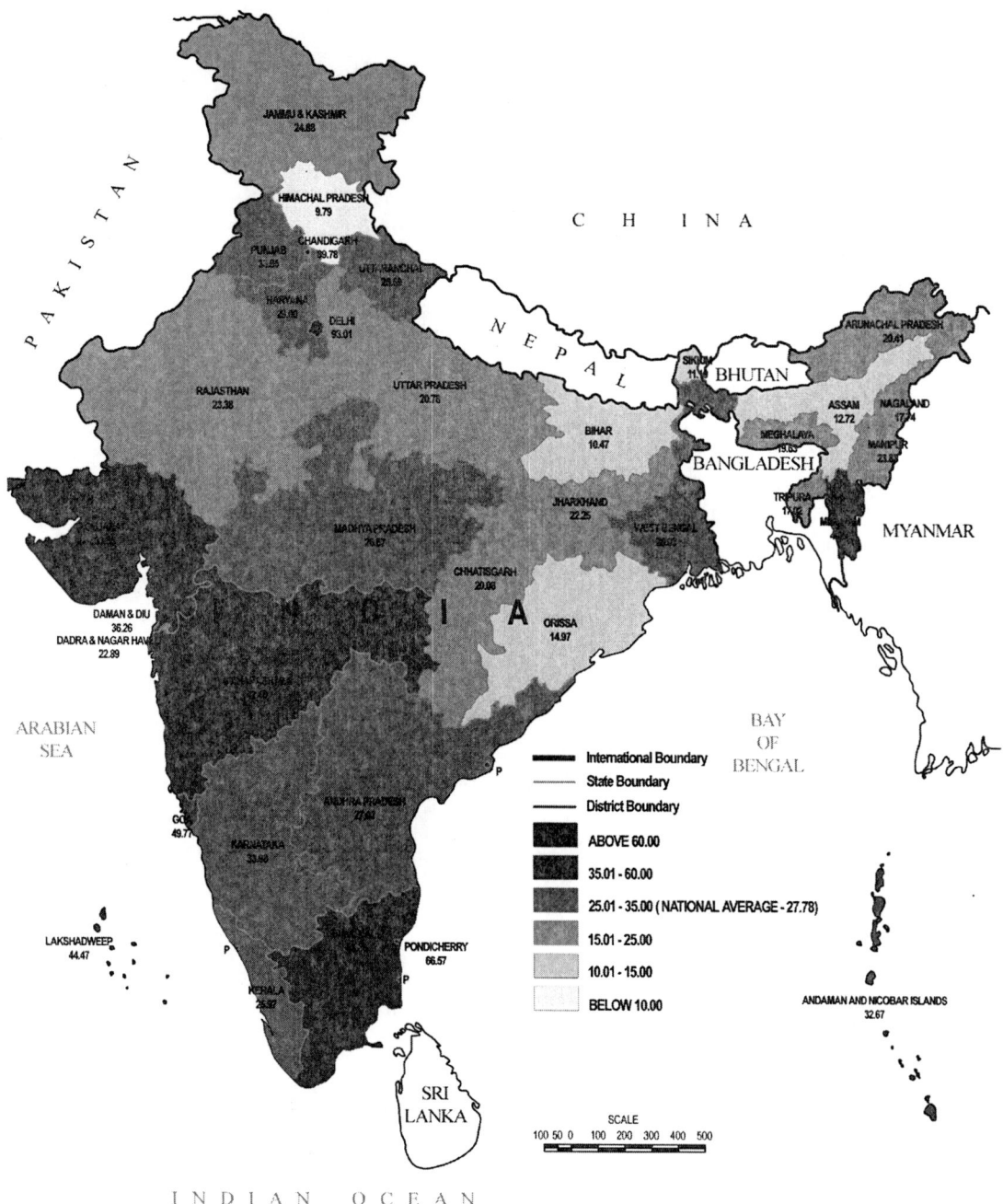

MAP 4.1: Level of Urbanization—India (2001)
Source: Census of India 2001.

post-independence period, as revealed through the census data presented for the last four decades in Table 4.1. West Bengal, Maharashtra, and Tamil Nadu, which had high per capita income, reported a large percentage of population residing in urban areas. This is due to the concentration of economic activities in the three metropolises of Calcutta, Bombay, and Madras (now Kolkata, Mumbai, and Chennai, respectively) and a few of their linked towns. That much of this urban growth was prompted by migration from rural areas in distress is a part of Indian economic history. After independence, the rapid increase in urbanization in these few states can be attributed to increased opportunities of manufacturing employment, infrastructural facilities, and levels of social development.

PATTERN OF GROWTH OF URBANIZATION ACROSS STATES

Importantly, a distinction has to be drawn between the pace and pattern of urban growth from the levels of urbanization. Since independence until 1991 (Table 4.2) the pace of growth has generally been high in relatively backward states. Bihar, Uttar Pradesh, Rajasthan, Orissa, and Madhya Pradesh figure at the top in the list of states arranged in a descending order. This puts a question mark on the relationship between urban growth and economic development. However, a few among the developed states, such as Maharashtra, Gujarat, and Haryana, too, recorded high or medium growth, although others like West Bengal, Tamil Nadu, and Punjab experienced low urban growth.

URBAN PROCESS: THE ISSUE OF DUALISM

The urban scenario in the post-independence period was, thus, characterized by dualism. The developed states attracted population to urban areas due to industrialization and

infrastructural investment. In the backward states too—particularly their backward districts and small and medium towns—the urban growth can partly be attributed to government investment in the district and taluka headquarters, programmes of urban industrial dispersal, and transfer of funds from the states to local bodies through a need-based or what is popularly known as 'a gap-filling approach'. A part of the RU migration into smaller towns is also explained in terms of push factors, owing to the lack of diversification in the agrarian economy.

During the 1990s, however, we see a significant departure from the earlier decades. Developed states like Tamil Nadu, Punjab, Haryana, Maharashtra, and Gujarat have registered urban growth above the national average. West Bengal is the only exception whose growth rate is not particularly impressive. In the backward states, on the other hand, urban growth has been either below the national average or at the most equal to that. The process of urbanization has, thus, become concentrated in developed regions with the exclusion of the backward states. Furthermore, the larger cities have recorded relatively higher growth when compared to smaller towns. This could partly be attributed to decentralization whereby the responsibilities of resource mobilization for infrastructural projects have been given to the local bodies. Large municipal bodies with a strong economic base, particularly those located in developed states, have had an advantage in this regard which is manifested in their high economic and demographic growth.

TRENDS AND PATTERN OF URBANIZATION ACROSS SIZE CATEGORIES OF TOWNS

The size class distribution of urban population and changes therein over the past two decades

TABLE 4.2
Annual Exponential Growth Rate of Urbanization Across States

States	1971–81	1981–91	1991–2001
Andhra Pradesh	3.94	3.55	1.37
Arunachal Pradesh	8.32	9.28	7.00
Assam	–	3.27	3.09
Bihar	4.34	2.65	2.57
Chhattisgarh	–	–	3.09
Delhi	4.56	3.79	4.14
Goa	4.37	3.96	3.32
Gujarat	3.42	2.90	2.80
Haryana	4.65	3.58	4.11
Himachal Pradesh	3.02	3.11	2.81
Jammu & Kashmir	–	3.78	6.87
Jharkhand	–	–	2.55
Karnataka	4.08	2.55	2.53
Kerala	3.19	4.76	0.74
Madhya Pradesh	4.45	3.71	2.71
Maharashtra	3.35	3.27	2.95
Manipur	9.70	2.98	1.21
Meghalaya	4.87	3.10	3.16
Mizoram	11.79	9.57	3.27
Nagaland	8.49	5.58	5.27
Orissa	5.21	3.08	2.61
Punjab	3.62	2.55	3.19
Rajasthan	4.52	3.31	2.71
Sikkim	9.55	–3.23	4.83
Tamil Nadu	2.45	1.76	3.56
Tripura	3.26	6.19	2.53
Uttar Pradesh	4.78	3.29	2.84
Uttaranchal	–	–	2.84
West Bengal	2.75	2.54	1.84
Union Territories			
Andaman & Nicobar Islands	6.38	4.10	4.40
Chandigarh	5.92	3.07	3.40
Dadra & Nagar Haveli	–	5.28	14.59
Daman & Diu	–	4.93	1.87
Lakshadweep	–	4.46	–0.77
Pondicherry	4.66	4.92	2.26
All India	3.79	3.09	2.73

Source: Computed from Census of India 1981, 1991, Paper-2; Census of India 2001.

(Table 4.3a) provide interesting insights into the development dynamics of the states. The smaller towns with population below 20,000 have been clubbed into one category for analysing the growth profile as also structure of urban population. The share of population in class I cities has been going up consistently, as noted in the previous chapter. The inter-state variation in the share is very high and reveals a regional pattern. Besides smaller states/UTs like Chandigarh, Delhi, Pondicherry, and Meghalaya, those that have a high concentration of urban population in class I cities are the economically prosperous states of West Bengal, Maharashtra, and Tamil Nadu. Three other developed states that had a high concentration in these cities are Gujarat, Karnataka, and Andhra Pradesh. Kerala also falls in this category due to its unique settlement pattern identifying a large number of class I cities. The less developed states like Rajasthan, Orissa, Madhya Pradesh, and Uttar Pradesh exhibit a low percentage of urban population in these class I cities. The shares of class II and class III towns, however, have remained stable in most of the states, as is the case at the national level. The only exceptions are the smaller states like Meghalaya, Nagaland, Himachal Pradesh, Goa, Andaman and Nicobar Islands, and Mizoram where the number of towns in different categories is small and shifting of a few towns makes a significant difference in the percentage shares. The shares of population in smaller towns (classes IV, V, and VI) have declined significantly during the 1980s, with the sole exceptions of Goa, Sikkim, and Tripura. The general trend in most of the states is towards concentration of population in the larger cities.

The pattern has not changed very significantly during the 1990s (Table 4.3b). The concentration in larger cities has been going up in most of the states.[1] The six states that reported a high share of population in class I cities in earlier years have generally maintained their position in 2001 as well. Even the less developed state of Kerala has registered an increase in this percentage figure. The only state where the share of the large cities has declined is Tamil Nadu and this is due to emergence of a large number of 'new' towns belonging to lower-order size categories. Further, the new states of Chhattisgarh and Jharkhand report high figures for the share of class I cities, much higher than that of their parent states of Madhya Pradesh and Bihar. The state of Uttaranchal, however, has lower concentration of population in these cities—much below the national average and even below the figure for the state of Uttar Pradesh. The population shares claimed by the class II and class III towns have remained stable in most of the states during the 1990s as well (Table 4.3b). The exceptions are once again the smaller states, wherein a shift of one or two towns has a significant impact on the size class distribution of urban population. In case of the smaller states, the percentage share has gone down in almost all the states (with a few exceptions of small north-eastern states), as is the case for the country as a whole.

GROWTH RATE OF COMMON TOWNS/UAs

The growth rates of urban centres in different size classes have been computed by taking the base-year classification for both initial as well as the terminal years, to take care of the problems of graduation of towns into higher categories during a decade. The rates for the

[1] Andaman and Nicobar Islands merit a special mention as the share has gone up from zero to 85 per cent due to the city of Port Blair graduating to a class I city.

TABLE 4.3a

Percentage of Population in Different Size Categories to Total Urban Population (1981 and 1991)

States/UTs	Class I		Class II		Class III		Class IV–VII		Total	
	1981	1991	1981	1991	1981	1991	1981	1991	1981	1991
Andhra Pradesh	53.69	66.88	16.17	12.60	20.95	16.53	9.19	3.99	100	100
Arunachal Pradesh	–	–	–	–	–	–	100	100	100	100
Assam	NA	37.56	NA	11.65	NA	25.61	NA	25.18	NA	100
Bihar	52.62	54.12	9.00	14.38	17.58	19.26	20.80	12.24	100	100
Delhi	99.32	99.38	–	–	–	–	0.68	0.62	100	100
Goa	–	–	65.61	51.84	8.05	6.59	26.34	41.57	100	100
Gujarat	57.92	66.43	14.53	12.73	13.37	10.52	14.18	10.32	100	100
Haryana	56.64	58.54	10.82	15.11	14.80	11.95	17.74	14.40	100	100
Himachal Pradesh	–	24.70	21.54	–	12.49	19.60	65.97	55.70	100	100
Jammu & Kashmir	65.80	NA	–	NA	11.74	NA	22.46	NA	100	NA
Karnataka	58.60	64.60	6.46	7.35	17.75	17.68	17.19	10.37	100	100
Kerala	53.13	66.34	9.52	7.22	31.86	19.08	5.49	7.36	100	100
Madhya Pradesh	46.84	50.38	18.00	13.94	12.24	12.82	22.92	22.86	100	100
Maharashtra	75.24	77.85	5.95	6.49	10.88	10.39	7.93	5.27	100	100
Manipur	41.72	39.66	–	–	11.18	17.96	47.10	42.38	100	100
Meghalaya	72.39	67.54	–	–	14.61	20.18	13.00	12.28	100	100
Mizoram	–	48.68	61.15	–	–	17.79	38.85	33.53	100	100
Nagaland	–	–	–	52.38	55.90	21.71	44.10	25.91	100	100
Orissa	41.63	44.43	12.76	14.65	21.83	19.73	23.78	21.19	100	100
Punjab	46.40	54.36	13.28	19.79	21.31	12.89	19.01	12.96	100	100
Rajasthan	46.52	50.09	10.05	13.67	22.02	21.31	21.41	14.93	100	100
Sikkim	–	–	–	–	71.93	67.52	28.07	32.48	100	100
Tamil Nadu	62.19	65.96	15.99	15.21	12.52	11.19	9.30	7.64	100	100
Tripura	58.60	37.62	–	–	9.22	27.59	32.18	34.79	100	100

(contd.)

TABLE 4.3a: contd.

States/UTs	Class I		Class II		Class III		Class IV–VII		Total	
	1981	1991	1981	1991	1981	1991	1981	1991	1981	1991
Uttar Pradesh	51.49	55.99	12.71	11.45	12.34	13.94	23.46	18.62	100	100
West Bengal	76.84	81.71	10.78	6.58	7.71	7.66	4.67	4.05	100	100
Union Territories										
Andaman & Nicobar Islands	–	–	–	100	100	–	–	–	100	100
Chandigarh	100	100	–	–	–	–	–	–	100	100
Dadra & Nagar Haveli	–	–	–	–	–	–	100	100	100	100
Daman & Diu	–	–	–	–	72.37	100	27.63	–	100	100
Lakshadweep	–	–	–	–	–	–	100	100	100	100
Pondicherry	79.55	77.64	–	11.97	13.74	3.93	6.71	6.46	100	100
All India	60.32	64.89	11.63	10.96	14.30	13.33	13.75	10.82	100	100

Notes: All–India average excludes Assam in 1981 and Jammu & Kashmir in 1991. Bihar, Madhya Pradesh, and Uttar Pradesh represent their undivided status. NA—Not available.

Source: Computed from the data of Paper-2, Rural–Urban Distribution, 1981, 1991.

TABLE 4.3b

Percentage of Population in Different Size Categories to Total Urban Population (2001)

States/UTs	Class I	Class II	Class III	Class IV	Class V	Class VI	Total
Andhra Pradesh	75.31	13.95	8.35	1.69	0.68	0.04	100
Arunachal Pradesh	–	–	37.66	43.23	15.40	3.72	100
Assam	44.34	14.37	18.56	13.74	8.44	0.54	100
Bihar		59.31	13.66	23.57	3.23	0.23	–
100							
Chhattisgarh	63.02	8.94	13.17	11.12	3.74	–	100
Delhi	99.78	–	–	0.12	0.10	–	100
Goa	15.65	28.90	9.20	29.55	14.60	2.09	100
Gujarat	76.50	9.67	9.47	3.55	0.67	0.14	100
Haryana	72.57	5.78	11.89	7.65	2.03	0.07	100
Himachal Pradesh	24.30	–	25.87	19.06	19.10	11.66	100
Jammu & Kashmir	63.03	14.70	3.89	10.02	5.85	2.51	100
Jharkhand	71.34	7.09	12.34	5.16	3.51	0.55	100
Karnataka	67.20	9.63	17.28	4.68	1.07	0.13	100
Kerala	68.82	11.32	14.05	4.98	0.82	–	100
Madhya Pradesh	55.77	12.00	15.95	12.13	4.01	0.15	100
Maharashtra	79.70	6.66	9.42	3.31	0.84	0.07	100
Manipur	43.12	–	19.41	17.12	17.66	2.69	100
Meghalaya	59.19	12.90	10.39	15.61	1.91	–	100
Mizoram	52.08	–	16.73	15.19	10.48	5.51	100
Nagaland	30.44	22.27	34.40	12.89	–	–	100
Orissa	48.41	17.12	18.20	12.65	3.17	0.45	100
Punjab	58.39	16.45	12.50	9.82	2.52	0.33	100
Rajasthan	57.23	13.94	20.80	6.92	1.00	0.11	100
Sikkim	–	–	48.60	24.45	9.05	17.90	100
Tamil Nadu	56.35	11.64	12.21	14.37	5.26	0.17	100

(contd.)

TABLE 4.3b: contd.

States/UTs	Class I	Class II	Class III	Class IV	Class V	Class VI	Total
Tripura	34.86	–	33.37	21.12	10.65	–	100
Uttar Pradesh	62.16	9.95	14.40	10.39	2.97	0.13	100
Uttaranchal	47.10	12.04	20.47	9.46	8.91	2.02	100
West Bengal	83.54	4.34	5.96	3.14	2.59	0.43	100
Union Territories							
Andaman & Nicobar Islands	86.07	–	–	–	13.93	–	100
Chandigarh	100.00	–	–	–	–	–	100
Dadra & Nagar Haveli	–	–	100.00	–	–	–	100
Daman and Diu	–	–	100.00	–	–	–	100
Lakshadweep	–	–	–	37.53	62.47	–	100
Pondicherry	78.01	11.47	10.52	–	–	–	100
All India	68.67	9.67	12.23	6.84	2.36	0.23	100

Source: Computed from Census of India 2001.

class I cities work out as generally higher than the smaller order towns in the developed states during the period 1971–91, as was noted for the country (Table 4.4a). In states such as Andhra Pradesh, Gujarat, Haryana, Karnataka, Maharashtra, Tamil Nadu, and Punjab,[2] the growth rates of these cities are significantly higher than that of all lower-order towns except those in Class VI category.[3] West Bengal is the only exception among the developed states where the growth rate of class I cities is below that of the lower-order towns. This, however, is the pattern observed for the less developed states like Bihar, Kerala, Madhya Pradesh, Rajasthan, and Uttar Pradesh. Here, the smaller towns have grown at similar or a higher rate than class I cities.

The growth pattern has remained similar during 1991–2001 as well (Table 4.4b). The developed states like Punjab, Gujarat, Maharashtra, and Tamil Nadu exhibit a pattern identical to that of the preceding two decades. Importantly, a few other backward states like Himachal Pradesh, Bihar, Rajasthan, Orissa, and Assam, too, exhibit this pattern that is, their class I cities growing at a faster rate than the lower order towns. The only exceptions, besides a few of the smaller states, are Uttar Pradesh, Madhya Pradesh, and Kerala among the backward states, and Haryana, Karnataka, and Andhra Pradesh among the developed states. The pattern in West Bengal remains similar to that in the previous decades.

[2] In case of Punjab, this holds good for 1981–91 only.

[3] It has been mentioned in Chapter III that class VI towns are of a special type as many of them come to exist with the establishment of a large public or private sector unit. Their socio-economic characteristics including demographic growth do not follow the pattern observed in case of different size classes of urban centres.

In analysing the dynamics of growth in urban centres we have considered three time spans, that is, 1971–81, 1981–91, and 1991–2001. The combined populations of the common towns in each of these size categories have been considered and their growth rates indicated in Tables 4.4a and 4.4b. In the next set of Tables, that is, 4.5a and 4.5b, the growth rates have been calculated somewhat differently. Here the individual exponential growth rate of each of the towns in a particular size category has been considered and on that basis averages for the relevant time span presented.

It is observed that the average growth rates for class I cities are higher than those of other size categories in most of the states during the 1980s and 1990s. The pattern is similar to what has been noted in Table 4.4. This reconfirms our thesis that the larger urban centres are experiencing higher demographic growth during the 1980s and 1990s, as was the case in earlier decades (Kundu 1983).

DISPARITY OF URBAN GROWTH IN DIFFERENT SIZE CATEGORIES

It is important to look at the disparity in growth rates to ascertain stability of growth in different size categories. Tables 4.6a and 4.6b give the coefficients of variation for the growth rates of urban centres belonging to the different size categories, during the 1980s and 1990s. Significantly, the class I cities show greater stability and consistency in growth, reflected in lower coefficients of variation during the 1980s. The disparity in their growth rates is noted to have gone down during the 1980s compared to the 1970s (Bhalla and Kundu 1984). As far as the lower-order size categories are concerned, the coefficients of variation in growth rates have remained stable or have gone up during the two decades.

TABLE 4.4a

Annual Exponential Growth Rate of Population in Common Towns/UAs during 1971–81 and 1981–91

States/UTs	Class I		Class II		Class III		Class IV–VI	
	1971–81	1981–91	1971–81	1981–91	1971–81	1981–91	1971–81	1981–91
Andhra Pradesh	3.80	4.00	3.69	3.35	3.76	2.81	3.55	2.58
Arunachal Pradesh	–	–	–	–	–	–	4.57	5.91
Assam	NA	NA	NA	NA	NA	NA	NA	NA
Bihar	4.48	2.14	2.40	1.97	4.34	2.51	3.59	2.84
Delhi	4.52	3.80	–	–	–	–	–	2.62
Goa	–	–	2.65	1.60	3.54	1.95	3.80	3.64
Gujarat	4.11	3.13	2.68	2.66	2.79	2.14	2.87	2.31
Haryana	5.16	3.42	4.10	2.77	3.39	2.84	2.99	3.51
Himachal Pradesh	–	–	2.42	4.09	–0.25	0.33	1.98	2.69
Jammu & Kashmir	NA	NA	NA	NA	NA	NA	NA	NA
Karnataka	4.44	2.95	3.59	2.99	3.19	1.85	2.88	1.90
Kerala	2.71	3.32	3.46	4.86	1.65	2.56	3.16	2.36
Madhya Pradesh	3.95	2.85	3.48	3.34	3.95	2.75	3.15	2.77
Maharashtra	3.48	3.28	3.08	2.41	2.66	2.47	2.34	2.62
Manipur	4.45	2.48	–	–	–	3.26	8.37	3.17
Meghalaya	3.53	2.41	–	–	–	2.59	6.80	6.67
Mizoram	–	–	–	7.28	8.53	–	10.51	7.20
Nagaland	–	–	–	–	4.66	4.93	5.34	4.47
Orissa	–	4.80	3.17	3.29	2.65	3.91	2.40	3.86
2.11								
Punjab	3.32	3.04	3.58	2.61	2.86	2.65	3.11	2.00
Rajasthan	4.29	3.28	3.38	2.68	3.84	3.21	3.31	2.63
Sikkim	–	–	–	–	–	–3.80	9.54	–1.70
Tamil Nadu	2.77	1.88	2.20	1.32	2.06	1.35	1.71	1.52
Tripura	2.76	1.76	–	–	–	2.19	1.59	1.69

(contd.)

TABLE 4.4: contd.

States/UTs	Class I		Class II		Class III		Class IV–VI	
	1971–81	1981–91	1971–81	1981–91	1971–81	1981–91	1971–81	1981–91
Uttar Pradesh	2.68	3.14	3.24	2.80	3.63	3.29	3.31	2.87
West Bengal	2.32	2.05	2.88	3.37	4.12	3.50	3.59	3.59
Union Territories								
Andaman & Nicobar Islands	–	–	–	–	6.38	4.10	–	–
Chandigarh	5.96	3.06	–	–	–	–	–	5.27
Dadra & Nagar Haveli	–	–	–	–	–	–	–	–
Daman & Diu	–	–	–	–	–	–	2.09	4.93
Lakshadweep	–	–	–	–	–	–	–	2.29
Pondicherry	4.84	4.68	–	–	5.09	3.54	1.86	3.70
All India	3.46	2.96	3.09	2.75	3.33	2.59	3.07	2.57

Notes: NA—Not available as Census was not held in Assam and Jammu & Kashmir in 1981 and 1991, respectively. Bihar, Madhya Pradesh, and Uttar Pradesh represent their undivided status.

Source: Paper-2, Rural–Urban Distribution 1991.

TABLE 4.4b

Annual Exponential Growth Rate of Population in Common Towns/UAs during 1991–2001

States/UTs	Class I	Class II	Class III	Class IV	Class V	Class VI
Andhra Pradesh	2.02	2.14	1.71	1.74	-0.03	–
Arunachal Pradesh	–	–	–	4.46	3.11	–
Assam	3.05	2.70	2.16	2.10	2.07	4.70
Bihar	3.23	2.74	2.60	2.33	2.95	1.47
Chhattisgarh	3.94	2.02	2.00	1.38	1.40	–
Delhi	4.18	–	–	–	–	–
Goa	–	1.82	2.37	1.61	0.75	2.18
Gujarat	3.60	1.98	2.10	1.99	1.87	-1.38
Haryana	4.12	4.80	3.30	2.84	3.84	5.58
Himachal Pradesh	2.70	–	2.41	2.30	1.86	2.69
Jammu & Kashmir	6.44	–	8.30	5.07	6.16	6.75
Jharkhand	2.79	2.48	3.05	1.78	0.98	-1.71
Karnataka	2.69	3.03	2.18	2.52	0.98	0.56
Kerala	1.10	1.38	1.12	1.68	2.12	–
Madhya Pradesh	2.67	2.84	2.72	2.27	2.04	-0.25
Maharashtra	2.91	2.72	2.05	2.55	2.41	3.23
Manipur	1.93	–	1.96	1.79	1.97	1.01
Meghalaya	1.82	–	2.24	4.24	3.15	–
Mizoram	3.92	–	2.69	3.29	2.41	1.80
Nagaland	–	5.38	2.84	7.38	5.37	–
Orissa	–	3.08	1.87	2.13	1.58	1.88
-0.64						
Punjab	2.99	2.34	2.23	2.26	2.59	6.45
Rajasthan	3.24	2.82	2.39	2.42	1.65	–
Sikkim	–	–	1.53	–	–	3.00
Tamil Nadu	1.71	0.97	1.31	1.16	1.31	-0.83

(contd.)

TABLE 4.4b: contd.

States/UTs	Class I	Class II	Class III	Class IV	Class V	Class VI
Tripura	–	–	1.35	2.39	2.63	1.85
Uttar Pradesh	2.87	2.46	2.83	2.36	2.42	2.83
Uttaranchal	3.19	2.46	2.13	1.87	2.31	2.73
West Bengal	1.99	2.43	2.23	1.60	1.68	0.52
Union Territories						
Andaman & Nicobar Islands	–	2.90	–	–	–	–
Chandigarh	3.40	–	–	–	–	–
Dadra & Nagar Haveli	–	–	–	6.24	–	–
Daman and Diu	–	–	1.87	–	–	–
Lakshadweep	–	–	–	–	–	–
Pondicherry	2.31	1.85	2.38	–	–	–
All India	2.76	2.37	2.27	2.19	2.22	3.26

Source: Computed from Census of India 2001 at the website.

TABLE 4.5a

The Average of Growth Rates (1981–91) of Towns as per their Size Class Distribution in 1981

States/UTs	1981–91					
	Class I	Class II	Class III	Class IV	Class V	Class VI
Andhra Pradesh	3.35	3.27	2.78	3.08	2.42	0.80
Arunachal Pradesh	–	–	–	–	7.07	3.82
Assam	10.70	5.12	3.79	4.83	5.77	6.49
Bihar	2.07	2.50	2.76	2.59	3.08	–
Chhattisgarh	2.86	3.06	2.97	2.45	3.57	3.84
Delhi	3.85	–	–	–	–	–
Goa	1.60	1.97	1.13	3.52	11.18	–
Gujarat	3.10	2.17	2.17	1.85	2.59	4.15
Haryana	2.92	2.83	2.69	3.96	3.08	3.02
Himachal Pradesh	–	4.13	0.35	2.74	3.04	2.98
Jammu & Kashmir	3.34	–	2.26	3.57	3.43	4.41
Jharkhand	2.68	1.45	2.13	2.15	1.57	–0.08
Karnataka	2.71	2.75	1.95	1.96	1.77	2.01
Kerala	3.35	4.79	2.58	1.21	1.34	–
Madhya Pradesh	2.60	3.32	2.66	2.77	3.08	1.79
Maharashtra	4.03	2.43	2.59	2.56	2.14	13.98
Manipur	2.59	–	–	2.52	3.69	2.08
Meghalaya	2.46	–	2.67	4.66	2.43	9.69
Mizoram	–	7.35	–	7.27	7.21	–
Nagaland	–	–	4.81	4.37	4.73	–
Orissa	3.11	2.59	2.38	2.07	2.23	5.22
Punjab	2.31	2.62	2.63	1.88	2.17	1.08
Rajasthan	3.32	2.65	3.21	2.72	2.26	–
Sikkim	–	–	–3.84	–	–	–1.23

(contd.)

TABLE 4.5a: contd.

States/UTs	1981–91					
	Class I	Class II	Class III	Class IV	Class V	Class VI
Tamil Nadu	1.43	1.30	1.44	1.45	1.81	2.54
Tripura	–	–	2.19	1.48	2.11	2.60
Uttar Pradesh	2.99	2.80	3.22	2.92	2.72	2.90
Uttaranchal	2.39	2.49	3.69	3.64	3.43	3.47
West Bengal	2.55	3.23	3.77	2.88	2.91	8.28
Union Territories						
Andaman & Nicobar Islands	–	–	4.12	–	–	–
Chandigarh	3.09	–	–	–	–	–
Dadra & Nagar Haveli	–	–	–	5.28	–	–
Daman & Diu	–	–	2.48	–	9.45	–
Lakshadweep	–	–	–	–	–	–
Pondicherry	4.68	–	2.28	5.57	–	–
All India	2.97	2.72	2.62	2.57	2.89	4.13

Note: The size class distribution is made on the basis of population in the base year and average of individual growth rates of the towns/cities is computed.

Source: Paper-2, Rural–Urban Distribution 1991.

TABLE 4.5b

The Average of Growth Rates (1991–2001) of Towns as per their Size Class Distribution in 1991

States/UTs	1991–2001					
	Class I	Class II	Class III	Class IV	Class V	Class VI
Andhra Pradesh	1.78	2.19	1.74	1.74	-0.02	–
Arunachal Pradesh	–	–	–	4.37	3.03	–
Assam	2.80	2.73	2.08	2.08	2.04	5.15
Bihar	2.69	2.79	2.53	2.39	2.87	1.47
Chhattisgarh	4.67	2.17	2.15	1.41	1.42	–
Delhi	4.18	–	–	–	–	–
Goa	–	1.87	2.37	1.65	0.75	2.16
Gujarat	3.12	1.88	2.09	1.96	1.86	1.99
Haryana	3.75	4.81	3.35	2.86	3.84	5.47
Jammu & Kashmir	7.71	–	8.34	4.98	6.16	6.75
Jharkhand	2.64	2.41	2.99	1.75	1.11	-1.71
Himachal Pradesh	2.70	–	2.41	2.40	1.99	2.68
Karnataka	2.21	2.96	2.15	2.64	0.87	0.55
Kerala	1.10	1.55	1.16	1.54	2.24	–
Madhya Pradesh	2.44	2.95	2.72	2.30	2.08	-0.25
Maharashtra	2.77	2.78	2.03	2.51	2.43	3.17
Manipur	1.93	–	1.92	1.80	1.96	1.21
Meghalaya	1.82	–	2.16	4.24	3.23	–
Mizoram	3.92	–	2.63	3.29	2.43	1.80
Nagaland	–	5.32	2.89	7.10	5.35	–
Orissa 0.63	–	3.04	1.84	2.14	1.55	1.90
Punjab	2.71	2.32	2.20	2.36	2.37	6.30
Rajasthan	2.82	2.78	2.42	2.42	1.63	–
Sikkim	–	–	1.53	–	–	2.95

(contd.)

TABLE 4.5b: contd.

States/UTs	1991–2001					
	Class I	Class II	Class III	Class IV	Class V	Class VI
Tamil Nadu	1.41	0.98	1.27	1.21	1.20	-1.01
Tripura	–	–	1.24	2.47	2.66	1.85
Uttar Pradesh	2.84	2.42	2.82	2.36	2.41	2.87
Uttaranchal	3.21	2.52	2.12	1.89	2.37	3.68
West Bengal	2.23	2.45	2.28	1.61	1.67	0.52
Union Territories						
Andaman & Nicobar Islands	–	2.90	–	–	–	–
Chandigarh	3.40	–	–	–	–	–
Dadra & Nagar Haveli	–	–	–	6.24	–	–
Daman & Diu	–	–	1.71	–	–	–
Lakshadweep	–	–	–	–	–	–
Pondicherry	2.31	1.85	2.80	–	–	–
All India	2.55	2.38	2.27	2.20	2.21	3.54

Note: The size class distribution is made on the basis of population in the base year and average of individual growth rates of the towns/cities is computed.

Source: Computed from Census of India 2001 at the website.

TABLE 4.6a

The Coefficients of Variation of Growth Rates (1981–91) of Towns as per their Size Class Distribution in 1981

States/UTs	1981–91					
	Class I	Class II	Class III	Class IV	Class V	Class VI
Andhra Pradesh	54.32	77.55	51.45	62.23	62.55	–
Arunachal Pradesh	–	–	–	–	44.70	–
Assam	–	47.31	71.46	101.06	106.95	154.27
Bihar	22.29	56.39	47.67	67.23	75.58	–
Chhattisgarh	27.54	59.50	30.73	33.30	44.29	–
Delhi	–	–	–	–	–	–
Goa	–	61.82	–	119.64	142.12	114.27
Gujarat	46.27	93.79	58.28	81.03	106.19	109.67
Haryana	57.25	44.55	46.59	214.86	65.79	55.11
Himachal Pradesh	–	–	215.03	60.66	109.03	90.28
Jammu & Kashmir	12.78	–	15.18	67.52	69.66	191.15
Jharkhand	45.24	129.78	47.03	75.69	129.91	–
Karnataka	43.52	86.19	61.00	69.56	92.38	111.59
Kerala	45.31	87.63	166.06	46.55	7.77	–
Madhya Pradesh	35.53	56.76	47.11	49.67	64.78	145.61
Maharashtra	57.94	45.67	62.36	65.93	82.69	212.12
Manipur	–	–	–	39.66	110.61	87.10
Meghalaya	–	–	–	–	–	70.49
Mizoram	–	–	–	–	47.48	–
Nagaland	–	–	27.67	45.08	22.53	–
Orissa 159.99	–	70.55	40.25	39.97	52.61	74.87
Punjab	84.06	27.07	93.98	90.91	71.35	78.40
Rajasthan	33.21	28.11	33.97	40.81	63.28	–
Sikkim	–	–	–	–	–	–260.08

(contd.)

TABLE 4.6a: contd.

States/UTs	1981–91					
	Class I	Class II	Class III	Class IV	Class V	Class VI
Tamil Nadu	65.32	50.99	74.10	87.46	119.59	108.49
Tripura	–	–	–	41.78	23.84	62.27
Uttar Pradesh	45.28	31.25	39.41	63.27	43.05	47.58
Uttaranchal	7.31	39.99	50.45	51.83	79.29	91.45
West Bengal	48.10	87.66	138.95	57.43	71.17	80.25
Union Territories						
Andaman & Nicobar Islands	–	–	–	–	–	–
Chandigarh	–	–	–	–	–	–
Dadra & Nagar Haveli	–	–	–	–	–	–
Daman & Diu	–	–	–	–	–	–
Lakshadweep	–	–	–	–	–	–
Pondicherry	–	–	92.10	–	–	–
All India	63.42	75.93	80.18	90.81	87.08	241.44

Source: Computed from Paper–2, Rural–Urban Distribution 1991.

TABLE 4.6b

The Coefficients of Variation of Growth Rates (1991–2001) of Towns as per their Size Class Distribution in 1991

States/UTs	1991–2001					
	Class I	Class II	Class III	Class IV	Class V	Class VI
Andhra Pradesh	64.60	92.40	62.20	97.30	–	–
Arunachal Pradesh	–	–	–	82.70	32.20	–
Assam	67.80	78.20	70.60	86.70	64.80	94.60
Bihar	35.60	51.10	42.00	54.60	24.80	–
Chhattisgarh	91.10	103.90	54.70	114.00	74.30	–
Delhi	–	–	–	–	–	–
Goa	–	41.10	–	56.50	138.40	51.00
Gujarat	47.10	75.10	83.30	97.30	104.20	428.60
Haryana	46.40	57.70	29.00	52.10	123.00	88.50
Himachal Pradesh	–	–	–	–	–	–
Jammu & Kashmir	68.00	–	37.53	38.22	67.16	77.70
Jharkhand	23.60	38.00	95.20	53.40	190.90	–9.40
Karnataka	41.30	71.20	51.50	150.20	230.30	269.70
Kerala	54.00	151.70	174.00	194.09	57.90	–
Madhya Pradesh	46.50	115.50	55.70	163.00	92.30	–
Maharashtra	50.10	118.20	63.90	127.90	211.00	78.90
Manipur	–	–	23.50	49.60	65.90	82.00
Meghalaya	–	–	15.50	1.90	31.40	–
Mizoram	–	–	14.20	14.80	25.40	96.80
Nagaland	–	35.20	32.30	54.70	33.90	–
Orissa 40.20		45.00	48.50	58.40	65.00	151.90–
Punjab	30.80	44.80	64.70	57.10	110.60	96.50
Rajasthan	34.80	38.90	39.10	54.40	104.30	–
Sikkim	–	–	–	–	–	67.80

(contd.)

TABLE 4.6b: contd.

States/UTs	1991–2001					
	Class I	Class II	Class III	Class IV	Class V	Class VI
Tamil Nadu	112.80	68.70	120.00	122.20	146.40	–104.00
Tripura	–	–	219.10	123.80	32.10	5.00
Uttar Pradesh	60.00	33.40	85.80	52.60	52.10	65.90
Uttaranchal	47.90	49.20	59.70	41.60	58.00	178.70
West Bengal	109.60	47.30	89.30	86.70	85.20	191.90
Union Territories						
Andaman & Nicobar Islands	–	–	–	–	–	–
Chandigarh	–	–	–	–	–	–
Dadra & Nagar Haveli	–	–	–	–	–	–
Daman & Diu	–	–	109.00	–	–	–
Lakshadweep	–	–	–	–	–	–
Pondicherry	–	–	97.20	–	–	–
All India	72.12	86.16	81.30	108.13	110.52	136.19

Source: Computed from Census of India 2001.

The growth scenario in the 1990s, however, makes a significant departure from the earlier trends. The coefficient of variation has gone up significantly for class I cities. This implies that although class I cities have maintained an edge in terms of growth rates, this may change. The disparity of growth within the size categories also projects temporal variation. For example, coefficients of variation became quite high in class I cities of developed states, especially in Tamil Nadu and West Bengal. In Tamil Nadu, cities like Tiruppur have grown by about 80 per cent while population in towns of Thoothukudi (Tuticorin) and Valparai has gone down by 10 per cent. Similar is the story of West Bengal wherein cities like Siliguri have grown by 120 per cent whereas the population in Nabadwip has decreased by 20 per cent during 1991–2001. The reasons for such variations among class I cities have to be sought mainly from economic growth and opportunities for specific cities. One can attribute these trends in class I cities to economic policies which permit easier access to national and international markets for some large cities only.

Major Findings

First, economic development of a particular region/state has been regarded as a significant factor in increasing urbanization, which is confirmed from the analysis of the urban scenario in the country since independence. The country being in its initial stage of economic development had very few growth centres in certain states. During the 1950s, Kolkata, Mumbai, and Chennai were the only three important metropolises which accommodated a very high share of urban population of the country. Their administrative, commercial, and manufacturing activities have continued to attract immigration. These cities have maintained their positions even after fifty years of independence.

Second, the study has demonstrated a distinctly different spatial pattern existing between the level of urbanization and pace of urban growth. The pattern and trend of urbanization in the backward states has historically been different from that of the relatively developed ones. Since independence, until 1991, the level of urbanization has generally been high in case of developed states like Maharashtra, Gujarat, Tamil Nadu, and Haryana although they experienced medium or low urban growth. In contrast, high urban growth was registered in relatively backward states, like Bihar, Uttar Pradesh, Rajasthan, Orissa, and Madhya Pradesh that had a low percentage of urban population. The 1990s, however, make a significant departure. Many of the developed states have registered urban growth above the national average. On the other hand, the backward states have experienced growth either below that of the country average or equal to that. Consequently, the disparity in terms of growth of urban population across the states has gone up during the 1990s.

Third, a changing pattern of urbanization in the size class distribution of towns across the states is observed during the 1990s. Until this decade, class I cities in developed states were noted to have recorded higher growth rates when compared to smaller towns, whereas in the less developed states the smaller towns have grown at similar or a higher rate than the class I cities. This pattern witnessed a change in the 1990s. Many of the backward states like Himachal Pradesh, Bihar, Rajasthan, Orissa, and Assam have reported high urban growth in their class I cities. However, the pattern in the developed states has remained similar to the 1980s. Furthermore, class I cities, million-plus cities, and capital cities are recording a higher growth rate than the other smaller categories. This has resulted in increasing co-efficient of variation within the class I towns during 1991–2001. Consequently, cities in class I category are showing significant disparity in their growth rates. It can be argued that international policies of linking a few 'fit' cities of the developing countries with the process of globalization have made the gap somewhat wider.

Fourth, the share of the medium towns or the class II and III towns is more stable in most of the states as also at the national level.

Lower category towns, that is, class IV–VI report a decline in their share in urban population as very few new towns have emerged in these categories while a large number of towns have either moved up to the next higher category or been declassified. The small towns, however, register similar or higher growth rates than class I cities in states like Bihar, Kerala, Madhya Pradesh, Rajasthan, and Uttar Pradesh. Possible reasons could be that in these states, the agrarian economy continues to be poor and in the existing large cities there is little additional employment.

V

Socio-economic Aspects of Urbanization
A State-level Scenario

The growth and distribution of urban population across the states and UTs have been analysed in detail in the previous chapters and a few of the differences have been highlighted. It has been observed that the pattern and trend of urbanization in the backward states has been different from that of the relatively developed ones. The present chapter examines this phenomenon in greater detail and attempts to identify the factors to explain the spatial pattern in the trend and processes of urbanization. The analysis has been carried out by taking seventeen major states of India as observational units, based on the information collected around the three census years of 1981, 1991, and 2001. More states could not be considered due to the difficulties in accessing data for the smaller states and UTs over the three time points.

URBANIZATION AND SELECTED DEVELOPMENTAL INDICATORS

The indicators in the process of socio-economic development of a state can broadly be placed into four categories. These are: (a) economic, (b) employment and poverty (c) infrastructure development, and (d) socio-demographic development. The economic indicators can further be classified into macro indicators such as per capita income, per capita foreign direct investment (FDI), agricultural development, such as productivity per hectare, size of landholding, and industrial indicators such as percentage share of industrial production, worker enterprise ratio etc. Employment and poverty dimension comprise WPR, unemployment rates, and poverty ratios taken separately for rural and urban areas. The infrastructural development indicators pertain to the facilities that promote the development and growth of other sectors, such as roads per 100 sq. km, railways per 100 sq. km, telephone lines per 100 persons, percentage of villages electrified, bank deposits, and credit to industry. The socio-demographic indicators constitute the demographic dimension relating to URGD, sex ratio in rural and urban areas, and indicators of social development like literacy in rural and urban areas, schooling facility (middle and higher secondary) per thousand persons, hospitals and dispensaries per thousand persons, and basic amenities for urban areas such as percentage of urban households, access to safe drinking water, sanitation facilities, and electricity use.

The socio-economic indicators selected for the state-level analysis (Tables 5.1 to 5.3) are listed in Box 5.1.

Box 5.1
Socio-economic Indicators

(A) Economic Indicators

Macro indicators

1. Percentage of urban population—*LoU*
2. Growth of urban population—*GR (U)*
3. Per capita income—*PCI*
4. Per capita flow of foreign direct investment—*PC_FDI*

Agricultural

5. Productivity per hectare in rupees—*Agri. Prod.*
6. Size of land holding in hectares—*Landholding*

Industrial

7. Industrial production as percentage of net state domestic product—*Industrial Prod.*
8. Worker enterprise ratio in rural areas—*WER (R)*
9. Worker enterprise ratio in urban areas—*WER (U)*

(B) Employment and Poverty Indicators

Employment

10. Workforce participation rate in 15+age group for rural areas—*WPR (R)*
11. Workforce participation rate in 15+age group for urban areas—*WPR (U)*
12. Percentage of regular workers to total workers in rural areas—*Reg. Workers (R)*
13. Percentage of regular workers to total workers in urban areas—*Reg. Workers (U)*
14. Unemployment rates in rural areas—*Unemploy (R)*
15. Unemployment rates in urban areas—*Unemploy (U)*

Poverty

16. Percentage of population below poverty line in rural area—*BPL (R)*
17. Percentage of population below poverty line in urban areas—*BPL (U)*
18. Average monthly per capita expenditure in rural areas—*Expenditure (R)*
19. Average monthly per capita expenditure in urban areas—*Expenditure (U)*

(C) Infrastructure Development Indicators

Physical Infrastructure

20. Roads per 100 square km—*Road*
21. Railways per 100 square km—*Railway*
22. Telephone lines per 100 persons—*Telephone*
23. Percentage of villages electrified—*Villages Elec.*

Financial Infrastructure

24. Per capita bank deposits—*Bank Deposits*
25. credit to industry per capita—*Credit Ind.*

(D) Socio-demographic Indicators

Demographic

26. Urban rural growth differential—*UR growth diff.*
27. Females per thousand males in rural areas—*Sex Ratio (R)*
28. Females per thousand males in urban areas—*Sex Ratio (U)*
29. Percentage of slum population in total urban population—*Slum Popln*

(contd.)

BOX 5.1 contd.

Social Development

  30. Literacy in rural areas—*Literacy (R)*
  31. Literacy in urban areas—*Literacy (U)*
  32. Hospitals and dispensaries per thousand persons—*Hospital*
  33. Middle and higher secondary schools per thousand person—*School*

Urban Basic Amenities

  34. Percentage of urban households having access to safe drinking water—*Water*
  35. Percentage of urban households having access to sanitation facilities—*Sanitation*
  36. Percentage of urban households having electricity connection—*Electricity*

LIMITATIONS OF DATA AVAILABILITY

Certain constraints in the analysis due to problems of non-availability of data have to be noted. The data on per capita FDI, for example, are available only for the year 2001 and not for the other two points of time. The value of agricultural productivity is obtained from the study by Bhalla and Singh (2001) for the 1980s and 1990s. In fact, the triennium averages of 1980–3 and 1992–5 are taken for the present analysis. This information is not available for the late 1990s or for the years of the present century. The employment figures for 1991 and 2001 are obtained from the 50th and 55th round surveys on employment and unemployment situation in India conducted by NSSO. Furthermore, the indicators relating to urban basic amenities could not be considered during 2001, due to unavailability of the data from population census.

The degree of interdependency between the level as well as growth of urbanization with the selected indicators has been examined by using the Pearson's coefficients of correlation, computed for the three time points (Tables 5.1, 5.2, and 5.3 respectively). A positive correlation of urbanization with any indicator signifies that the states for which the indicator obtains higher values, urbanization also shows higher values. Conversely, a negative correlation implies that the states that have high values in these indicators would in general report low levels of urbanization.

URBANIZATION AND ECONOMIC INDICATORS

PER CAPITA INCOME: 1981

The all-India average of per capita net state domestic product or per capita income in 1981 was Rs 1630. The states showing much higher per capita income were Delhi, Maharashtra, Gujarat, Punjab, and Haryana. On the other hand, Bihar, Orissa, Uttar Pradesh, and Rajasthan reported per capita income of less than Rs 1400. West Bengal, Tamil Nadu, and Karnataka constitute the moderately developed states in terms of per capita income but their level of urbanization is high. The only major exception is Himachal Pradesh wherein the per capita income was higher than the average per capita income of the country but the percentage of urban population was only 7.6 per cent—much below the national average of 23.73 per cent.

The coefficient of variation in the level of urbanization across the states has been estimated to be 73.4 per cent, which is very high. The correlation of the level of urbanization with per capita income is also very high viz. 0.846 which is significant at one per cent level. This confirms the fact that the economically

TABLE 5.1

Interdependence among Indicators of Urbanization and Socio-economic Development at State Level (1981)

(1)	LoU	GR (U)	PCI	Agri. prod.	Land-holding	Industrial prod.	BPL (R)	BPL (U)	Expend-iture (R)	Expend-iture (U)	Road	Railway	Tele-phone
	(2)	(3)	(4)	(5)	(6)	(7)	(8)	(9)	(10)	(11)	(12)	(13)	(14)
LoU	1	0.075	.846(**)	0.075	0.113	0.138	-0.439	-0.072	.678(**)	0.386	.864(**)	.878(**)	0.011
GR (U)	0.075	1 ·	0.028	-0.445	0.319	-0.336	-0.021	0.3	0.034	-0.279	0.166	0.118	-0.023
PCI	.846(**)	0.028	1	0.162	0.261	0.078	-.650(**)	-0.423	.843(**)	.641(**)	.754(**)	.791(**)	-0.056
Agri. prod.	0.075	-0.445	0.162	1	-0.376	-0.096	-0.173	-0.064	0.32	0.047	0.207	0.217	-0.065
Landholding	0.113	0.319	0.261	-0.376	1	0.01	-0.437	-0.127	0.188	0.044	-0.165	-0.084	0.222
Industrial prod.	0.138	-0.336	0.078	-0.096	0.01	1	0.351	0.341	-0.358	-0.166	-0.18	-0.083	0.003
BPL (R)	-0.439	-0.021	-.650(**)	-0.173	-0.437	0.351	1	.656(**)	-.842(**)	-.665(**)	-0.424	-0.378	-0.124
BPL (U)	-0.072	0.3	-0.423	-0.064	-0.127	0.341	.656(**)	1	-.574(*)	-.743(**)	-0.142	-0.193	0.042
Expenditure (R)	.678(**)	0.034	.843(**)	0.32	0.188	-0.358	-.842(**)	-.574(*)	1	.748(**)	.766(**)	.707(**)	-0.042
Expenditure (U)	0.386	-0.279	.641(**)	0.047	0.044	-0.166	-.665(**)	-.743(**)	.748(**)	1	0.457	0.32	0.032
Roads	.864(**)	0.166	.754(**)	0.207	-0.165	-0.18	-0.424	-0.142	.766(**)	0.457	1	.888(**)	-0.197
Railway	.878(**)	0.118	.791(**)	0.217	-0.084	-0.083	-0.378	-0.193	.707(**)	0.32	.888(**)	1	-0.206
Telephone	0.011	-0.023	-0.056	-0.065	0.222	0.003	-0.124	0.042	-0.042	0.032	-0.197	-0.206	1
Bank deposits	.950(**)	0.12	.874(**)	0.07	0.007	-0.031	-.495(*)	-0.233	.782(**)	.531(*)	.949(**)	.918(**)	-0.105
Credit industry	.965(**)	0.015	.906(**)	0.068	0.083	0.215	-0.428	-0.188	.691(**)	.491(*)	.842(**)	.868(**)	-0.027
Village elec.	.517(*)	-0.196	.649(**)	.614(**)	0.137	0.035	-.568(*)	-0.19	.693(**)	0.474	0.454	0.413	0.089
U-R growth diff.	0.359	.905(**)	0.254	-0.223	0.129	-0.26	-0.052	0.36	0.207	-0.17	0.462	0.369	-0.064
Sex ratio (R)	-.607(**)	-0.41	-.670(**)	0.073	-0.318	0.195	.511(*)	0.321	-.617(**)	-0.218	-.554(*)	-.765(**)	0.164
Sex ratio (U)	-0.154	-0.26	-0.342	.573(*)	-0.11	0	0.08	0.43	-0.176	-0.361	-0.157	-0.306	0.239
Literacy (R)	0.298	-0.465	0.398	.698(**)	-0.389	0.001	-0.236	-0.173	.499(*)	.501(*)	.486(*)	0.286	-0.02
Literacy (U)	0.185	-.661(**)	0.322	.497(*)	-0.337	0.125	-0.144	-0.283	0.351	.594(*)	0.289	0.119	0.01
Hospitals	.609(**)	-0.363	.705(**)	.482(*)	-0.128	0.162	-0.43	-0.257	.714(**)	.655(**)	.670(**)	.556(*)	-0.161
Schools	-0.25	-0.016	-0.263	-0.377	0.233	0.087	0.145	0.147	-0.355	-0.079	-0.357	-0.466	0.427
Water	0.431	-0.071	.638(**)	-0.282	.507(*)	0.1	-.593(*)	-.643(**)	.494(*)	.537(*)	0.19	0.407	0.072
Sanitation	0.411	-0.309	.509(*)	0.204	-0.012	0.254	-0.199	-0.323	0.389	0.292	0.318	.564(*)	-0.078
Electricity	0.236	-0.211	.622(**)	0.041	0.461	-0.141	. -.758(**)	-.795(**)	.667(**)	.775(**)	0.162	0.212	0.063

(contd.)

TABLE 5.1 contd.

(1)	Bank deposits (15)	Credit Industry (16)	Vill. electrified (17)	UR growth diff. (18)	Sex ratio (R) (19)	Sex ratio (U) (20)	Literacy (R) (21)	Literacy (U) (22)	Hospital (23)	School (24)	Water (25)	Sanitation (26)	Electricity (27)
LoU	.950(**)	.965(**)	.517(*)	0.359	-.607(**)	-0.154	0.298	0.185	.609(**)	-0.25	0.431	0.411	0.236
GR (U)	0.12	0.015	-0.196	.905(**)	-0.41	-0.26	-0.465	-.661(**)	-0.363	-0.016	-0.071	-0.309	-0.211
PCI	.874(**)	.906(**)	.649(**)	0.254	-.670(**)	-0.342	0.398	0.322	.705(**)	-0.263	.638(**)	.509(*)	.622(**)
Agri. prod.	0.07	0.068	.614(**)	-0.223	0.073	.573(*)	.698(**)	.497(*)	.482(*)	-0.377	-0.282	0.204	0.041
Landholding	0.007	0.083	0.137	0.129	-0.318	-0.11	-0.389	-0.337	-0.128	0.233	.507(*)	-0.012	0.461
Industrial prod.	-0.031	0.215	0.035	-0.26	0.195	0	0.001	0.125	0.162	0.087	0.1	0.254	-0.141
BPL (R)	-.495(*)	-0.428	-.568(*)	-0.052	.511(*)	0.08	-0.236	-0.144	-0.43	0.145	-.593(*)	-0.199	-.758(**)
BPL (U)	-0.233	-0.188	-0.19	0.36	0.321	0.43	-0.173	-0.283	-0.257	0.147	-.643(**)	-0.323	-.795(**)
Expenditure (R)	.782(**)	.691(**)	.693(**)	0.207	-.617(**)	-0.176	.499(*)	0.351	.714(**)	-0.355	.494(*)	0.389	.667(**)
Expenditure (U)	.531(*)	.491(*)	0.474	-0.17	-0.218	-0.361	.501(*)	.594(*)	.655(**)	-0.079	.537(*)	0.292	.775(**)
Roads	.949(**)	.842(**)	0.454	0.462	-.554(*)	-0.157	.486(*)	0.289	.670(**)	-0.357	0.19	0.318	0.162
Railway	.918(**)	.868(**)	0.413	0.369	-.765(**)	-0.306	0.286	0.119	.556(*)	-0.466	0.407	.564(*)	0.212
Telephone	-0.105	-0.027	0.089	-0.064	0.164	0.239	-0.02	0.01	-0.161	0.427	0.072	-0.078	0.063
Bank deposits	1	.945(**)	0.455	0.394	-.645(**)	-0.311	0.371	0.244	.665(**)	-0.29	0.436	0.435	0.311
Credit industry	.945(**)	1	.536(*)	0.283	-.591(*)	-0.268	0.376	0.307	.680(**)	-0.235	.505(*)	.494(*)	0.339
Village elec.	0.455	.536(*)	1	0.051	-0.228	0.309	.607(**)	0.479	.689(**)	-0.338	0.198	0.154	0.468
UR growth diff.	0.394	0.283	0.051	1	-0.446	-0.173	-0.209	-0.464	-0.103	-0.148	-0.128	-0.273	-0.241
Sex ratio (R)	-.645(**)	-.591(*)	-0.228	-0.446	1	.547(*)	0.188	0.336	-0.157	0.442	-.671(**)	-.511(**)	-0.413
Sex ratio (U)	-0.311	-0.268	0.309	-0.173	.547(*)	1	0.347	0.224	0.046	0.063	-.643(**)	-0.369	-0.392
Literacy (R)	0.371	0.376	.607(**)	-0.209	0.188	0.347	1	.904(**)	.839(**)	-0.078	-0.177	0.267	0.217
Literacy (U)	0.244	0.307	0.479	-0.464	0.336	0.224	.904(**)	1	.760(**)	0.034	-0.062	0.281	0.301
Hospitals	.665(**)	.680(**)	.689(**)	-0.103	-0.157	0.046	.839(**)	.760(**)	1	-0.26	0.181	.518(*)	0.395
Schools	-0.29	-0.235	-0.338	-0.148	0.442	0.063	-0.078	0.034	-0.26	1	-0.003	-0.337	0.06
Water	0.436	.505(*)	0.198	-0.128	-.671(**)	-.643(**)	-0.177	-0.062	0.181	-0.003	1	.512(*)	.804(**)
Sanitation	0.435	.494(*)	0.154	-0.273	-.511(*)	-0.369	0.267	0.281	.518(*)	-0.337	.512(*)	1	0.332
Electricity	0.311	0.339	0.468	-0.241	-0.413	-0.392	0.217	0.301	0.395	0.06	.804(**)	0.332	1

Notes: ** Correlation is significant at the 0.01 level (2-tailed). * Correlation is significant at the 0.05 level (2-tailed).

Source: Computed by Authors.

TABLE 5.2

Interdependence among Indicators of Urbanization and Socio-economic Development at State Level (1991)

(1)	LoU (2)	GR (U) (3)	PCI (4)	Agri. prod. (5)	Land-holding (6)	Indus-trial prod. (7)	WPR (R) (8)	WPR (U) (9)	Workers (R) (10)	Workers (U) (11)	Un-employ. (R) (12)	Un-employ. (U) (13)	BPL (R) (14)	BPL (U) (15)	Expend-iture (R) (16)	Expend-iture (U) (17)
LoU	.1	0.123	.835(**)	0.161	0.014	0.198	0.062	0.247	.867(**)	0.172	-0.144	-0.392	-.599(**)	-0.053	.756(**)	.559(*)
GR (U)	0.123	1	0.094	0.012	-0.148	-0.218	-0.159	-0.081	0.253	-0.23	0.295	0.177	-0.206	-0.127	0.326	0.23
PCI	.835(**)	0.094	1	0.18	0.237	0.152	0.035	0.308	.758(**)	0.405	-0.279	-.543(*)	-.716(**)	-0.404	.850(**)	.703(**)
Agri. prod.	0.161	0.012	0.18	1	-0.305	-0.081	-0.468	0.269	0.135	-0.425	0.357	0.366	-0.285	-0.233	0.357	0.009
Landholding	0.014	-0.148	0.237	-0.305	1	0.031	0.367	0.242	-0.189	0.12	-0.479	-.569(*)	-0.272	0.002	0.071	-0.12
Industrial prod.	0.198	-0.218	0.152	-0.081	0.031	1	0.258	0.161	-0.152	0.109	-0.34	-0.164	0.211	0.384	-0.244	-0.145
WPR (R)	0.062	-0.159	0.035	-0.468	0.367	0.258	1	.603(*)	-0.195	0.252	-.613(**)	-0.599(*)	-0.285	0.399	-0.15	0.1
WPR (U)	0.247	-0.081	0.308	0.269	0.242	0.161	.603(*)	1	-0.058	-0.019	-0.409	-0.445	-.524(*)	0.187	0.222	0.12
Workers (R)	.867(**)	0.253	.758(**)	0.135	-0.189	-0.152	-0.195	-0.058	1	0.276	0.132	-0.216	-.540(*)	-0.367	.826(**)	.721(**)
Workers (U)	0.172	-0.23	0.405	-0.425	0.12	0.109	0.252	-0.019	0.276	1	-0.154	-0.288	-0.138	-0.4	0.144	.605(*)
Unemploy. (R)	-0.144	0.295	-0.279	0.357	-0.479	-0.34	-.613(**)	-0.409	0.132	-0.154	1	.833(**)	0.3	-0.204	-0.071	-0.095
Unemploy. (U)	-0.392	0.177	-.543(*)	0.366	-.569(*)	-0.164	-.599(**)	-0.445	-0.216	-0.288	.833(**)	1	.550(*)	0.06	-0.379	-0.371
BPL (R)	-.599(*)	-0.206	-.716(**)	-0.285	-0.272	0.211	-0.285	-.524(*)	-.540(*)	-0.138	0.3	.550(*)	1	0.425	-.825(**)	-.681(**)
BPL (U)	-0.053	-0.127	-0.404	-0.233	0.002	0.384	0.399	0.187	-0.367	-0.4	-0.204	0.06	0.425	1	-.545(*)	-.622(**)
Expenditure (R)	.756(**)	0.326	.850(**)	0.357	0.071	-0.244	-0.15	0.222	.826(**)	0.144	-0.071	-0.379	-.825(**)	-.545(*)	1	.767(**)
Expenditure (U)	.559(*)	0.23	.703(**)	0.009	-0.12	-0.145	0.1	0.12	.721(**)	.605(*)	-0.095	-0.371	-.681(**)	-.622(**)	.767(**)	1
Road	.875(**)	0.323	.702(**)	0.156	-0.236	-0.149	-0.163	-0.014	.968(**)	0.141	0.115	-0.19	-.531(*)	-0.215	.815(**)	.673(**)
Railway	.841(**)	0.089	.739(**)	0.271	-0.159	-0.07	-0.381	-0.119	.927(**)	0.143	0.075	-0.18	-0.434	-0.343	.775(**)	.527(*)
Telephone	.951(**)	0.204	.849(**)	0.098	-0.071	0.029	-0.006	0.104	.953(**)	0.299	-0.07	-0.375	-.635(**)	-0.25	.836(**)	.741(**)
Bank deposits	.926(**)	0.196	.852(**)	0.084	-0.081	-0.002	-0.068	0.033	.965(**)	0.324	-0.078	-0.366	-.610(**)	-0.299	.847(**)	.755(**)
Credit industry	.966(**)	0.115	.887(**)	0.111	-0.047	0.165	0.007	0.149	.921(**)	0.358	-0.094	-0.381	-.583(*)	-0.224	.786(**)	.698(**)

(contd.)

TABLE 5.2: contd.

(1)	LoU (2)	GR (U) (3)	PCI (4)	Agri. prod. (5)	Land-holding (6)	Industrial prod. (7)	WPR (R) (8)	WPR (U) (9)	Workers (R) (10)	Workers (U) (11)	Un-employ. (R) (12)	Un-employ. (U) (13)	BPL (R) (14)	BPL (U) (15)	Expenditure (R) (16)	Expenditure (U) (17)
Villages elec.	0.372	0.145	.538(*)	0.393	0.125	0.01	0.243	.492(*)	0.289	0.096	-0.002	-0.232	-.688(**)	-0.364	.500(*)	0.474
U-R growth diff.	-.644(**)	0.303	-.522(*)	0.145	0.019	0.176	0.025	0.106	-.744(**)	-0.348	0.201	0.424	0.303	0.173	-.497(*)	-0.444
Sex ratio (R)	-.508(*)	0.025	-.610(**)	0.081	-0.257	0.081	0.262	0.159	-.588(*)	-0.131	0.293	.506(*)	0.252	0.312	-.546(*)	-0.266
Sex ratio (U)	-0.007	0.246	-0.226	.551(*)	-0.127	0.059	0.107	0.467	-0.248	-.665(**)	0.231	0.339	-0.143	0.395	-0.065	-0.323
Literacy (R)	0.316	0.353	0.337	.604(*)	-0.392	-0.054	-0.27	0.179	0.369	0.04	0.429	0.288	-0.41	-0.404	.511(*)	.540(*)
Literacy (U)	0.067	0.226	0.118	0.413	-0.388	-0.072	-0.168	0.089	0.174	0.244	.530(*)	0.425	-0.204	-0.421	0.236	0.472
Hospital	.552(*)	0.386	.527(*)	0.352	-0.181	0.154	-0.082	0.159	.511(*)	0.134	0.179	-0.007	-.537(*)	-0.349	.624(**)	.654(**)
School	-0.268	-0.186	-0.296	-.508(*)	0.392	0.004	0.316	-0.131	-0.343	0.168	0.013	-0.08	0.2	0.189	-0.439	-0.216
Water	0.351	-0.362	.598(*)	-0.342	.499(*)	0.259	0.361	0.239	0.229	.530(*)	-.793(**)	-.855(**)	-0.374	-0.224	0.32	0.384
Sanitation	0.076	0.082	0.183	0.384	-0.074	-0.016	-.597(*)	-0.302	0.232	0.07	0.445	0.26	-0.096	-.677(**)	0.258	0.187
Electricity	0.27	-0.098	.661(**)	0.063	.491(*)	0.098	0.406	.554(*)	0.149	0.457	-.568(*)	-.689(**)	-.711(**)	-0.451	.524(*)	.596(*)

(contd.)

TABLE 5.2: contd.

(1)	Road (18)	Railway (19)	Tele- phone (20)	Bank deposits (21)	Credit ind. (22)	Villages elec. (23)	UR growth diff. (24)	Sex ratio (R) (25)	Sex ratio (U) (26)	Lit- eracy (R) (27)	Lit- eracy (U) (28)	Hos- pital (29)	School (30)	Water (31)	Sani- tation (32)	Electri- city (33)
LoU	.875(**)	.841(**)	.951(**)	.926(**)	.966(**)	0.372	-.644(**)	-.508(*)	-0.007	0.316	0.067	.552(*)	-0.268	0.351	0.076	0.27
GR (U)	0.323	0.089	0.204	0.196	0.115	0.145	0.303	0.025	0.246	0.353	0.226	0.386	-0.186	-0.362	0.082	-0.098
PCI	.702(**)	.739(**)	.849(**)	.852(**)	.887(**)	.538(*)	-.522(*)	-.610(**)	-0.226	0.337	0.118	.527(*)	-0.296	.598(*)	0.183	.661(**)
Agri. prod.	0.156	0.271	0.098	0.084	0.111	0.393	0.145	0.081	.551(*)	.604(*)	0.413	0.352	-.508(*)	-0.342	0.384	0.063
Landholding	-0.236	-0.159	-0.071	-0.081	-0.047	0.125	0.019	-0.257	-0.127	-0.392	-0.388	-0.181	0.392	.499(*)	-0.074	.491(*)
Industrial prod.	-0.149	-0.07	0.029	-0.002	0.165	0.01	0.176	0.081	0.059	-0.054	-0.072	0.154	0.004	0.259	-0.016	0.098
WPR (R)	-0.163	-0.381	-0.006	-0.068	0.007	0.243	0.025	0.262	0.107	-0.27	-0.168	-0.082	0.316	0.361	-.597(*)	0.406
WPR (U)	-0.014	-0.119	0.104	0.033	0.149	.492(*)	0.106	0.159	0.467	0.179	0.089	.511(*)	-0.131	0.239	-0.302	.554(*)
Workers (R)	.968(**)	.927(**)	.953(**)	.965(**)	.921(**)	0.289	-.744(**)	-.588(*)	-0.248	0.369	0.174	.511(*)	-0.343	0.229	0.232	0.149
Workers (U)	0.141	0.143	0.299	0.324	0.358	0.096	-0.348	-0.131	-.665(**)	0.04	0.244	0.134	0.168	.530(*)	0.07	0.457
Unemploy. (R)	0.115	0.075	-0.07	-0.078	-0.094	-0.002	0.201	0.293	0.231	0.429	.530(*)	0.179	0.013	-.793(**)	0.445	-.568(*)
Unemploy. (U)	-0.19	-0.18	-0.375	-0.366	-0.381	-0.232	0.424	.506(*)	0.339	0.288	0.425	-0.007	-0.08	-.855(**)	0.26	-.689(**)
BPL (R)	-.531(*)	-0.434	-.635(**)	-.610(**)	-.583(*)	-.688(**)	-.784(**)	-.732(**)	-0.143	-0.41	-0.204	-.537(*)	0.2	-0.374	-0.096	-.711(**)
BPL (U)	-0.215	-0.343	-0.25	-0.299	-0.224	-0.364	0.173	0.312	0.395	-0.404	-0.421	-0.349	0.189	-0.224	-.677(**)	-0.451
Expenditure (R)	.815(**)	.775(**)	.836(**)	.847(**)	.786(**)	.500(*)	-.497(*)	-.546(*)	-0.065	.511(*)	0.236	.624(**)	-0.439	0.32	0.258	.524(*)
Expenditure (U)	.673(**)	.527(*)	.741(**)	.755(**)	.698(**)	0.474	-0.444	-0.266	-0.323	.540(*)	0.472	.654(**)	-0.216	0.384	0.187	.596(*)
Road	1	.879(**)	.951(**)	.952(**)	.898(**)	0.242	-.676(**)	-.494(*)	-0.105	0.416	0.167	.561(*)	-0.351	0.119	0.077	0.087
Railway	.879(**)	1	.869(**)	.899(**)	.866(**)	0.15	-.784(**)	-.526(*)	-0.272	0.247	0.005	0.373	-0.466	0.293	0.329	0.077
Telephone	.951(**)	.869(**)	1	.991(**)	.982(**)	0.382	-.691(**)	-.526(*)	-0.159	0.396	0.167	.611(**)	-0.259	0.339	0.103	0.306
Bank deposits	.952(**)	.899(**)	.991(**)	1	.970(**)	0.318	-.731(**)	-.591(*)	-0.25	0.352	0.123	.560(*)	-0.321	0.375	0.132	0.297
Credit industry	.898(**)	.866(**)	.982(**)	.970(**)	1	0.395	-.681(**)	-.538(*)	-0.18	0.368	0.16	.584(*)	-0.265	0.4	0.134	0.334

(contd.)

TABLE 5.2: contd.

(1)	Road	Railway	Tele-phone	Bank deposits	Credit ind.	Villages elec.	U-R growth diff.	Sex ratio (R)	Sex ratio (U)	Lit-eracy (R)	Lit-eracy (U)	Hos-pital	School	Water	Sani-tation	Electri-city
	(18)	(19)	(20)	(21)	(22)	(23)	(24)	(25)	(26)	(27)	(28)	(29)	(30)	(31)	(32)	(33)
Villages elec.	0.242	0.15	0.382	0.318	0.395	1	0.077	0.061	0.339	.554(*)	.518(*)	.546(*)	0.032	0.109	0.197	.637(**)
U-R growth diff.	−.676(**)	−.784(**)	−.691(**)	−.731(**)	−.681(**)	0.077	1	.723(**)	.554(*)	0,19	0.293	0.037	0.212	−.527(*)	−0.008	−0.075
Sex ratio (R)	−.494(*)	−.732(**)	−.526(*)	−.591(*)	−.538(*)	0.061	.723(**)	1	.607(**)	0.3	.505(*)	0.132	0.331	−.643(**)	−0.202	−0.201
Sex ratio (U)	−0.105	−0.272	−0.159	−0.25	−0.18	0.339	.554(*)	.607(**)	1	0.422	0.326	0.307	−0.026	−.622(**)	−0.116	−0.147
Literacy (R)	0.416	0.247	0.396	0.352	0.368	.554(*)	0.19	0.3	0.422	1	.893(**)	.886(**)	−0.163	−0.349	0.35	0.248
Literacy (U)	0.167	0.005	0.167	0.123	0.16	.518(*)	0.293	.505(*)	0.326	.893(**)	1	.737(**)	0.026	−0.402	0.37	0.189
Hospital	.561(*)	0.373	.611(**)	.560(*)	.584(*)	.546(*)	0.037	0.132	0.307	.886(**)	.737(**)	1	−0.093	−0.102	0.318	0.356
School	−0.351	−0.466	−0.259	−0.321	−0.265	0.032	0.212	0.331	−0.026	−0.163	0.026	−0.093	1	−0.043	−0.11	−0.019
Water	0.119	0.293	0.339	0.375	0.4	0.109	−.527(*)	−.643(**)	−.622(**)	−0.349	−0.402	−0.102	−0.043	1	−0.029	.679(**)
Sanitation	0.077	0.329	0.103	0.132	0.134	0.197	−0.008	−0.202	−0.116	0.35	0.37	0.318	−0.11	−0.029	1	0.031
Electricity	0.087	0.077	0.306	0.297	0.334	.637(**)	−0.075	−0.201	−0.147	0.248	0.189	0.356	−0.019	.679(**)	0.031	1

Notes: ** Correlation is significant at the 0.01 level (2–tailed). * Correlation is significant at the 0.05 level (2–tailed).
Source: Computed by Authors.

TABLE 5.3

Interdependence among Indicators of Urbanization and Socio-economic Development at State Level (2001)

(1)	LoU	Urban GR	PCI	FDI	Land-holding	Indus-trial prod.	WER (R)	WER (U)	WPR (R)	WPR (U)	Work-ers (R)	Work-ers (U)	Un-employ. (R)	Un-employ. (U)	BPL (R)	BPL (U)
	(2)	(3)	(4)	(5)	(6)	(7)	(8)	(9)	(10)	(11)	(12)	(13)	(14)	(15)	(16)	(17)
LoU	1.00	0.42	.844(**)	.915(**)	0.03	0.19	0.19	.750(**)	-0.24	0.31	.790(**)	.526(*)	-0.13	-0.46	-.520(*)	-0.24
GR (U)	0.42	1.00	0.43	0.44	0.30	-0.04	0.35	.539(*)	-0.13	-0.07	0.44	.545(*)	-0.46	-.538(*)	-0.12	-0.29
PCI	.844(**)	0.43	1.00	.667(**)	0.25	0.31	0.21	.738(**)	-0.05	0.40	.621(**)	.633(**)	-0.25	-.560(*)	-.725(**)	-0.47
FDI	.915(**)	0.44	.667(**)	1.00	-0.12	-0.05	0.17	.806(**)	-0.33	0.01	.868(**)	.577(*)	-0.06	-0.28	-0.38	-0.19
Landholding	0.03	0.30	0.25	-0.12	1.00	0.13	-0.04	0.03	0.45	0.26	-0.20	0.00	-.614(**)	-.701(**)	-0.27	-0.14
Industrial prod.	0.19	-0.04	0.31	-0.05	0.13	1.00	-0.15	-0.05	0.43	0.41	-0.30	0.11	-0.24	-0.31	0.05	0.29
WER (R)	0.19	0.35	0.21	0.17	-0.04	-0.15	1.00	0.20	-0.43	-0.08	.488(*)	0.28	0.21	0.03	-0.07	-0.46
WER (U)	.750(**)	.539(*)	.738(**)	.806(**)	0.03	-0.05	0.20	1.00	-0.37	-0.21	.765(**)	.669(**)	-0.20	-0.32	-0.44	0.29
WPR (R)	-0.24	-0.13	-0.05	-0.33	0.45	0.43	-0.43	-0.37	1.00	0.44	-.580(*)	-0.01	-0.43	-0.42	-0.06	0.06
WPR (U)	0.31	-0.07	0.40	0.01	0.26	0.41	-0.08	-0.21	0.44	1.00	-0.06	0.03	-0.01	-0.41	-0.40	0.06
Workers (R)	.790(**)	0.44	.621(**)	.868(**)	-0.20	-0.30	.488(*)	.765(**)	-.580(*)	-0.06	1.00	.592(*)	0.13	-0.10	-0.47	-.522(*)
Workers (U)	.526(*)	.545(*)	.633(**)	.577(*)	0.00	0.11	0.28	.669(**)	-0.01	0.03	.592(*)	1.00	-0.15	-0.29	-0.42	-.538(*)
Unemploy. (R)	-0.13	-0.46	-0.25	-0.06	-.614(**)	-0.24	0.21	-0.20	-0.43	-0.01	0.13	-0.15	1.00	.858(**)	0.33	0.12
Unemploy. (U)	-0.46	-.538(*)	-.560(*)	-0.28	-.701(**)	-0.31	0.03	-0.32	-0.42	-0.41	-0.10	-0.29	.858(**)	1.00	.523(*)	0.22
BPL (R)	-.520(*)	-0.12	-.725(**)	-0.38	-0.27	0.05	-0.07	-0.44	-0.06	-0.40	-0.47	-0.42	0.33	.523(*)	1.00	.646(**)
BPL (U)	-0.24	-0.29	-0.47	-0.19	-0.14	0.29	-0.46	0.29	0.06	0.06	-.522(*)	-.538(*)	0.12	0.22	.646(**)	1.00
Expenditure (R)	.595(*)	0.26	.707(**)	.555(*)	0.06	-0.28	0.19	.645(**)	-0.38	0.11	.744(**)	0.44	-0.09	-0.25	-.844(**)	-.676(**)
Expenditure (U)	0.14	0.09	.494(*)	0.05	0.01	0.10	0.09	0.26	0.20	0.24	0.21	.616(**)	-0.11	-0.18	-.647(**)	-.684(**)
Road	.844(**)	0.33	.572(*)	.954(**)	-0.23	-0.22	0.22	.753(**)	-.505(*)	-0.06	.931(**)	0.46	0.11	-0.09	-0.39	-0.24
Railway	.827(**)	0.42	.574(*)	.852(**)	-0.16	-0.20	0.37	.769(**)	-.671(**)	-0.11	.898(**)	0.40	0.03	-0.18	-0.34	-0.38
Telephone	.895(**)	0.36	.827(**)	.898(**)	-0.04	-0.06	0.19	.816(**)	-0.31	0.14	.895(**)	.629(**)	-0.05	-0.30	-.669(**)	-0.45

(contd.)

TABLE 5.3: contd.

(1)	LoU (2)	Urban GR (3)	PCI (4)	FDI (5)	Land-holding (6)	Indus-trial prod. (7)	WER (R) (8)	WER (U) (9)	WPR (R) (10)	WPR (U) (11)	Work-ers (R) (12)	Work-ers (U) (13)	Un-employ. (R) (14)	Un-employ. (U) (15)	BPL (R) (16)	BPL (U) (17)
Bank deposits	.904(**)	0.40	.739(**)	.959(**)	-0.09	-0.08	0.22	.851(**)	-0.41	-0.01	.922(**)	.599(*)	-0.05	-0.26	-.517(*)	-0.37
Credit industry	.955(**)	0.46	.788(**)	.972(**)	-0.06	0.08	0.23	.849(**)	-0.32	0.07	.875(**)	.641(**)	-0.10	-0.34	-0.47	-0.29
Villages elec.	.504(*)	0.10	.755(**)	0.30	0.31	0.25	0.02	0.26	0.37	.637(**)	0.29	0.40	-0.29	-.553(*)	-.836(**)	-0.39
UR growth diff.	.684(**)	.805(**)	.649(**)	.637(**)	0.01	0.01	0.36	.586(*)	-0.14	0.29	.648(**)	.667(**)	-0.10	-0.40	-0.30	-0.33
Sex ratio (R)	-.542(*)	-.742(**)	-0.43	-.575(*)	-0.32	0.13	-0.33	-.668(**)	0.41	0.26	-.569(*)	-0.37	.518(*)	.551(*)	0.22	0.34
Sex ratio (U)	-0.10	-.657(**)	-0.17	-0.26	-0.29	0.14	-0.12	-.583(*)	0.09	.574(*)	-0.24	-.505(*)	.556(*)	0.35	0.03	0.36
Slum popln.	0.293	0.217	0.438	0.213	0.193	0.411	-0.138	0.391	0.217	0.181	0.059	.512(*)	-0.366	-0.447	-0.277	-0.04
Literacy (R)	0.38	-0.15	.522(*)	0.33	-0.30	-0.05	0.10	0.35	-0.23	0.29	.506(*)	0.40	0.45	0.22	-.545(*)	-0.41
Literacy (U)	-0.02	-0.27	0.20	0.00	-0.35	-0.10	0.19	0.09	-0.09	0.07	0.22	0.34	.599(*)	.483(*)	-0.21	-0.38
Hospital	.486(*)	0.13	.675(**)	0.40	0.02	0.45	-0.01	.530(*)	0.11	0.06	0.32	.485(*)	-0.13	-0.18	-0.43	-0.33
School	-0.27	0.00	-0.18	-0.22	0.44	0.15	0.03	-0.24	.513(*)	0.02	-0.40	-0.19	-0.13	-0.09	0.29	0.27

(contd.)

TABLE 5.3: contd.

(1)	Expenditure (R) (18)	Expenditure (U) (19)	Road (20)	Railway (21)	Telephone (22)	Bank deposits (23)	Credit ind. (24)	Villages elec. (25)	UR growth diff. (26)	Sex ratio (R) (27)	Sex ratio (U) (28)	Slum popln. (29)	Literacy (R) (30)	Literacy (U) (31)	Hospital (32)	School (33)
LoU	.595(*)	0.14	.844(**)	.827(**)	.895(**)	.904(**)	.955(**)	.504(*)	.684(**)	-.542(*)	-0.10	0.293	0.38	-0.02	.486(*)	-0.27
GR (U)	0.26	0.09	0.33	0.42	0.36	0.40	0.46	0.10	.805(**)	-.742(**)	-.657(**)	0.217	-0.15	-0.27	0.13	0.00
PCI	.707(**)	.494(*)	.572(*)	.574(*)	.827(**)	.739(**)	.788(**)	.755(**)	.649(**)	-0.43	-0.17	0.438	.522(*)	0.20	.675(**)	-0.18
FDI	.555(*)	0.05	.954(**)	.852(**)	.898(**)	.959(**)	.972(**)	0.30	.637(**)	-.575(*)	-0.26	0.213	0.33	0.00	0.40	-0.22
Landholding	0.06	0.01	-0.23	-0.16	-0.04	-0.09	-0.06	0.31	0.01	-0.32	-0.29	0.193	-0.30	-0.35	0.02	0.44
Industrial prod.	-0.28	0.10	-0.22	-0.20	-0.06	-0.08	0.08	0.25	0.01	0.13	0.14	0.411	-0.05	-0.10	0.45	0.15
WER (R)	0.19	0.09	0.22	0.37	0.19	0.22	0.23	0.02	0.36	-0.33	-0.12	-0.138	0.10	0.19	-0.01	0.03
WER (U)	.645(**)	0.26	.753(**)	.769(**)	.816(**)	.851(**)	.849(**)	0.26	.586(*)	-.668(**)	-.583(*)	0.391	0.35	0.09	.530(*)	-0.24
WPR (R)	-0.38	0.20	-.505(*)	-.671(**)	-0.31	-0.41	-0.32	0.37	-0.14	0.41	0.09	0.217	-0.23	-0.09	0.11	.513(*)
WPR (U)	0.11	0.24	-0.06	-0.11	0.14	-0.01	0.07	.637(**)	0.29	0.26	.574(*)	0.181	0.29	0.07	0.06	0.02
Workers (R)	.744(**)	0.21	.931(**)	.898(**)	.895(**)	.922(**)	.875(**)	0.29	.648(**)	-.569(*)	-0.24	0.059	.506(*)	0.22	0.32	-0.40
Workers (U)	0.44	.616(**)	0.46	0.40	.629(**)	.599(*)	.641(**)	0.40	.667(**)	-0.37	-.505(*)	.512(*)	0.40	0.34	.485(*)	-0.19
Unemploy. (R)	-0.09	-0.11	0.11	0.03	-0.05	-0.05	-0.10	-0.29	-0.10	.518(*)	.556(*)	-0.366	0.45	.599(*)	-0.13	-0.13
Unemploy. (U)	-0.25	-0.18	-0.09	-0.18	-0.30	-0.26	-0.34	-.553(*)	-0.40	.551(*)	0.35	-0.447	0.22	.483(*)	-0.18	-0.09
BPL (R)	-.844(**)	-.647(**)	-0.39	-0.34	-.669(**)	-.517(*)	-0.47	-.836(**)	-0.30	0.22	0.03	-0.277	-.545(*)	-0.21	-0.43	0.29
BPL (U)	-.676(**)	-.684(**)	-0.24	-0.38	-0.45	-0.37	-0.29	-0.39	-0.33	0.34	0.36	-0.04	-0.41	-0.38	-0.33	0.27
Expenditure (R)	1.00	.533(*)	.654(**)	.605(*)	.826(**)	.727(**)	.623(**)	.608(**)	0.42	-0.39	-0.17	0.094	.697(**)	0.32	0.44	-0.42
Expenditure (U)	.533(*)	1.00	0.02	-0.06	0.37	0.18	0.16	.652(**)	0.29	0.18	-0.11	0.159	.657(**)	.670(**)	.590(*)	-0.11
Road	.654(**)	0.02	1.00	.891(**)	.904(**)	.960(**)	.922(**)	0.23	.550(*)	-.523(*)	-0.17	0.056	0.44	0.08	0.33	-0.33
Railway	.605(*)	-0.06	.891(**)	1.00	.803(**)	.889(**)	.864(**)	0.11	.560(*)	-.718(**)	-0.26	0.098	0.25	-0.09	0.23	-.485(*)
Telephone	.826(**)	0.37	.904(**)	.803(**)	1.00	.969(**)	.937(**)	.559(*)	.628(**)	-0.47	-0.21	0.193	.607(**)	0.23	.587(*)	-0.33

(contd.)

TABLE 5.3: contd.

(1)	Expenditure (R)	Expenditure (U)	Road	Railway	Telephone	Bank deposits	Credit ind.	Villages elec.	UR growth diff.	Sex ratio (R)	Sex ratio (U)	Slum popln.	Literacy (R)	Literacy (U)	Hospital	School
	(18)	(19)	(20)	(21)	(22)	(23)	(24)	(25)	(26)	(27)	(28)	(29)	(30)	(31)	(32)	(33)
Bank deposits	.727(**)	0.18	.960(**)	.889(**)	.969(**)	1.00	.973(**)	0.38	.599(*)	-.592(*)	-0.30	0.199	0.46	0.10	.494(*)	-0.34
Credit Ind.	.623(**)	0.16	.922(**)	.864(**)	.937(**)	.973(**)	1.00	0.40	.668(**)	-.592(*)	-0.27	0.291	0.40	0.05	.528(*)	-0.28
Villages elec.	.608(**)	.652(**)	0.23	0.11	.559(*)	0.38	0.40	1.00	0.36	0.01	0.17	0.309	.557(*)	0.32	.502(*)	-0.09
UR growth diff.	0.42	0.29	.550(*)	.560(*)	.628(**)	.599(*)	.668(**)	0.36	1.00	-0.48	-0.27	0.188	0.27	0.08	0.29	-0.16
Sex ratio (R)	-0.39	0.18	-.523(*)	-.718(**)	-0.47	-.592(*)	-.592(*)	0.01	-0.48	1.00	.694(**)	-0.316	0.25	.523(*)	-0.01	0.24
Sex ratio (U)	-0.17	-0.11	-0.17	-0.26	-0.21	-0.30	-0.27	0.17	-0.27	.694(**)	1.00	-0.276	0.26	0.25	-0.18	-0.04
Slum popln.	0.094	0.159	0.056	0.098	0.193	0.199	0.291	0.309	0.188	-0.316	-0.276	1.00	0.011	-0.167	0.071	-0.322
Literacy (R)	.697(**)	.657(**)	0.44	0.25	.607(**)	0.46	0.40	.557(*)	0.27	0.25	0.26	0.011	1.00	.823(**)	.497(*)	-0.30
Literacy (U)	0.32	.670(**)	0.08	-0.09	0.23	0.10	0.05	0.32	0.08	.523(*)	0.25	-0.167	.823(**)	1.00	0.42	-0.02
Hospital	0.44	.590(*)	0.33	0.23	.587(*)	.494(*)	.528(*)	.502(*)	0.29	-0.01	-0.18	0.071	.497(*)	0.42	1.00	0.07
School	-0.42	-0.11	-0.33	-.485(*)	-0.33	-0.34	-0.28	-0.09	-0.16	0.24	-0.04	-0.322	-0.30	-0.02	0.07	1.00

Notes: ** Correlation is significant at the 0.01 level (2–tailed). * Correlation is significant at the 0.05 level (2-tailed).

Source: Computed by Authors.

better-off states tend to have higher percentage of urban population in the country.

PER CAPITA INCOME: 2001

For the period 2001, the pattern has altered but the correlations are high and positive as before. Indeed, the developed states have been maintaining their urban status. However, Kerala improved its position in terms of per capita income, crossing the all-India average of Rs 9660. But in terms of urbanization it shows a mixed trend. The percentage of urban population in the state had gone up from 18.7 per cent in 1981 to 26.4 per cent (higher than the all-India average) in 1991 but has subsequently come down to 25.9 per cent in 2001. Looking at the interdependence between per capita income and level of urbanization for 2001, the correlation coefficient has also exhibited a highly significant positive value of 0.844 which confirms the phenomenon that the developed states constitute a higher percentage of urban population than the poorer ones.

GROWTH OF URBAN
POPULATION: 1981–91

As emphasized in the earlier chapter, the level of urbanization, usually expressed as a percentage of urban population is different from the rates of urban growth. The poorer states like Orissa, Bihar, Uttar Pradesh, Madhya Pradesh, and Rajasthan have experienced a high growth of urban population during the 1970s. The rates were above 4.5 per cent, which is much higher than the average urban growth in the country (3.8 per cent) or for the developed states such as Gujarat, Maharashtra, Punjab, and Tamil Nadu (3 per cent). The states of Delhi, Haryana, and Karnataka have shown a high growth of urban population (4.6 per cent, 4.7 per cent, and 4.1 per cent, respectively).

The high-ranking states in terms of per capita income have thus obtained low ranks in terms of growth of urban population and vice versa. The correlation coefficient of 0.028 shows the relationship between growth and per capita income as insignificant. Similar is the correlation coefficient for the period 1981–91 which works out as 0.094. The low correlation has been attributed to the dual pattern existing in the urban economy during the 1970s and 1980s.

GROWTH OF URBAN
POPULATION: 1991–2001

Growth of urbanization concentrated in developed states during the 1990s has been mentioned before. The correlation coefficient between per capita income and growth of urban population is 0.43. This is statistically significant at one per cent level. One can see that several of the developed states have reported growth of urban population, which is at par with the national average of 2.7 or slightly higher than that. Correspondingly, the growth rates of urban population in the backward states have gone down; these are often similar to the national urban growth rate or slightly below that. This can possibly be attributed to the process of liberalization which has resulted in the shift of population to urban centres in developed states which have received a large part of the industrial and infrastructural investment.

FOREIGN DIRECT INVESTMENT

Analysing the data for FDI from 1990–1 to 2000–1, it may be noted that the inflow varies widely across the states. Gujarat, Maharashtra, Delhi, Tamil Nadu, and Karnataka are the states that benefited the most whereas Assam, Bihar, Orissa, Rajasthan, and Uttar Pradesh lagged far behind the national average. The correlation coefficient is as high as 0.915. In other words, the states exhibiting a high percentage of urban population in the base year received higher FDIs, compared to other states. Another important dimension is that the correlation between per capita flow of FDI and infrastructure indicators like road, railways, and telecom are positive and very strong, suggesting that these investments directly or indirectly became instrumental in infrastructural development. It also shows that the states providing better basic infrastructure facilities have been able to receive higher FDI.

Strikingly, flow of FDI is strongly correlated with URGD, which means wider the gap between urban to rural, greater the flow of FDIs. Undoubtedly, this will accentuate the disparity and make the rich states richer relative to the poorer states. The relationship of flow of FDI is also positively related with the growth of urban population, although the value of correlation coefficient (0.44) in 2001 is not statistically significant at one per cent level. Thus, while urban infrastructural development in the country during the 1990s has facilitated FDI, it has also led to a widening of regional inequality.

AGRICULTURE

The correlation between agricultural productivity and level of urbanization is not statistically significant, reflecting a pattern during the two decades ending 1981 as well as 1991.[1] The coefficient of correlation between per capita income and agricultural productivity is also statistically insignificant, implying

[1] The value of agricultural productivity indicator has not been taken for 2001 because of inaccessibility of data.

that the relative performance of other sectors has influenced urbanization much more. However, district-level analysis in Punjab (see Chapter VI) has shown some direct correlation between urbanization and agricultural productivity. The level and tempo of urbanization has increased with an increase in agriculture and agro industries. In some districts of Haryana and Punjab which are regarded as frontline for their agricultural performance contributing more than one per cent to the country's total wheat and rice production, both the level of urbanization and growth rates are high or even higher than the state averages. In the developed states of Maharashtra, Tamil Nadu, Gujarat, and West Bengal and others such as Andhra Pradesh, Uttar Pradesh, and Orissa, the increase in agricultural productivity has been accompanied by increased urbanization. The details of such complementarity are as discussed next.

Rice

The share of some of the districts in the country's total rice production and their respective levels of urbanization as compared to that of the state have been shown in Table 5.4a. The Krishna district in Andhra Pradesh, for example, has maintained a consistently higher level of urbanization ranging from 32 to 36 per cent as compared to the state average ranging from 23 to 27 per cent. Similarly, the level of urbanization in the Ludhiana district of Punjab is about 42 per cent in 1981 and nearly 50 per cent in 1991 compared to the Punjab state figure of 27 and 29, respectively. If it is the dominance of the Ludhiana city in that district is considered a distorting factor, one can also refer to the figures for the Patiala district which again are above the state average. In Tamil Nadu, the Chengalpattu district is another important rice producing district

TABLE 5.4a
Frontline Districts of Rice Production and Urbanization

State/District	Share in India's production (%)	Level of urbanization			Annual expn. growth rate	
	1988–91	1981	1991	2001	1981–91	1991–2001
Andhra Pradesh	13.85	23.34	25.72	27.08	3.09	1.37
Districts						
West Godavari	1.75	20.77	20.83	19.69	2.05	0.26
Krishna	1.52	32.54	35.83	32.37	2.89	0.30
East Godavari	1.44	22.21	23.85	23.33	2.76	0.50
Guntur	1.38	27.53	28.93	27.95	2.27	0.37
Madhya Pradesh	6.82	20.29	23.21	26.67	3.71	2.71
Districts						
Raipur	1.57	17.19	19.75	30.45	3.76	1.73
Bilaspur	1.17	13.84	17.08	24.16	4.62	NA
Orissa	7.72	11.79	13.43	14.97	3.08	2.61
Districts						
Sambalpur	1.08	15.49	17.18	27.37	2.68	1.62
Cuttack	1.07	10.28	12.31	27.40	3.53	1.91
Punjab	8.32	27.68	29.72	33.95	2.55	3.19
Districts						
Sangrur	1.30	22.81	24.56	29.26	2.62	3.36
Patiala	1.24	29.59	30.48	34.98	2.23	3.22
Ludhiana	1.06	42.04	49.95	55.80	4.61	3.08
Tamil Nadu	7.99	32.95	34.20	43.86	1.76	3.56
Districts						
Thanjavur	2.02	23.06	22.94	33.92	1.04	2.78
Chengalpattu MGR	1.05	38.93	44.83	53.98	3.86	3.75
West Bengal	14.62	26.47	27.39	28.03	2.54	1.89
Districts						
Medinipur	2.13	8.49	10.00	10.48	3.77	1.91
Bardhaman	1.93	29.39	35.43	37.17	3.99	1.94
Birbhum	1.14	8.28	8.89	8.58	2.80	1.19
Bankura	1.12	7.63	8.31	7.37	2.49	0.12
Murshidabad	1.05	9.36	10.41	12.48	3.54	3.96
West Dinajpur	1.00	11.17	13.33	12.45	4.41	1.62

Note: NA—not available.

Source: Census of India 1981, 1991, Series-1, Paper-2; Census 2001; CMIE September 1995.

whose level of urbanization ranges from about 39 per cent in 1981 to 54 per cent in 2001 as compared to Tamil Nadu's average of about 33 per cent and 44 per cent, respectively. In Orissa, the Sambalpur district shows a similar comparison indicating a positive association-ship between agricultural growth and the level of urbanization.

Wheat

Karnal of Haryana (25.95: 21.88 in 1981 and 27.6:24.79 in 1991), Patiala, Amritsar, Ludhiana of Punjab (29.59,32.97,42.04:27.68 in 1981 and 30.48,34.14,49.95:29.72 in 1991 and also 34.98,40, and 55.8: 33.95 in 2001), Moradabad and Aligarh of Uttar Pradesh (26.95,23: 17.95 in 1981 and 27.46, 25.2: 19.89 in 1991 and also 31.02,28.87: 20.78 in 2001)—the leading wheat producing districts of the country have indi-cated a comparatively high level and growth of urban population that are similar or above the averages of the respective states (Table 5.4b).

Groundnut

Similarly, frontline districts in groundnut pro-duction like Rajkot and Jamnagar of Gujarat (41.29, 37.44: 31.1 in 1981 and also 47.03, 39.74: 34.4 in 1991 and also 50.52, 44.54: 37.35 in 2001) and Chengalpattu of Tamil Nadu (38.93: 32.95 in 1981 and 44.83: 34.2 in 1991 and also 53.98: 43.86 in 2001) have shown such signifi-cant complementarity with level and tempo of urbanization.

Overall, the correlation between the growth of urban population and agricultural produc-tivity has been noted as negative (–0.44) during the 1970s (Table 5.1). During the period 1981–91, there is no correlation between agri-cultural productivity and growth of urban population. It is important to mention here that agriculture did very badly during the 1990s

and its impact on reorganization of population and other economic activities is likely to be minimal. However, one cannot be dismissive about the correlation between agricultural productivity and urbanization on the basis of data available so far. The impact of agricultural productivity, increased farm income, conse-quent demand for non-farm foods and ser-vices, off-farm employment, and resulting urbanization merits further study.

INDUSTRIAL PRODUCTION

Industrial production as percentage of aggre-gate state domestic product shows positive correlation with the level of urbanization in all the three periods, and size of enterprise (worker enterprise ratio) in rural and urban areas has been correlated with the level and growth of urbanization separately.[2] The cor-relation coefficients, however, work out as negative when we relate industrialization with the growth of urban population during the 1970s and 1980s. It has already been argued that urban growth is characterized by dualism and both developed and backward states had experienced high growth of population in ur-ban areas. The pattern, however, has changed during the 1990s. The correlation coefficient is no longer negative as the capacity of indus-trially backward states to attract migrants has gone down over the years. Worker enterprise ratio in urban areas correlates positively and in a highly (statistically) significant manner, with both the level as well as growth of urban population in 2001. This further confirms the proposition that industrialization contin-ues to be a significant though not uniform factor in explaining the level and growth of urbanization across the states in the 1990s.

[2] The worker enterprise ratio has been taken from the Economic Census 1998 and used for the period 2001.

TABLE 5.4b
Frontline Districts of Wheat Production and Urbanization

State/District	Share in India's production (%)	Level of urbanization			Annual expn. growth rate	
	1988–91	1981	1991	2001	1981–91	1991–2001
Haryana	11.68	21.88	24.79	29.00	3.58	4.11
Districts						
Hissar	1.75	19.38	21.18	34.96	2.98	3.28
Kaithal	1.20	11.94	14.74	19.36	3.96	4.17
Karnal	1.17	25.95	27.60	26.56	2.91	2.64
Kurukshetra	1.05	20.72	24.25	26.06	3.58	3.37
Sirsa	1.04	20.44	21.16	26.36	2.78	4.26
Jind	1.02	15.14	17.27	20.34	3.34	3.80
Rohtak	1.00	19.28	21.63	35.06	2.76	2.62
Punjab	22.26	27.68	29.72	33.95	2.55	3.19
Districts						
Sangrur	3.02	22.81	24.56	29.26	2.62	3.36
Firozpur	2.80	22.85	23.94	25.81	2.51	1.90
Faridkot	2.60	23.87	25.35	33.89	2.41	2.22
Patiala	2.41	29.59	30.48	34.98	2.23	3.22
Amritsar	2.40	32.97	34.14	40.00	1.68	3.65
Ludhiana	2.11	42.04	49.95	55.80	4.61	3.08
Bhatinda	2.09	22.68	22.58	29.78	1.71	2.80
Jalandhar	1.53	35.32	36.31	47.45	1.87	3.24
Gurdaspur	1.20	21.69	23.10	25.46	2.17	3.23
Rajasthan	7.34	21.05	22.88	23.38	3.31	2.71
District						
Ganganagar	1.72	20.61	21.08	25.28	2.77	3.02
Uttar Pradesh	35.13	17.95	19.89	20.78	3.29	2.83
Districts						
Moradabad	1.25	26.95	27.46	31.02	2.84	0.32
Aligarh	1.15	23.00	25.20	28.87	3.36	0.42
Hardoi	1.06	11.06	11.76	11.98	2.48	2.33
Budaun	1.03	16.14	17.68	18.16	3.04	2.56
Bulandsahar	1.02	19.34	20.96	23.05	2.62	1.29

Note: NA—not available.

Sources: Census of India 1981, 1991, Series–1, Paper-2; Census 2001; CMIE September 1995.

TABLE 5.4c

Frontline Districts of Groundnut Production and Urbanization

State/District	Share in India's production (%)	Level of urbanization			Annual expn. growth rate	
	1988–91	1981	1991	2001	1981–91	1991–2001
Andhra Pradesh	25.81	23.32	26.84	27.08	3.55	1.37
Districts						
Anantapur	6.93	20.81	23.51	25.28	3.42	2.07
Chittoor	3.68	16.88	19.82	21.69	3.34	2.26
Kurnool	3.09	24.49	25.85	22.57	2.63	0.31
Cuddapah	2.85	19.40	24.00	23.33	3.72	0.97
Mahbubnagar	1.65	10.93	11.11	10.59	2.45	0.82
Vizianagram	1.09	15.94	17.20	18.36	2.30	1.25
Gujarat	22.24	31.10	34.40	37.35	2.90	2.88
Districts						
Junagadh	6.28	30.46	32.55	29.05	1.96	2.23
Rajkot	3.64	41.29	47.03	50.52	3.11	3.01
Jamnagar	3.51	37.44	39.74	44.54	1.63	3.28
Amreli	3.27	20.42	21.53	22.45	2.01	1.49
Bhavnagar	2.04	33.29	35.05	37.85	2.48	1.53
Kachchh	1.47	26.13	30.29	30.72	3.19	2.17
Karnataka	11.03	28.89	30.91	33.98	2.55	2.53
Districts						
Chitradurga	1.40	23.50	27.02	18.15	3.43	2.31
Tumkur	1.37	13.77	16.59	19.64	3.38	2.82
Raichur	1.32	19.27	20.92	25.42	3.34	2.33
Dharwad	1.10	35.25	34.95	54.98	1.64	2.00

(contd.)

TABLE 5.4c: contd.

State/District	Share in India's production (%) 1988–91	Level of urbanization			Annual expn. growth rate	
		1981	1991	2001	1981–91	1991–2001
Maharashtra	11.78	35.03	38.73	42.40	3.27	2.95
Districts						
Kolhapur	1.32	25.32	26.40	29.65	2.33	2.81
Satara	1.17	13.04	12.91	14.24	1.72	2.32
Dhule	1.11	19.52	20.53	26.07	2.61	2.24
Orissa	6.00	11.79	13.43	14.97	3.08	2.61
District						
Cuttack	1.82	10.28	12.31	27.40	3.53	1.91
Tamil Nadu	14.55	32.95	34.20	43.86	1.76	3.56
Districts						
S. Arcot	2.76	15.70	15.76	22.56	1.52	4.29
N. Arcot (A)	1.75	30.80	31.76	37.85	1.63	3.18
Salem	1.60	28.93	28.86	46.35	1.26	5.08
Chengalpattu MGR	1.40	38.93	44.83	53.98	3.86	3.75
Tiruvannamalai	1.26	11.54	12.10	18.36	1.60	5.00
Periyar	1.04	22.01	24.77	46.20	2.34	7.30

Note: NA—not available.

Source: Census of India 1981, 1991, Series-1, Paper-2; Census 2001; CMIE September 1995.

Urbanization and Employment/Poverty

Employment

The WPR for the fifteen-plus age group shows no significant correlation (rural as well as urban) with the level as well as growth of urban population in 1991 and 2001. Similarly, unemployment rate adjusted for usual status does not reveal any significant relationship with the level of urbanization, though the correlations are negative in both rural and urban and in 1991 as well as 2001. The correlation coefficient observed is −0.538 which is significant at 5 per cent level. It implies that urban unemployment rate has diminished in the states as a result of rapid urban growth. Unfortunately, rural unemployment rate has not exhibited a similar correlation. It is, therefore, difficult to argue that urbanization per se would lead to growth in employment rate or bring down the unemployment rate. In fact, there is a complex interaction among various forces that are linked with urban growth, affecting employment scenario in more than one way. As a result, there emerges no clear relationship between the two. Interestingly, the correlation of rural WPR with infrastructural indicators like roads and railways works out as significantly negative in 2001. This implies that the states where roads and railways are not developed, rural workforce participation tends to be high. This implies that high WPR could be due to excessive dependence on agriculture and cannot be taken as a development indicator.

There is, nonetheless, no denial of the fact that urbanization results in growth of regular jobs. The states with high levels of urbanization or experiencing high urban growth have indeed provided job opportunities which are somewhat stable and of long-term nature. Both the level and growth of urban population correlates positively with the percentage of regular workers in urban areas at both the time points, 1991 and 2001. Importantly, the correlation has improved over time. One would infer that the regular (urban) jobs have come up more in the urbanized states in the 1990s. Furthermore, the impact is not restricted to the rural areas only. In case of rural areas, the correlation coefficients are much higher than urban areas.

Informal Sector in Urban Areas

The informal sector includes urban street vendors, hawkers, and small-scale informal industries, etc. The informal sector plays a significant role in poverty reduction, providing an opportunity to raise incomes by such population. The informal sector is characterized by ease of entry, reliance on indigenous resources, family ownership of enterprises, small scale of operation, labour intensive, and skills acquired outside formal education/training systems.

Attempts have been made by several cities in developing countries to support the informal sector by (a) amending restrictive urban regulations; (b) making land-use standards more realistic and meaningful to the majority of the population; (c) providing adequate land for the location of informal enterprises and markets; and (d) developing basic infrastructure to benefit the informal enterprises.

In view of the existence and rapid growth of a large informal sector in large cities, there is a need to provide for enabling framework by amending zoning regulations, land use standards, and building bye-laws for the operation of informal sector in urban areas. Special schemes and programmes have been implemented by the Government of India through various departments like industry, labour, urban employment, and poverty alleviation and others, to develop small and micro enterprises with particular focus on the urban poor.

POVERTY

In the context of poverty, it is seen that apart from Bihar, Madhya Pradesh, Rajasthan, and Uttar Pradesh, the incidence of poverty is high in Orissa and Assam as well. It has already been mentioned that the level of urbanization correlates positively with economic development at all the time points under consideration. One would, therefore, expect a negative correlation between urbanization and rural poverty. This is indeed the case. The value was −0.439 in 1981 and became −0.599 in 2001. The correlations work out as negative even with urban poverty but the values are somewhat lower. Another indicator, linked to poverty, is average monthly per capita expenditure. In rural areas, it exhibits highly positive correlation with the level of urbanization during the entire period, as expected. The correlation, however, is not so high in case of urban areas and this has gone down further in 2001. This may be attributed to the growing slum population in urban areas.

As per expert group (Planning Commission 1993) methodology, at the macro level, the percentage of people below the poverty line has gone down from 54.9 per cent in 1973–4 to 51.8 per cent in 1977–8 to 44.8 per cent in 1983, then to 39.3 per cent in 1987–8 and finally to 36.3 per cent in 1993–4. As per the modified methodology, the corresponding figures are 54.9 per cent, 51.3 per cent, 44.5 per cent, 38.9 per cent and 36 per cent, respectively. Even though the two sets of estimates are marginally different, but the declining trend is well established.

The head count ratio (HCR) of the poor in urban areas has been significantly below (5 percentage points) that in rural areas during the 1970s and 1980s based on the NSS data. The gap between the two poverty levels narrowed down so much that in 1987–8, urban poverty works out higher than rural poverty. The figure for rural areas was again higher than that of urban areas but RU poverty differential in the late 1990s (1997) was noted as less than that of the 1970s. Based on sample data from NSS, it may be concluded that the poverty scenario has changed significantly since the mid-1990s. The poverty levels in developed states like Maharashtra, Tamil Nadu, and Gujarat have surprisingly been high. Industrial growth in recent years did not lead to any significant decline in poverty in these states. Based on NSS data, the poverty scenario has changed significantly in the mid-1990s. The percentage of people below poverty line in rural areas has increased by one percentage point in 1994–5 compared to that of the previous year. It remained at that level until 1997. Correspondingly, the figures have gone up by around two percentage points in urban areas. There is thus evidence that the poverty level increased during 1993–8 and thus the trend of decline has been stalled in the mid-1990s.

The proportion of people living below the poverty line in many states is now higher in urban areas than in rural areas. Developed states, such as Punjab and Karnataka, and the less developed states like Andhra Pradesh, Kerala, Madhya Pradesh, Uttar Pradesh, and Rajasthan, have reported higher levels of urban poverty than rural poverty for a number of years.

The poverty data analysis indicated below is taken from two full rounds of NSS, 43rd round (July 1987 to June 1988) and 50th round (July 1993 to June 1994). From the NSS survey, towns were classified into five groups as per population size: (i) less than 50,000 (S1),

(ii) 50,000 to 200,000 (S2), (iii) 200,000 to 400,000 (S3), (iv) 400,000 to 1,000,000 (S4), and (v) above 1,000,000 (S5).

It was observed that the highest incidence of urban poverty was mostly in the small cities. With the increase in size of the town, the incidence of poverty declined steadily. In 1987–8, the HCR in S1 towns was 47.40 per cent and in S5 towns was 26.73 per cent and in 1993–4 it was 43.16 per cent and 20.57 per cent, respectively. The HCR in 1987–8 in S2 towns was 43.22 per cent, in S3 towns was 34.53 per cent, and in S4 towns was 31.76 per cent. These figures in 1993–4 were 34.19 per cent, 33.67 per cent, and 26.83 per cent, respectively.

URBANIZATION AND INFRASTRUCTURE

The data have been taken from the CMIE report for the three periods. All these indicators of physical as well as financial infrastructure, viz., roads, railway lines, telephone connections, village electrification, bank deposits, and credit to industry exhibit highly significant correlations with urbanization level at all the three points of time under consideration. Excepting village electrification all are also showing very high correlation values with per capita income and expenditure. Moreover, correlations have remained almost the same, suggesting that no substantial changes have occurred in the ranking of the states. In other words, the poorer states have not been able to improve their position relative to rich states. The relationship of infrastructural facilities with growth of urban population are also positive and generally significant at the three points. This implies that the process of urbanization is directly related to improvement in infrastructural facilities across the states.

URBANIZATION AND SOCIO-DEMOGRAPHIC INDICATORS

SEX RATIO

Sex ratio has negative correlation with urbanization, implying that RU migration is generally male selective, resulting in a reduction in the female–male ratio. Its correlation with urban growth turns out as highly significant during the 1990s suggesting that the urbanization process has been backed up by male-dominant migration streams. Rural sex ratio also relates negatively and significantly with the level of urbanization and it has been maintained at all the three time points. This may be explained in terms of RU linkages in the relatively urbanized states. Here, the migrants are attractive not only in the urban centres but also in the rural peripheries. Furthermore, the rural economy in these urbanized states on an average seems to be doing better than the others; thereby attracting the male migrants in large numbers.

BASIC AMENITIES

The levels of urban basic amenities like access to safe drinking water, sanitation facilities, and electricity are positively correlated with urbanization although the values are statistically insignificant. It is thus not possible to argue that the more urbanized states provide basic amenities to a larger percentage of their urban population. On the other hand, the correlation of these indicators with urban growth has become negative over the years. It appears that the growth of urban population over the decades has led to increased pressure on basic amenities and resulted in deterioration in standards of living.

The correlation of percentage of urban population with hospitals per thousand persons is highly positive. But its value has decreased continuously from 0.609 in 1981 to 0.552 in 1991 and then to 0.486 in 2001. Furthermore, its correlation with middle/ higher secondary schools has been negative and has been maintained as such in 2001 as well. This apparently reflects the pressure of the growing urban population on the limited infrastructure. It has been argued before that urbanization in the later years has been backed up by industrialization. Unfortunately, a similar relationship does not exist between indicators of urbanization, social development, and access to basic services.

SLUMS

The existence and rapid growth of slum settlements has been noted as a general urban phenomenon in recent years. The previous censuses had not gathered any information regarding this aspect of urbanization. For the first time, the Census 2001 has collected demographic data regarding the slum settlements in all urban centres with a population of 50,000 or more throughout the country. The total slum population in the country works out as above 40 million accounting for 14.12 per cent of the total urban population. The states reporting high share of slum population in total urban population are Maharashtra, Andhra Pradesh, and Haryana, constituting 25.9 per cent, 25.1 per cent, and 23 per cent of the urban population respectively. West Bengal and Delhi too have exhibited moderately higher shares of slum population than the national average. The important point to note here is that these states are relatively well off economically and have higher levels of urbanization than other states. Evidently, the correlations between the indicators of urbanization (level and growth) and slum population are positive which confirms the fact that slum settlements have generally increased in highly urbanized states.

Importantly, some of the developed states, which are also highly urbanized, like Gujarat, Karnataka, Punjab, and Tamil Nadu have reported shares of slum population, which are much below the national average. One would, therefore, like to look into the structural conditions of the states which influences RU migration, thereby increasing slum population. Analysing the interdependence between the indicators of socio-economic development and share of slum population, it has been found that indicators on per capita income and industrialization have exhibited highly positive correlation with regular workers in urban areas. On the other hand, it has shown negatively high correlation with urban unemployment rate. This shows that increase in job opportunities is conducive for growing slum population. On the contrary, existence of high unemployment rate in the state discourages RU migration, and thereby, does not provide a conducive atmosphere for increase in slum population in the state. These facts confirm the generally perceived conclusion that increasing slum population has been prompted by rapid industrialization and growing job opportunities in selected pockets of the country.

Some aspects of slum demography as brought out by the Census 2001 are revealing. The female–male ratio in the slums of some of the states for example, Tamil Nadu and Andhra Pradesh are higher in comparison to the state's urban sex ratio. The age–sex composition is also reflective of the general pattern obtaining in the country (Table 5.5). These facts confirm that Indian slums are not to be generalized as male-dominant and transient settlements. In most cases they are established communities with demographic characteristics in common with the city.

An attempt has been made to examine city-wise concentrations of slum population.

TABLE 5.5
Socio-demographic Characteristics of Slums (2001)

States/India	Slum population	% of slum population to total urban population	Sex ratio	Literacy	% of 0–6 popn to total slum population
India	40,297,341	14.12	875	63.62	13.73
A&N Islands	16,265	13.97	835	68.05	12.95
Andhra Pradesh	5,149,272	25.11	975	61.90	12.44
Assam	84,644	2.50	886	68.20	11.95
Bihar	507,383	5.85	885	53.91	16.88
Chandigarh	107,098	13.24	707	44.18	20.33
Chhattisgarh	788,127	18.88	935	65.50	14.82
Delhi	2,025,890	15.80	780	56.46	15.93
Goa	14,529	2.17	936	50.88	14.37
Gujarat	1,346,709	7.13	811	56.02	15.14
Haryana	1,421,839	23.25	824	62.83	14.99
Jammu & Kashmir	270,084	10.78	898	57.45	10.52
Jharkhand	309,557	5.17	897	63.97	14.57
Karnataka	1,267,759	7.07	965	58.07	14.21
Kerala	45,337	0.55	1029	73.97	12.15
Madhya Pradesh	2,388,517	14.83	904	64.27	15.07
Maharashtra	10,644,605	25.95	829	69.85	13.68
Meghalaya	110,714	24.46	997	77.68	11.81
Orissa	635,150	11.56	910	63.34	13.19
Pondicherry	72,275	11.15	1032	65.59	12.88
Punjab	1,151,864	13.97	841	64.33	12.79
Rajasthan	1,206,123	9.13	900	54.89	17.08
Tamil Nadu	2,530,289	9.29	983	69.35	11.20
Tripura	29,378	5.41	988	77.41	9.78
Uttar Pradesh	4,156,020	12.04	867	54.36	15.75
Uttaranchal	195,604	9.01	881	59.01	15.16
West Bengal	3,822,309	17.00	850	67.03	10.62

Notes: a. Crude literacy rate has been calculated (to make the data comparable, same method has been applied in case of total urban population also).

b. In case of Himachal Pradesh, Sikkim, Arunachal Pradesh, Nagaland, Manipur, Mizoram, Daman & Diu, Dadra & Nagar Haveli, and Lakshadweep no slum population has been reported at the Census of India, 2001.

c. Delhi includes eleven census towns and Uttar Pradesh one.

d. Seven towns, one each in Bihar, Maharashtra, and Meghalaya, two each in Gujarat and Madhya Pradesh include population of outgrowths/UAs.

Source: Census of India 2001.

Variation of concentration of slums in cities can be attributed to a combination of many factors like industrial development, nature and structure of industry, rate of unemployment, basic amenities, and planning controls. Cities like Greater Mumbai (48.88 per cent), Faridabad (46.55 per cent), Meerut (43.87 per cent), and Nagpur (35.42 per cent) tend to indicate a combination of some of these factors acting in favour of the growth of slums (Table 5.6). Specific case studies on slums in Indian cities though have been undertaken but in the light of the 2001 Census more comprehensive studies on slums need to be attempted. It has traditionally been assumed that a considerable share of city's growth can be attributed to growth of slums and such growth is accelerated by the growth of migration. All these components encourage further research on slums to actually appraise its relevance in recent urbanization of the country. The city specific share of migration in the urban growth is given in Table 5.7.

Before the mid-1970s there was no systematic time series data available on slum population on a countrywide scale. It was only after the findings of nationwide sample survey of slums conducted by the NSSO in 1976–7 and published in 1980, that a tentative, though restricted, estimate of slum population of Class I cities in the country became available. Another set of data on slum population released in 1981 related to the estimate computed by the National Building Organization (NBO).

The Town and Country Planning Organization (TCPO) prepared 'A Compendium on Indian Slums' in 1985 giving estimates of slum population at the all-India level, state-wise and town-wise. Another compendium was brought out in 1996 by TCPO which presents the slum population estimates for 1991 but

also the estimates for 2001. According to TCPO estimates, the slum population in the country as of 1991 was of the order of about 46.3 million, constituting nearly 21 per cent of the total urban population of the country. Slum population for the year 2001 is estimated at about 61.8 million constituting, 21.24 per cent of the total urban population. The slum population as per the 2001 Census is only 40 million, accounting for 14.12 per cent of the total population.

As per TCPO estimates, the distribution of estimated slum population (2001) indicates the preponderance of slum dwellers in the twenty-three metropolitan cities of the country which accommodated about 26.57 per cent of the total population of these cities. The Census 2001 has indicated a percentage of 26.37 per cent only, with Lucknow not reporting any figure of slum population. As per TCPO estimates, among the states, Maharashtra emerges with the highest number of slum dwellers accommodating about 10.7 million persons in 2001, which constitutes about 25.80 per cent of its urban population. Other states, having fairly a large slum population are Uttar Pradesh (7.7 million), West Bengal (6.5 million), Andhra Pradesh (6.0 million), Tamil Nadu (4.3 million), Bihar (3.5 million), while those which accounted for a smaller share of slum population included Assam (0.5 million), Haryana (1 million), Karnataka (1.7 million), Kerala (1.6 million), and Orissa (1.1 million). As per census these figures are much lower except Maharashtra which is nearly equal to the TCPO estimates for 2001 census.

MIGRATION

In the absence of data on migration for 2001, an attempt has been made to evaluate the role

TABLE 5.6
Slum Population in Municipal Corporations of Million-plus Cities

Municipal corporation	Population 2001	% of slum population
Greater Mumbai	11,914,398	48.88
Delhi	9,817,439	18.89
Kolkata	4,580,544	32.55
Bangalore	4,292,223	8.04
Chennai	4,216,268	25.60
Ahmedabad	3,515,361	12.51
Hyderabad	3,449,878	17.43
Pune	2,540,069	20.92
Kanpur	2,532,138	14.57
Surat	2,433,787	16.68
Jaipur	2,324,319	15.07
Nagpur	2,051,320	35.42
Indore	1,597,441	16.25
Bhopal	1,433,875	8.81
Ludhiana	1,395,053	22.56
Patna	1,376,950	0.25
Vadodara	1,306,035	8.21
Lucknow	2,207,340	NA
Agra	1,259,979	9.67
Kochi	596,473	1.32
Varanasi	1,100,748	12.55
Nashik	1,076,967	13.21
Meerut	1,074,229	43.87
Faridabad	1,054,981	46.55
Coimbatore	923,085	6.49
Madurai	922,913	19.06
Vishakhapatnam	969,608	17.65
Jabalpur	951,469	28.95
Jamshedpur	570,349	NA
Asansol	486,304	NA
Dhanbad	198,963	NA
Allahabad	990,298	NA
Amritsar	975,695	NA
Vijaywada	825,436	31.97
Rajkot	966,642	15.57

Notes: NA—not available.
Population of cities' municipal corporations instead of their UAs is taken into consideration for calculation of share of slum population. Without the UAs, few smaller municipal corporations have reported a population which is less than a million.

Source: Census of India 2001.

TABLE 5.7
Share of Migration in Urban Growth

	Bombay	Calcutta	Delhi	Madras	Bangalore	Hyderabad
1981						
Population (in million)	8.24	9.19	5.73	4.29	2.92	2.55
Increase in 1971–81 (in million)	2.27	1.77	2.08	1.12	1.26	0.75
Migration (in million)	1.55	0.69	1.16	0.68	0.5	0.25
Percentage	68.28	38.98	55.77	60.71	39.68	33.33
1991						
Population (in million)	12.57	10.91	8.38	5.36	4.09	4.28
Increase in 1981–91 (in million)	4.33	1.72	2.65	1.07	1.16	1.73
Migration (in million)	1.81	0.61	1.36	0.57	0.51	0.55
Percentage	41.80	35.47	51.32	53.27	43.97	31.79

Source: Census of India 1981 and 1991.

of migration in urban growth considering the data of earlier censuses. Leading metropolitan cities—the magnets of migration in the country—have exhibited varying features of the share of migration in the marginal increase of their urban population during two decades 1971–81 and 1981–91. The analysis in Table 5.7 indicates:

• Out of these six large metropolises, Bangalore has indicated a steady increase in the share of migration in the city's urban growth.

• The rest of the five cities, on the other hand, have shown a decline in the share of migration though the degree of decline has got considerable variation.

Only further studies on detailed disaggregated data on various streams of migration will help explain the factors causing differentials behind the share of migration in urban growth.

VI

Socio-economic Aspects of Urbanization
A District-level Analysis for Four Select States

NEED FOR MACRO-LEVEL ANALYSIS

This chapter analyses the relationship between urbanization and other related developmental indicators at the district level for four selected states of Maharashtra, Punjab, Bihar, and Rajasthan, on lines similar to the analysis at the national and state levels in the previous chapter. The macro or state-level analysis basically helped in getting a broad overview of urbanization. This, however, could not capture the micro-level details pertaining to the processes of urbanization and explanatory factors. Averaging of values at the country and state levels tends to overshadow the attributes and regional specificity that are observable at the district level. The study has, therefore, been supplemented with this chapter incorporating a district-level analysis (Maps 6.1 and 6.2).

This chapter analyses the pattern of urbanization across the districts and examines the nature of interdependence between the level and trend of urbanization and the socio-economic indicators of development at the micro level over the three decades, 1971–81, 1981–91, and 1991–2001. Two developed states (Maharashtra and Punjab) and two less developed states (Bihar and Rajasthan) have been included in the spatio–temporal analysis. It is hoped that the analysis will be able to bring

forth the significant differences in the nature and pattern of urbanization and at the same time highlight their association with the process of economic development.

TRENDS OF URBANIZATION IN FOUR SELECT STATES

MAHARASHTRA
Level of Urbanization
Maharashtra is economically one of the developed states in the country. Availability of good infrastructure network including ports and widespread industrial enterprises have contributed significantly to the development of the state in recent decades. The level of urbanization, which by itself is an important indicator of development, has shown strong positive association with industrialization. In fact, Maharashtra had the highest percentage of urban population among all the large states in 1991, as was the position even earlier. However, according to the 2001 Census, Tamil Nadu has a higher percentage of urban population.[1]

An analysis of disaggregated figures of the

[1] This has encouraged researchers to examine the definitions of 'urban centre' as adopted at the state level in 1991 and 2001. This point has been examined at length in Chapter II.

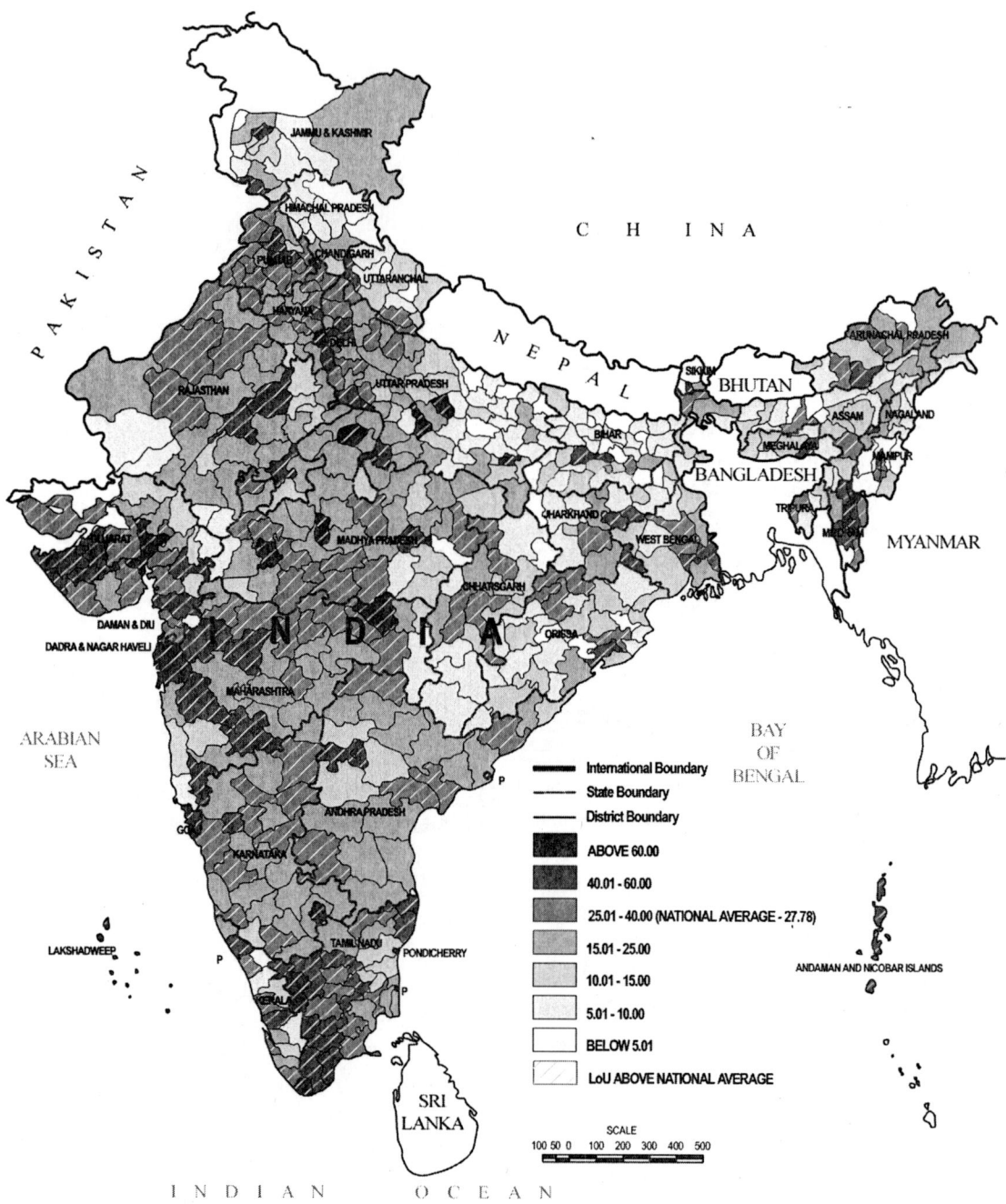

MAP 6.1: Level of Urbanization—Districts (2001)

Source: Census of India 2001.

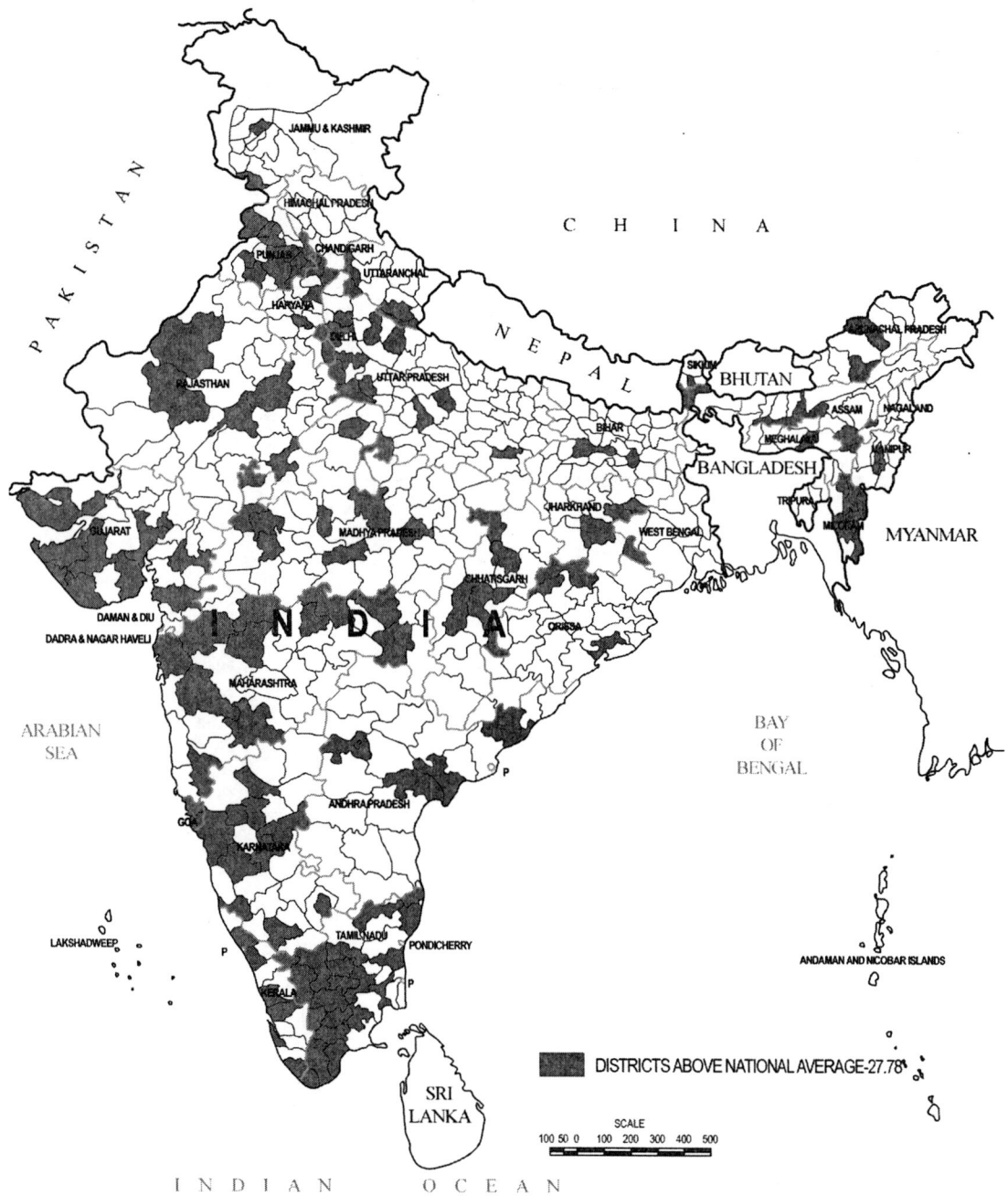

MAP 6.2: Districts above National Average (2001)
Source: Census of India 2001.

percentage of urban population at the district level within Maharashtra indicates high disparity. The data obtained from the past three censuses substantiate this fact. In 1981, for example, the industrially developed districts such as Nagpur (56.75), Pune (47.53), and Thane (44.34) reported a share of urban population much above the state average (35.03), Greater Bombay being the exception. On the other

hand, out of the total twenty-six districts, eleven districts in 1981 reported figures below 20 per cent. The lowest among them were Ratnagiri (8.73), Ahmadnagar (12.95), Satara (13.04), and Bhandara (13.1). Therefore, the coefficient of variation of the level of urbanization across districts worked out to be as high as 71.6 per cent, reflecting a high degree of dispersion (Table 6.1a).

TABLE 6.1a
Trends and Pattern of Urbanization Across Districts in Maharashtra (1981)

Districts	Towns (UAs)	Annl. exp. gr. rate (1971–81)	% Urban popln
Dhule	7	3.30	19.52
Jalgaon	14(1)	2.70	25.14
Buldana	9	2.29	18.49
Akola	9	2.52	24.89
Amrawati	10	2.48	29.25
Wardha	6	1.92	24.98
Nagpur	14(1)	3.28	56.75
Bhandara	7	2.88	13.10
Chandrapur	8	4.48	17.38
Yavatmal	8	3.01	15.09
Nanded	10	3.60	18.74
Parbhani	12	3.48	19.87
Aurangabad	10(1)	4.90	24.87
Nashik	16(1)	3.13	31.02
Thane	25(4)	5.84	44.34
Greater Bombay	1	3.21	100.00
Raigarh	14	3.19	14.12
Pune	18(2)	3.93	47.53
Ahmadnagar	8(1)	3.32	12.95
Bid	7	4.32	16.26
Osamabad	12	3.71	12.64
Solapur	11(1)	2.19	29.65
Satara	11	1.58	13.04
Ratnagiri	12	0.22	8.73
Kolhapur	12(1)	3.45	25.32
Sangli	5(1)	3.17	21.48
Mean		3.16	26.35
SD		1.10	18.86
CV		34.78	71.57
State	276(14)	3.39	35.03

Notes: Number of UAs is shown within the bracket in the district where they exist. The total number of towns/UAs, obtained by counting UAs as a single unit, is shown outside the bracket.
Source: Census of India 1981, Paper-2, Rural–Urban Distribution.

The 1991 Census also reveals a similar pattern of urbanization (Table 6.1b). The highly urbanized districts in 1981 such as Nagpur, Pune, and Thane have maintained a higher percentage of urban population in 1991 as well, being 61.48, 50.76, and 64.74, respectively. The

TABLE 6.1b
Trends and Pattern of Urbanization Across Districts in Maharashtra (1991)

Districts	Towns (UAs)	Annl. exp. gr. rate (1981–91)	% Urban popln
Dhule	5	2.61	20.53
Jalgaon	14(1)	2.83	27.42
Buldana	10	3.30	20.63
Akola	7	3.33	28.68
Amravati	10	2.92	33.01
Wardha	3	2.03	26.61
Nagpur	18(2)	3.22	61.48
Bhandara	7	1.38	13.15
Gadchiroli	3	14.85	8.71
Chandrapur	11(1)	7.00	28.04
Yavatmal	9(1)	3.09	17.21
Nanded	11(1)	4.32	21.71
Parbhani	10	3.77	22.50
Jalna	4	3.68	16.92
Aurangabad	7(1)	6.08	32.78
Nashik	15(1)	3.86	35.52
Thane	22(3)	8.23	64.74
Greater Bombay	1(1)	1.84	100.00
Raigarh	18	4.33	17.84
Pune	33(1)	3.50	50.76
Ahmadnagar	12(2)	4.16	15.84
Bid	6	3.52	17.96
Latur	5	4.72	20.42
Osamabad	7	3.97	15.22
Solapur	8(1)	1.91	28.81
Satara	9	1.72	12.91
Ratnagiri	7	1.37	8.97
Sindhudurg	3	2.22	7.60
Kolhapur	8(1)	2.33	26.40
Sangli	7(1)	2.42	22.84
Mean		*3.82*	*27.51*
SD		*2.60*	*19.38*
CV		*68.20*	*70.46*
State	290(18)	3.32	38.73

Notes: Note: Number of UAs is shown within the bracket in the district where they exist. The total number of towns/UAs, obtained by counting UAs as a single unit, is shown outside the bracket.
Source: Census of India 1991, Paper-2, Rural–Urban Distribution.

figures, in fact, reveal significant upward revision during the 1980s. In comparison, the growth of urban population in the backward districts is low. The districts of Ratnagiri (8.97), Ahmadnagar (15.84), Satara (12.91), and Bhandara (13.15) with their share of urban population in 1991 continue to be low as before. Of the four new districts (Jalna, Gadchiroli, Latur, and Sindhudurg), which have come up during 1991 Census, Sindhudurg and Gadchiroli show very low share of urban population, viz., 7.6 per cent and 8.7 per cent respectively. The process of urbanization in the state has thus maintained the high degree of disparity across the districts, the coefficient of variation being 70.5 per cent in 1991.

The urbanization pattern across the districts has not changed even in 2001 (Table 6.1c). The highly urbanized districts have shown a very high share of urban population, much above the state's average (42.4). The developed districts have thus been able to maintain their relative positions in all the three censuses. Greater Mumbai comprises 100 per cent of urban population in all the censuses. The less urbanized districts of Gadchiroli (6.93), Sindhudurg (9.56), Ratnagiri (11.33), Satara (14.24), and Bhandara (15.44) are stagnant in terms of their positions in urban hierarchy. The highly urbanized districts have continued to reveal higher shares of urban population in subsequent censuses whereas the less urbanized or the backward districts have experienced marginal improvements over the three decades, thereby maintaining the level of disparity. The coefficient of variation in the percentage of urban population works out as 67.6 across the districts.

Urban Growth Rate

The annual growth rate of urban population during the three decades under consideration,

however, reveals interesting departures from the existing pattern of urbanization. The highly urbanized districts of Nagpur (3.28), Pune (3.93), and Thane (5.84) had experienced high urban growth during the period 1971–81. The growth rates of Thane and Pune were much above the state average of 3.39 per cent whereas Nagpur was closely similar. The exceptionally high urban growth in Thane can be explained by the fact that here growth has taken place as an extension of Greater Bombay UA. Another responsible factor is the emergence of new towns in the area. Out of thirty-three new towns of Maharashtra, Thane alone claims eleven, constituting 10.84 per cent of the district's urban population in 1981. Earlier, all these new towns were census towns and their inclusion reflects a marked increase in the workforce engaged in non-agricultural activities in large villages in the neighbourhood of metro cities of Maharashtra. What is more interesting is that the growth rates of several backward districts such as Bid (4.32), Kolhapur (3.45), and Osamabad (3.71) in 1971–81 are also above the state average and are quite comparable to those of the developed districts. Furthermore, a few other backward districts like Dhule, Sholapur, and Parbhani, have experienced growth rates around the state average although their share of urban population is very low.

During 1981–91, the developed districts maintained their high urban growth. The backward districts like Aurangabad, Osamabad, Bid, too, maintained their growth rates at a level higher than the state average of 3.32 per cent. The new district of Gadchiroli reported an exceptionally high growth of urban population of 14.85 per cent.

The 2001 Census reports a decline in the overall urban growth rate in the state from 3.32 per cent in 1981–91 to 2.95 per cent in

TABLE 6.1c
Trends and Pattern of Urbanization Across Districts in Maharashtra (2001)

Districts	Towns (UAs)	Annl. exp. gr. rate (1991–2001)	% Urban popln
Dhule	2	2.24	26.07
Jalgaon	16(1)	1.85	28.60
Buldana	11	1.98	21.26
Akola	8	2.44	38.48
Amrawati	10	2.26	34.51
Wardha	7	1.36	26.40
Nagpur	25(2)	2.50	64.36
Bhandara	6	1.84	15.44
Gadchiroli	2	−0.19	6.93
Chandrapur	14	3.03	32.37
Yavatmal	13(1)	2.52	18.67
Nanded	13	3.08	24.02
Parbhani	8	2.87	32.53
Jalna	4	2.87	19.07
Aurangabad	9(1)	4.04	37.19
Nashik	15(1)	3.47	38.83
Thane	27(2)	5.53	72.58
Mumbai (suburb)	1	2.41	100.00
Raigarh	26	4.87	24.24
Pune	21(1)	4.02	58.07
Ahmadnagar	17(2)	4.10	19.66
Bid	6	1.68	17.90
Latur	5	3.60	23.58
Osamabad	8	1.85	15.84
Solapur	9	2.77	31.80
Satara	14	2.32	14.24
Ratnagiri	8	3.31	11.33
Sindhudurg	5	2.66	9.56
Kolhapur	15(2)	2.81	29.65
Sangli	8(1)	2.31	24.52
Gondiya	2	0.96	11.95
Hingoli	4	2.72	15.62
Nandurbar	4	2.55	15.47
Wasim	4	2.16	17.48
Mean		*2.67*	*28.77*
SD		*1.08*	*19.44*
CV		*40.44*	*67.58*
State	347(15)	2.95	42.40

Notes: No. of UAs is shown within the bracket in the district where they exist. The total no. of towns/UAs, obtained by counting UAs as a single unit, is shown outside the bracket.

Source: Census of India 2001, Paper-2, Rural-Urban Distribution.

1991–2001. The district of Thane (5.53) has also experienced a reduction in growth rate of urban population than the earlier two decades. But, urban population in Pune has grown at a rate of 4.02, which is higher than the growth rate during the 1980s mainly due to industrialization and tertiary activities. The growth rate of urban population in relatively backward districts during the 1990s has also registered a decline from that of earlier decades. However, districts like Aurangabad, Ahmadnagar, Ratnagiri, and Latur, have recorded growth higher than the state average.

Coefficient of Variation

The coefficient of variation across the districts with regard to growth of urban population during the 1970s was 34.8 per cent which went up to 68.2 per cent during the 1980s and came down to 40.4 per cent in the 1990s (Tables 6.1a, 6.1b, and 6.1c). All this is possibly due to the phenomenally high growth rate recorded by the new district of Gadchiroli during the 1980s and, a negative growth rate recorded by it during the 1990s. This does not fall in line with the pattern observed in the state and, thus, disturbs the coefficient of variation. However, the level of urbanization across the districts correlates highly with the growth of urban population during the 1990s. This suggests that urbanization has been mostly in the highly urbanized districts in the state.

Size Class-wise Distribution of Towns

Looking at the size class distribution of towns in Maharashtra, it characterizes a high degree of concentration of urban population in class I cities in 1981, claiming over 75.24 per cent of the total urban population in the state. This figure has gone up to 77.8 per cent and 79.7 per cent in 1991 and 2001, respectively. With increasing share of urban population in the larger towns, it is understandable that the smaller towns (classes IV–VI) have lost their share over time, viz., from 7.9 per cent in 1981 to 5.3 per cent in 1991 and 4.2 per cent in 2001. This figure is much lower than the national average of 9.4 per cent in this category. Moreover, the growth of class I towns has also been higher than the growth rates registered by smaller towns in the state[2] in all the three decades under consideration (See Chapter IV, Tables 4.3 and 4.4).

In Maharashtra, a large number of towns (twenty-three) both in backward as well as developed districts have been declassified in 2001. However, all these declassified towns were census towns in 1991 and fulfilled the necessary criteria in 1991. The declassification of these seems to be due to a decline in the share of non-agricultural workforce. This reflects a process of adjustment of economic forces within a district resulting in spatial reorganization of economic activities.

PUNJAB

Punjab is the other developed state analysed in this chapter. It has been at the core of the 'Green Revolution' and high agricultural growth since the 1960s. Linkages established with the national and international system, as members of the country's armed forces and migrations abroad, have enabled significant investments in agriculture and associated agro-based industries. Remittances from the state's Non-resident Indians (NRIs) have also facilitated investment in industrial and

---

[2] The class VI category, however, has a number of new townships set up by public enterprises, and military establishments and therefore does not fall in the size class pattern in terms of the growth rate. In most states, these towns have much higher growth rates than the state average, as is the case in Maharashtra.

commercial enterprises. Level of urbanization has grown simultaneously with the increase in non-agricultural activities.[3]

The urban structure in Punjab, inherited from the colonial period, has been relatively balanced compared to other states.[4] It remained so until the 1970s.[5] The balanced urban structure has often been attributed to the fact that agriculture has provided the main impetus to development since the beginning of the century. Further, the Green Revolution in the 1960s gave a boost to agro-processing activities in Punjab, resulting in modernization and commercialization of the agricultural sector. This led to a growth in the demand for agricultural implements and the consequent establishment of a number of engineering units. Arguably, when urban centres emerge to meet the economic needs of an agrarian economy, their spacing tends to be more even (Bhalla and Kundu 1982). The balanced pattern of urbanization in Punjab can also be seen in the fact that the average distance between towns

---

[3] See Gopal Krishan (1998).

[4] The present structure of urbanization in Punjab must be seen in the historical context of its growth. Since independence, it has gone through three phases of population change: (a) replacement of a large number of Muslims by the non-Muslims at the time of partition in 1947; (b) population redistribution during 1947–66 mainly with extension of irrigation facilities and reclamation of new agricultural lands; and (c) spatial containment of the population due to a check on agricultural out-migration since its reorganization in 1966. Further, regional disparities in population density narrowed down in the post-independence period, blurring the demographic distinction between the former British administered and princely ruled parts of the Punjab (Bhalla and Kundu 1982).

[5] The percentage of the population in class I cities was just one-third of the total urban population in 1951. The medium towns—with population between fifty and one hundred thousand—and small towns— with population less than fifty thousand—also claimed one third each (Bhalla and Kundu 1982).

---

is just twenty-two km, which is the lowest among the states. This compares favourably with the national figure of thirty-one km.

Level of Urbanization

The Census of 1981 reported five districts out of total twelve—Ludhiana (42.04), Jalandhar (35.32), Amritsar (32.97), Kapurthala (29.97), and Patiala (29.59)—having higher percentage of urban population than the state average (27.7). The lowest figure was for Hoshiarpur, with only 14.42 per cent population residing in urban areas, which was significantly below the state average figure. Most of the districts reported urbanization figures around the state average of 27.7 per cent. Understandably, the disparity across the districts works out quite low: 28.3 per cent only, as shown in Table 6.2a. Ludhiana had the highest percentage (49.95) of urban population in 1991 as well (Table 6.2b). Further, the other developed districts like Jalandhar, Amritsar, and Patiala maintained their positions, with percentage figures as high as 36.31, 34.14, and 30.48 per cent, respectively, as shown in Table 6.2b. Hoshiarpur did not show any relative improvement. In Kapurthala district, the percentage of urban population decreased from 29.97 in 1981 to 25.79 in 1991, mainly due to the large-scale declassification of towns in Punjab, specifically in this district. Overall, the ranks in terms of level of urbanization across the districts have not changed much during the 1970s and 1980s, and as a result, the coefficient of variation has remained stable at 31 per cent.

Ludhiana has maintained the lead by reporting the highest percentage of urban population in the 2001 Census as well. Districts like Jalandhar (47.45), followed by Amritsar (40) and Patiala (34.98) have retained their high ranking in the level of urbanization. In fact, the level of urbanization has increased in

TABLE 6.2a
Trends and Pattern of Urbanization Across Districts in Punjab (1981)

Districts	Towns (UAs)	Annl. exp. gr. rate (1971–81)	% Urban popln
Gurdaspur	11(3)	2.68	21.69
Amritsar	11(1)	2.87	32.97
Firozpur	10(3)	2.36	22.85
Ludhiana	9	4.31	42.04
Jalandhar	16	3.34	35.32
Kapurthala	8	4.70	29.97
Hoshiyarpur	10	3.43	14.42
Rupnagar	9(1)	6.36	21.59
Patiala	13(2)	3.80	29.59
Sangrur	14(7)	3.23	22.81
Bhatinda	12(1)	4.82	22.68
Faridkot	11(1)	4.10	23.87
Mean		*3.83*	*26.65*
SD		*1.11*	*7.53*
CV		*29.00*	*28.26*
State	134(19)	3.70	27.70

Note: Number of UAs is shown within the bracket in the district where they exist. The total number of towns/UAs, obtained by counting UAs as a single units, is shown outside the bracket.
Source: Census of India 1981, Paper-2, Rural–Urban Distribution.

TABLE 6.2b
Trends and Pattern of Urbanization Across Districts in Punjab (1991)

Districts	Towns (UAs)	Annl. exp. gr. rate (1981–91)	% Urban popln
Gurdaspur	13(4)	2.17	23.10
Amritsar	10(1)	1.68	34.14
Firozpur	10(3)	2.51	23.94
Ludhiana	8(1)	4.61	49.95
Jalandhar	15	1.87	36.31
Kapurthala	3(1)	0.13	25.79
Hoshiyarpur	8	2.11	15.50
Rupnagar	9(2)	4.04	25.57
Patiala	13(3)	2.23	30.48
Sangrur	12(4)	2.62	24.56
Bhatinda	10	1.71	22.58
Faridkot	9(3)	2.41	25.35
Mean		*2.34*	*28.11*
SD		*1.14*	*8.79*
CV		*48.51*	*31.28*
State	120(22)	2.52	29.72

Note: Number of UAs is shown within the bracket in the district where they exist. The total number of towns/UAs, obtained by counting UAs as a single unit, is shown outside the bracket.
Source: Census of India 1991, Paper-2, Rural–Urban Distribution.

the developed districts rapidly over the two decades whereas the backward districts have not shown significant increases during the period. The developed districts thus seem to have a high percentage of urban population as also high increase over the decades. It may be noted that a backward district like Faridkot has matched a percentage of urban population with the state average (33.95). However, the disparity across the districts has gone up marginally to 34.4 per cent during the 1990s (Table 6.2c).[6]

Urban Growth Rate

In the context of urban growth rates, Punjab presents an interesting contrast to the other states. The growth rate of the population in large cities has been higher than that in the small and medium towns in the country during the 1970s. This is also true in the case of most of the developed states. However, this is not so in Punjab. Here, the annual exponential growth rate of population for towns with population between 50,000 and 100,000 was

TABLE 6.2c
Trends and Pattern of Urbanization Across Districts in Punjab (2001)

Districts	Towns (UAs)	Annl. exp. gr. rate (1991–2001)	% Urban popln
Gurdaspur	14(4)	3.23	25.46
Amritsar	13(1)	3.65	40.00
Kapurthala	7(1)	3.86	32.59
Jalandhar	14(1)	3.24	47.45
Hoshiyarpur	12	2.69	19.66
Nawanshahr	4(1)	3.26	13.80
Rupnagar	11(2)	4.39	32.46
Fatehgarhsahib	5(1)	4.07	28.08
Ludhiana	12	3.08	55.80
Moga	4(1)	1.77	20.04
Firozpur	9(2)	1.90	25.81
Muktsar	4	2.58	25.52
Faridkot	3(2)	2.22	33.89
Bhatinda	9(1)	2.80	29.78
Mansa	5	5.12	20.68
Sangrur	17(1)	3.36	29.26
Patiala	14(1)	3.22	34.98
Mean		*3.20*	*30.31*
SD		*0.87*	*10.43*
CV		*27.07*	*34.40*
State	157(19)	3.20	33.95

Notes: Number of UAs is shown within the bracket in the district where they exist. The total number of towns/UAs, obtained by counting UAs as a single unit, is shown outside the bracket.
Source: Census of India 2001, Paper-2, Rural–Urban Distribution.

[6] Punjab has only three towns declassified in all the seventeen districts in 2001 (which was twelve earlier). Gurudaspur had two of these towns.

3.6 per cent during 1971–81, which is higher than that of the class I cities. The small towns with population of between 5000 and 10,000 grew at the same rate as the class I cities viz., 3.3 per cent. Growth in agriculture and agro-based industries, established through demand and supply linkages, has contributed to the emergence and growth of small towns. As a consequence, the pattern of urbanization here is not top heavy, as is the case in the country as a whole. Some of the districts like Patiala, Amritsar, Ludhiana, and Jalandhar, which are highly productive in agriculture and which contribute nearly 2 per cent or more to the country's wheat production have shown levels as well as growth rates of urbanization higher than the state average. Punjab has thus been an example of urbanization prompted by agricultural growth which is becoming apparent in the neighbouring state of Haryana as well. Other similar examples as mentioned before are Godavari and Krishna districts in Andhra Pradesh, as also the Thanjavur and Chengalpattu districts in Tamil Nadu.

The growth of small and medium-scale industries in Punjab during the 1970s has a distinct regional pattern. The major factor behind this growth process is the emergence of an urban industrial corridor along Ludhiana, Jalandhar, and Amritsar highway. Besides the linear physical growth of small and medium towns in the corridor, industrial units have tended to concentrate in the districts of Ludhiana, Jalandhar, and Amritsar, contributing over 60 per cent of the registered manufacturing units. This industrial corridor, however, had some spread along the Grand Trunk (GT) road from Ludhiana to Delhi. Many of the towns in this corridor specialize in steel industry. Their location in this region is partly due to proximity to Delhi and other supply and demand centres in the country. Further, raw materials for the industry being heavy, the location of the units nearer Delhi has reduced the operating cost. The

state, thus, has experienced an impressive growth of industrial activities, dotting the two sides of the GT Road right from Delhi to Amritsar during the 1970s. All these made Punjab an economically dynamic region with industries getting located not only in a handful of large cities but also in a number of small and medium towns (Gopal Krishan 1998).

Analysing the pattern of urban growth at sub-state level, the districts may be placed in two categories that is, developed and relatively less developed. Many among the less developed districts like Bhatinda (4.82), Faridkot (4.10), and Rupnagar (6.36) have shown growth rates higher than the state average during 1971–81 (Table 6.2a). But, high growth rates are noted even in case of developed districts like Kapurthala (4.7) and Ludhiana (4.31) that have a high concentration of industrial and business activities. It is satisfying to note that the disparity across the districts during the 1970s in terms of growth of urban population is not so high (29 per cent).

The 1980s, however, mark a significant change in terms of the growth profile across the towns in different size classes and districts. The decade has been described as 'the lost decade' or 'a period of missed opportunities' for Punjab. To a large extent, the state suffered significantly due to the disturbed socio-political conditions and widespread terrorism. Many of the small towns experienced deceleration in population growth during the 1980s compared to the previous decade, as these were considered less safe than the larger cities. As a consequence, the demographic growth in large cities was higher than that in other categories of towns during the 1980s. Understandably, the share of population in class I cities has gone up sharply—from 46 per cent to 54 per cent during 1981–91.

During the 1980s, districts like Ludhiana (4.61) and Rupnagar (4.04) have reported much higher growth rates than all other districts and the state average (2.52). Significantly, the 2001 Census has indicated a decline in the growth rate of urban population in many of the districts. The decline in urban growth in case of the backward districts seems to be significant and this marks a departure from the pattern of the 1970s. Kapurthala is an exception as its growth rate declined from 4.7 in 1981 to 0.13 in 1991. As a result of this growth pattern, the disparity across the districts has gone up, the coefficient of variation being as high as 48.5 per cent.

Census 2001 reports acceleration in growth of urban population during 1991–2001 compared to the previous decade. The growth pattern during this decade is somewhat similar to that of the 1971–81. The annual exponential growth of population in class I cities is as high as 3.0 per cent which is higher than that of all other size categories.[7] At the district level, however, it is difficult to argue that the developed districts have experienced higher urban growth than the state average or the other way round. The correlation of urban growth with indicators of the level of urbanization and economic development works out as statistically insignificant. The correlation has also been weakened by the new district of Mansa witnessing the highest growth rate of 5.12 per cent. This is followed by Rupnagar (4.39) and Fatehgarhsahib (4.07). The growth rate of the industrial district of Ludhiana has come down from 4.61 during the 1980s to 3.08

[7] The class VI category, however, has a number of new townships set up by public enterprises and military establishments, and therefore do not fall in the size class pattern in terms of the growth rate. In most states, these towns have much higher growth rate than the state average, as is the case in Punjab.

during the 1990s. All these have led to a decline in the coefficient of variation in urban growth across the districts from 48.5 per cent to 27.1 per cent.

The growth differential between the headquarters of the district and other urban centres in the district is well pronounced in Punjab. The district headquarters of Gurudaspur and Amritsar have registered similar or little lower growth rates than the other towns in the districts during the 1980s. The urban growth rates of these two districts were 2.68 and 2.87 while their headquarters grew by 2.1 and 2.70 per cent respectively. This gap has become wider during 1991–2001 as the district headquarter of Gurudaspur has grown by 2.03 per cent as compared to the figure of 3.23 per cent for the district. Similarly, Amritsar district has indicated a growth rate of 3.65 whereas its headquarter has shown 3.03 per cent annual growth. This is largely because governmental activities or investment is a marginal factor in the urban growth in the state of Punjab.

The share of urban population in class I cities has been increasing from 46.4 per cent in 1981 to 54.4 per cent in 1991 and 58.4 per cent in 2001 in the state of Punjab. However, despite the higher demographic growth in Class I cities, their share of the total urban population in 2001 is still much below the national average of 68.7 per cent. The other developed states like Maharashtra and West Bengal had about 80 per cent of their urban population in such cities. The share of the towns having population between 50,000 and 100,000 has gone up from 14 per cent to 20 per cent during 1981–91 but decreased to 16.5 per cent during 2001. Furthermore, in the case of towns with less than 50,000 people the share has declined from about 40 per cent in 1981 to 26 per cent in 1991 and to around 25 per cent in 2001. And yet this is above the national figure of 22 per cent.

BIHAR

Well endowed with minerals and other raw materials, undivided Bihar has been, in theory, conducive for industrial development. Availability of water and cheap labour has encouraged entrepreneurs to establish industrial units in and around Jamshedpur and Bokaro. Leaving aside these industrial towns and a few administrative cities like Patna and Ranchi (now in Jharkhand after bifurcation), urbanization and economic development in other sub-regions of the state have been insignificant.

Level of Urbanization

Barring a few districts of the state like Dhanbad (50.7), Patna (36.87), Singhbhum (32.09), and Ranchi (20.93) that have high levels of urban and industrial development, all the other districts reported urban population below 15 per cent in 1981. Dhanbad with 50.7 per cent of its population living in urban areas—a figure comparable with any developed district in a developed state in the country—presents a sharp contrast within the state. Furthermore, the district has recorded addition of towns in each census since 1971. Five new towns of Dhanbad in 1981 accounted for 3.89 per cent of the district's urban population. However, there has been large-scale declassification of census towns suggesting that a large number of them are losing workforce engaged outside agriculture. The coefficient of variation works out to a very high 88.59 per cent, which is the highest among all the states taken up for detailed empirical investigation (Table 6.3a). This pattern has remained unchanged during 1981–91, the districts having high percentage of urban population retaining their position

after a decade (Table 6.3b). All other districts have urban population below 15 per cent of the population in the district. The disparity has increased to 92.68 across the districts during eighties.

The district-level data for the state of undivided Bihar for the year 2001 have been presented in two parts giving information separately for Bihar and Jharkhand (Table 6.3c). Bifurcation of the state took place in the year 2000. Jharkhand comprises the mining and industrial areas of Chhotanagpur region and thus has supposedly better prospects for urban industrial growth than Bihar. Among all the districts of the new state of Bihar, only two districts namely, Patna and Munger record urban population over 25 per cent. In Jharkhand, on the other hand, as many as five out of eighteen districts report a higher urban figure. Interestingly, the number of new towns in Jharkhand is high, especially in Dhanbad and Singhbhum districts, whereas Bihar reports only three new towns in 2001. The Dhanbad–Singhbhum–Hazaribagh region, due to its mining and ancillary industrial activities, has had a large number of new urban centres that have broadened the base of urbanization. The coefficient of variation for the districts in the undivided state of Bihar would work out to be 96.2 per cent in 2001, even higher than that noted in 1991.

Urban Growth Rate

In terms of growth rates, the spatial pattern across districts is very interesting. All the urbanized and relatively developed districts like Dhanbad, Ranchi, Patna, and Purbi Singhbhum report a growth rate less than the state average of 2.70 during 1981–91. In contrast, the backward districts report high growth of urban population during this period. The figures for Godda (4.6) and Hazaribagh (4.35) work out

TABLE 6.3a
Trends and Pattern of Urbanization Across Districts in Bihar (1981)

Districts	Towns (UAs)	Annl. exp. gr. rate (1971–81)	% Urban popln
Pashchimi Champaran	4	2.10	7.33
Purbi Champaran	4(1)	5.13	4.65
Sitamarhi	4(1)	5.58	4.52
Madhubani	3	5.24	3.11
Purnia	7(1)	5.21	7.96
Katihar	3(1)	5.16	9.42
Saharsa	8	4.62	5.72
Darbhanga	1	2.87	8.77
Muzaffarpur	1	4.07	8.06
Gopalganj	3	8.39	4.99
Siwan	3	4.16	4.41
Saran	4	5.43	8.17
Vaishali	2	3.27	6.48
Samastipur	6	4.33	4.16
Begusarai	3(1)	3.73	10.55
Bhagalpur	5	3.13	11.62
Santhal Pargana	11(1)	3.30	6.88
Munger	13	2.69	14.07
Nalanda	5	6.08	13.62
Patna	9(1)	4.97	36.87
Bhojpur	9	4.12	10.78
Rohtas	4	4.06	9.73
Aurangabad	5	5.36	6.94
Gaya	5	3.48	10.82
Nawada	3	3.79	6.65
Dhanbad	11(2)	5.14	50.70
Giridih	6(2)	3.08	14.20
Hazaribagh	7(2)	4.67	15.11
Palamu	5	4.27	5.64
Ranchi	9(1)	5.84	20.93
Singhbhum	16(1)	3.61	32.09
Mean		*4.41*	*11.77*
SD		*1.25*	*10.43*
CV		*28.27*	*88.59*
State	179(15)	4.39	12.46

Notes: Number of UAs is shown within the bracket in the district where they exist. The total number of towns/UAs, obtained by counting UAs as a single unit, is shown outside the bracket.

Source: Census of India 1981, Paper-2, Rural–Urban Distribution.

TABLE 6.3b
Trends and Pattern of Urbanization Across Districts in Bihar (1991)

Districts	Towns (UAs)	Annl. exp. gr. rate (1981–91)	% Urban popln
Pashchimi Champaran	5	4.87	10.09
Purbi Champaran	6(1)	4.27	5.68
Sitamarhi	4(1)	4.23	5.58
Madhubani	5	3.48	3.63
Araria	3	2.43	6.34
Kishanganj	3	2.20	10.02
Purnia	3(1)	2.09	8.37
Katihar	2	2.41	9.41
Madhepura	3	2.88	6.52
Saharsa	5	4.32	6.82
Darbhanga	3	2.14	8.70
Muzaffarpur	2	3.64	9.30
Gopalganj	4	3.50	5.67
Siwan	3	3.69	5.25
Saran	4	3.24	9.14
Vaishali	4	2.86	6.69
Samastipur	5	4.26	4.96
Begusarai	3(1)	1.42	9.79
Khagaria	2	2.94	6.00
Bhagalpur	5(1)	2.36	12.71
Munger	5	1.83	16.60
Nalanda	5	2.82	14.77
Patna	6(1)	2.05	37.96
Bhojpur	5	2.35	11.37
Rohtas	6	2.50	10.22
Jehanabad	2	5.05	6.31
Aurangabad	5	3.17	7.67
Gaya	3(1)	1.85	13.34
Nawada	3	2.57	6.95
Godda	1	4.60	2.75
Sahibgang	3	1.31	7.30
Dumka	3	2.86	6.12
Deoghar	3(1)	3.39	13.63
Dhanbad	18(3)	2.61	51.30
Giridih	9(2)	3.30	15.44
Hazaribagh	14(5)	4.35	18.07
Palamu	7	1.91	5.34
Lohardaga	1	3.07	11.00
Gumla	2	2.42	4.45

(contd.)

TABLE 6.3b: contd.

Districts	Towns (UAs)	Annl. exp. gr. rate (1981–91)	% Urban popln
Ranchi	15(2)	2.32	33.12
Purbi Singhbhum	6(1)	1.99	52.92
Pashchimi Singhbhum	15	2.70	15.82
Mean		*2.96*	*12.22*
SD		*0.95*	*11.32*
CV		*31.95*	*92.68*
State	211(21)	2.70	13.17

Notes: Number of UAs is shown within the bracket in the district where they exist. The total number of towns/UAs, obtained by counting UAs as a single units, is shown outside the bracket.
Source: Census of India 1991, Paper-2, Rural–Urban Distribution.

TABLE 6.3c
Trends and Pattern of Urbanization Across Districts in Bihar & Jharkhand (2001)

Districts	Towns (UAs)	Annl. exp. gr. rate (1991–2001)	% Urban popln
Bihar			
Pashchimi Champaran	5	2.65	10.17
Purbi Champaran	6(1)	2.57	6.39
Sheohar	1	3.09	4.15
Sitamarhi	4(1)	2.82	5.74
Madhubani	4	2.32	3.48
Supaul	3	2.62	5.04
Araria	3	2.76	6.24
Kishanganj	3	2.74	9.97
Purnia	3(1)	3.02	8.74
Katihar	3(1)	2.69	9.13
Madhepura	2	2.58	4.46
Saharsa	1	2.85	8.23
Darbhanga	1	2.69	8.12
Muzaffarpur	3	2.37	9.30
Gopalganj	4	2.32	6.07
Siwan	3	2.21	5.45
Saran	5	2.34	9.17
Vaishali	2	2.34	6.88
Samastipur	4(1)	2.28	3.62
Begusarai	2(1)	2.55	4.58
Khagaria	2	2.57	5.97
Bhagalpur	4(1)	2.41	18.59
Banka	2	2.21	3.50
Munger	5	1.85	27.88

(contd.)

TABLE 6.3c: contd.

Districts	Towns (UAs)	Annl. exp. gr. rate (1981–91)	% Urban popln
Lakhisarai	2	2.15	14.68
Shekhpura	2	2.23	15.48
Nalanda	5	1.71	14.92
Patna	8(1)	2.64	41.80
Bhojpur	6	2.20	13.98
Buxer	2	2.55	9.18
Kaimur	1	2.67	3.23
Rohtas	5	2.45	13.34
Jehanabad	2	2.52	7.40
Aurangabad	3	2.64	8.42
Gaya	4(1)	2.63	13.71
Nawada	3	2.86	7.66
Jamui	2	2.84	7.38
Jharkhand			
Garhwa	2	4.30	4.13
Palamu	4	1.89	5.97
Chatra	1	2.99	5.31
Hazaribagh	19(2)	2.40	23.23
Kodarama	2	2.68	17.37
Giridih	3(1)	1.25	6.41
Deoghar	4(1)	2.45	13.76
Godda	1	4.48	3.53
Sahibganj	2	3.55	10.58
Pakur	1	3.17	5.13
Dumka	4	2.29	6.52
Dhanbad	12(2)	2.69	52.39
Bokaro	9(2)	2.15	45.31
Ranchi	8(1)	2.90	35.09
Lohardaga	1	3.75	12.68
Gumla	2	3.44	5.48
Pashchimi Singhbhum	15(1)	2.16	16.86
Purbi Singhbhum	12(1)	2.47	54.97
Mean		*2.62*	*12.49*
SD		*0.55*	*12.01*
CV		*20.94*	*96.18*
State			
(Bihar+Jharkhand)	215(20)	2.60	13.35
Bihar	120(9)	2.57	10.47
Jharkhand	95(11)	2.55	22.25

Notes: Number of UAs is shown within the bracket in the district where they exist. The total number of towns/UAs, obtained by counting UAs as a single unit, is shown outside the bracket.
Source: Census of India 2001, Paper-2, Rural–Urban Distribution.

as much higher than the state average. The coefficients of variation work out as 28.27 per cent and 31.9 per cent during the 1970s and 1980s, implying that difference in terms of growth across the districts is rather low.

The growth pattern during 1991–2001 across districts in the state of Bihar is markedly different from that in Jharkhand. All the districts report urban growth around the state average, with little disparity. This is due to the fact that there is no large industrial centre, region or corridor in the state that could attract urban industrial growth. The state of Jharkhand, however, presents a sharp contrast to this scenario. Here, the relatively less urbanized districts like Garhwa, Godda, Sahibganj, Pakur, Lohardaga, and Gumla have recorded phenomenal urban growth. Further micro-level studies are needed to determine whether the rapid growth of urban population in these districts can be attributed to their low urban base, dispersed infrastructural development, or distress migration from their rural areas.

Urbanization in the state of Bihar has remained far behind the national average during the three decades covered in the present analysis. After bifurcation, the urbanization level has gone down from 13.17 (for undivided Bihar) in 1991 to 10.47 (for the new state of Bihar) in 2001. This is because a large majority of urban centres, particularly, the class I category have come under Jharkhand. As a consequence, the percentage of urban population in class I cities in Bihar is much below that of Jharkhand, the two figures being 59 and 71, respectively. Surprisingly, the share of smaller towns (classes IV–VI) in Bihar was low and has gone down significantly from 12.2 per cent in 1981 to 9 per cent in 1991 and 3.4 per cent in 2001. The corresponding figure for the new state of Jharkhand, however, is as high as 9 per cent in 2001, which is about the national average.

SIZE CLASS WISE DISTRIBUTION

The growth of urban population across the size categories is different from that of other states. Class I cities have recorded a growth rate of 4.5 per cent which was higher than the smaller towns (classes IV, V, and VI) during the 1970s. The latter, however, have even recorded a growth rate higher than the towns having population 50,000 to 100,000. Importantly, during the 1980s, the smaller towns have grown at a rate higher than all other category towns. The same pattern holds good for the 1990s as well. Unfortunately, however, the smaller towns have not been able to record any significant improvement in their share in urban population over the decades.

RAJASTHAN

Rajasthan, part of old Rajputana of medieval India comprised many kingdoms with different administrative and development experiences. Important urban centres of the state can be identified as the historical cities of Jodhpur, Udaipur, Ajmer, and Jaipur, which were the headquarters of the princely states. A cross-sectional analysis of the urbanization data at the district level provides interesting insights into the development dynamics in the state.

Level of Urbanization

As per the 1981 census, Rajasthan had five districts with the percentage share of urban population much above the state average of 20.9 per cent. These are Ajmer (42.8), Bikaner (39.48), Jaipur (36.39), Jodhpur (34.77), and Kota (32.18). These places have historical importance and reflect features of any developed district in the country. At the lowest end of the spectrum, we have urban population reported in the backward districts of Banswara (6.22) and Dungarpur (6.46) in 1981. The disparity in levels of urbanization in the state; thus, works out to 53.14 per cent (Table 6.4a).

A few of the developed districts have maintained their relative positions in the following decade as well. In fact, the districts of Bikaner (39.72), Jaipur (39.46), Jodhpur (35.11), and Kota (36.44) reflect significant increases in their share of urban population in 1991. Correspondingly, the increase in case of backward districts like Banswara and Dungarpur was meagre. The overall disparity in the level, computed through the coefficient of variation, has, however, come down to 47.3 per cent in 1991. This implies that the districts in the

TABLE 6.4a
Trends and Pattern of Urbanization Across Districts in Rajasthan (1981)

Districts	.Towns (UAs)	Annl. exp. gr. rate (1971–81)	% Urban popln
Ganganagar	14	5.89	20.61
Bikaner	5(1)	3.23	39.48
Churu	11(2)	2.87	29.22
Jhunjhunun	14(1)	4.40	20.74
Alwar	5	4.06	11.18
Bharatpur	12	4.48	17.90
Sawai Madhopur	7(2)	3.72	13.42
Jaipur	15(3)	5.08	36.39
Sikar	9	4.52	20.25
Nagaur	10	4.25	14.56
Jodhpur	4	4.32	34.77
Jaisalmer	2	2.42	13.55
Barmer	3	5.36	8.78
Jalor	4	9.02	8.06
Sirohi	5	2.33	17.90
Pali	12	7.69	18.42
Ajmer	8	3.41	42.80
Tonk	6	2.76	18.36
Bundi	6(1)	4.21	16.99
Bhilwara	6	4.82	14.39
Udaipur	8	4.62	15.07
Dungarpur	2	3.45	6.46
Banswara	2(1)	5.08	6.22
Chittaurgarh	8(1)	5.07	13.18
Kota	10	5.71	32.18
Jhalawar	7	4.42	11.66
Mean		*4.51*	*19.33*
SD		*1.49*	*10.27*
CV		*33.06*	*53.14*
State	195(12)	4.59	20.90

Notes: Number of UAs is shown within the bracket in the district where they exist. The total number of towns/UAs, obtained by counting UAs as a single unit, is shown outside the bracket.
Source: Census of India 1981, Paper-2, Rural–Urban Distribution.

middle level have interchanged their positions with more spatially balanced urban growth (Table 6.4b).

The 2001 Census has reported certain features that contrast sharply with those observed in 1991. The level of urbanization has increased more rapidly in urbanized districts than in backward districts (Table 6.4c). Ajmer (40.09), Jaipur (49.38), and Kota (53.42) have experienced substantial increase in urban population

TABLE 6.4b
Trends and Pattern of Urbanization Across Districts in Rajasthan (1991)

Districts	Towns (UAs)	Annl. exp. gr. rate (1981–91)	% Urban popln
Ganganagar	15(1)	2.77	21.08
Bikaner	4	3.60	39.72
Churu	12(1)	2.57	28.94
Jhunjhunun	14(2)	2.57	20.74
Alwar	9(1)	2.31	14.05
Bharatpur	11(1)	3.21	19.48
Dholpur	3	3.68	17.21
Sawai Madhopur	7(2)	3.46	14.90
Jaipur	18(2)	3.98	39.46
Sikar	9	3.29	21.10
Nagaur	11(1)	3.67	16.01
Jodhpur	4(1)	2.53	35.11
Jaisalmer	2	4.89	15.62
Barmer	4	3.89	10.11
Jalor	4	1.32	7.28
Sirohi	5(1)	2.74	19.52
Pali	13	3.19	21.76
Ajmer	8(1)	1.31	40.77
Tonk	6(2)	2.80	19.56
Bundi	6(1)	2.51	17.41
Bhilwara	7	5.00	19.54
Udaipur	10(1)	3.28	17.09
Dungarpur	3	3.68	7.29
Banswara	5(1)	4.81	7.73
Chittaurgarh	6	3.55	15.62
Kota	11	4.03	36.44
Jhalawar	8	5.00	15.79
Mean		*3.32*	*20.72*
SD		*0.97*	*9.80*
CV		*29.23*	*47.32*
State	215(19)	3.31	22.88

Notes: Number of UAs is shown within the bracket in the district where they exist. The total number of towns/UAs, obtained by counting UAs as a single unit, is shown outside the bracket.
Source: Census of India 1991, Paper-2, Rural–Urban Distribution.

TABLE 6.4c
Trends and Pattern of Urbanization Across Districts in Rajasthan (2001)

Districts	Towns (UAs)	Annl. exp. gr. rate (1991–2001)	% Urban popln
Ganganagar	11(1)	3.02	25.28
Hanumangarh	6	3.32	20.01
Bikaner	3	2.12	35.52
Churu	12(2)	1.83	27.86
Jhunjhunun	11(2)	1.95	20.64
Alwar	10(1)	2.90	14.53
Bharatpur	10(1)	2.42	19.47
Dholpur	2(1)	3.15	17.95
Karauli	3	3.06	14.25
Sawai Madhopur	5(2)	3.38	19.05
Dausa	5	2.55	10.31
Jaipur	10	3.80	49.38
Sikar	9(2)	1.97	20.64
Nagaur	12(2)	3.31	17.20
Jodhpur	3(2)	2.40	33.75
Jaisalmer	2	3.68	15.25
Barmer	2	0.07	7.40
Jalor	3	2.79	7.59
Sirohi	5(1)	1.67	17.22
Pali	11	1.89	21.48
Ajmer	7(2)	2.17	40.09
Tonk	7(1)	2.85	20.90
Bundi	7(1)	2.13	18.61
Bhilwara	8	2.87	20.64
Rajasamand	5	2.70	13.05
Udaipur	9	2.14	18.62
Dungarpur	3	2.28	7.24
Banswara	3(1)	1.85	7.15
Chittaurgarh	8	2.22	16.04
Kota	11(1)	3.06	53.42
Baran	6	3.42	16.94
Jhalawar	7	1.08	14.25
Mean		*2.50*	*20.68*
SD		*0.78*	*11.14*
CV		*31.26*	*53.85*
State	216(23)	2.71	23.38

Notes: Number of UAs is shown within the bracket in the district where they exist. The total number of towns/UAs, obtained by counting UAs as a single unit, is shown outside the bracket.
Source: Census of India 2001, Paper-2, Rural–Urban Distribution.

as compared to all other districts. Banswara (7.15) and Dungarpur (7.24) have not improved their relative positions even during the 1990s. Furthermore, one of the backward districts—Barmer—has registered a sharp decline in urban share, from 10.11 per cent in 1991 to 7.4 per cent in 2001. Understandably, the disparity level for the 1990s has gone up from 47.3 per cent in the previous decade to 53.85 per cent.

Growth Rate of Urban Population

The growth rates of urban population in most of the backward districts of the state like Pali (7.69), Jalore (9.02), Banswara (5.08), and Chittaurgarh (5.07), are high during 1971–81. The developed districts of Kota (5.71) and Jaipur (5.08), too, have experienced high urban growth but that can be attributed to the emergence of a large number of new towns in these districts. The coefficient of variation works out to a modest 33.06 per cent only, which is less than what was observed in case of the level of urbanization. During 1981–91, the traditional growth centres like Jaipur and Jodhpur reported comparatively low urban growth than the previous decade. Backward districts like Bhilwara and Jhalawar, on the other hand, picked up the tempo, registering growth rates above 5 per cent; which was much above the state average of 3.3 per cent. As a result of this spatially balanced urban development, the coefficient of variation declined from 33 per cent in the 1970s to 29.23 per cent during the 1980s.

During 1991–2001, the pattern of growth once again reported a departure from that of the previous decade. The less urbanized districts like Jhalawar (1.08), Banswara (1.85), and Sirohi (1.67) have registered lower growth rates than those reported by the developed districts such as Jaipur (3.8), Jodhpur (2.4), and Kota (3.06). The coefficient of variation across the

districts has shown a marginal increase to 31.26 per cent during the 1990s as urban growth concentrated in urbanized districts.

Size Class Distribution of Towns

The share of urban population in class I cities in Rajasthan has gone up from 46 per cent to 50 per cent during 1981–91 but the figures still remain below the national average. The share has gone up further to 57.2 during the 1990s. The percentage of urban population in class II towns in the state has, also gone up. The smaller towns (classes IV–VI) have, however, reported a substantial decline from 21.4 per cent in 1981 to 14.9 per cent in 1991 and 8 per cent in 2001. The growth rates of larger towns have remained above the growth rates of smaller towns during 1971–81. But, the difference has narrowed down during the 1980s, with a general decline in the growth rates. The 1990s again report widening of the gap between the growth rates of class I and smaller towns.

INTERDEPENDENCIES BETWEEN URBANIZATION AND DEVELOPMENTAL INDICATORS IN SELECT STATES

A number of indicators have been considered in the district-level analysis as has been done for analysing the pattern of interdependence at the state level. These include (1) the level of urbanization (LoU) and (2) growth of urban population GR (U). The indicators of socio-economic development that are included in the analysis[8] can be broadly categorized into the following.

[8] Data for all these indicators for three consecutive time points are not available, specially for districts in Bihar and Rajasthan and a few more in other states. Correlation matrices for the four states are, therefore, of different sizes, varying with the number of indicators. The value of agricultural productivity is obtained

(a) Economic Development Indicators[9]

(3) Size of industrial enterprise—*Ind. enterprise*

(4) Value of agricultural output per hectre—*Agri. output*

(b) Infrastructural Development Indicators[10]

(5) Road length per 100 sq. km—*Road*

(6) Railway lines per 100 sq. km—*Railway*

(7) Telephone connections per 100 persons—*Telephone*

(8) Per capita bank deposits—*Bank deposits*

(9) Per capita industrial credit—*Ind. credit*

(c) Socio-demographic Development Indicators[11]

(10) Females per thousand males in urban areas—*Sex ratio (U)*

(11) Literacy in rural areas—*Literacy (R)*

(12) Literacy in urban areas—*Literacy (U)*

(13) Middle and higher secondary schools per thousand persons—*School*

(14) Hospitals and dispensaries per thousand persons—*Hospital*

MAHARASHTRA

Levels of urbanization across districts in the state of Maharashtra exhibit strong correlation with the developmental indicators at all the three points of time. The same is generally true for the growth of urban population as well. This relates very strongly and positively to the size of factories in 2001, much more than the urbanization level. The relationship was not significant in earlier years (See Tables 6.5a, 6.5b, and 6.5c). The improvement in the relationship during 1991–2001 can be taken to suggest an increase in urbanization due to the increasing industrial activity in the post-liberalization phase. As already mentioned in Chapter V, Maharashtra has attracted a large volume of FDI during this period.

The correlation of the indicators of urbanization (level and growth) with agricultural productivity does not show any significant relationship in the early 1980s or early 1990s. However, there was a positive relationship between the two during the early 1980s, which subsequently became negative over a decade in the early 1990s. Hence, positive and strong interdependence of level of urbanization with factory size on the one hand (as shown above) and its inverse relationship with agricultural productivity, on the other, reflects the shifting of occupational structure over time, along with increasing level of urbanization in the state of

___

from the study by Bhalla and Singh (2000) for the 1980s and 1990s. In fact, the triennium averages of 1980–3 and 1992–5 are taken for the present analysis. This information is not available for the late 1990s or for the years of the present century.

[9] Due to non-availability of information on per capita income at the district level the same has not been included in the analysis. We could not even include indicators on the percentage of workers in industrial or commercial activities, as the results from the Census of 2001 are yet to become available. The only economic indicator on which information is available for the latest year is the (3) size of industrial enterprise.

[10] Under infrastructure, development indicators pertaining to (5) road, (6) railways, (7) telecom have been considered and (8) per capita bank deposits, (9) credit to industry, have also been taken up to comprise the category of financial infrastructure.

[11] Under socio-demographic development, only three indicators viz. education, health, and gender discrimination have been taken into consideration. Indicators on these have been captured through (11) rural literacy rate, (12) urban literacy rate, (13) middle and higher schools, (14) hospital and dispensaries per thousand populations, and female–male ratio.

TABLE 6.5a

Interdependence among Indicators of Urbanization and Socio-economic Development at District Level in Maharashtra (1981)

	LoU	GR (U)	Ind. enterprise	Agri. output	Road	Railway	Telephone	Bank deposits	Ind. credit	Literacy (U)	Sex ratio (U)	Hospital
LoU	1.00	0.22	0.07	0.34	−0.38	.815(**)	.906(**)	.882(**)	.876(**)	0.33	−.762(**)	.843(**)
GR (U)	0.22	1.00	0.04	0.118	−0.11	−0.06	0.11	0.05	0.26	−0.34	−.580(**)	−0.04
Ind. enterprise	0.07	0.04	1.00	−0.034	0.01	0.04	0.07	0.04	0.10	0.19	−0.22	0.06
Agri. output	0.34	0.118	−0.034	1.00	−0.076	0.335	0.334	0.338	0.332	−0.236	−0.281	0.18
Road	−0.38	−0.11	0.01	−0.076	1.00	−.406(*)	−0.34	−0.36	−0.30	0.09	0.18	−0.14
Railway	.815(**)	−0.06	0.04	0.335	−.406(*)	1.00	.952(**)	.971(**)	.862(**)	0.29	−.621(**)	.663(**)
Telephone	.906(**)	0.11	0.07	0.334	−0.34	.952(**)	1.00	.992(**)	.952(**)	0.38	−.767(**)	.779(**)
Bank deposits	.882(**)	0.05	0.04	0.338	−0.36	.971(**)	.992(**)	1.00	.933(**)	0.37	−.735(**)	.755(**)
Ind. credit	.876(**)	0.26	0.10	0.332	−0.30	.862(**)	.952(**)	.933(**)	1.00	.399(*)	−.844(**)	.719(**)
Literacy (U)	0.33	−0.34	0.19	−0.236	0.09	0.29	0.38	0.37	.399(*)	1.00	−0.20	.539(**)
Sex ratio (U)	−.762(**)	−.580(**)	−0.22	−0.281	0.18	−.621(**)	−.767(**)	−.735(**)	−.844(**)	−0.20	1.00	−.546(**)
Hospital	.843(**)	−0.04	0.06	0.18	−0.14	.663(**)	.779(**)	.755(**)	.719(**)	.539(**)	−.546(**)	1.00

Notes: * Correlation is significant at the 0.05 level (2-tailed). ** Correlation is significant at the 0.01 level (2-tailed).

Source: Computed by Authors.

TABLE 6.5b

Interdependence among Indicators of Urbanization and Socio-economic Development at District Level in Maharashtra (1991)

	LoU	GR (U)	Ind. enterprise	Agri. output	Road	Railway	Telephone	Bank deposits	Ind. credit	Literacy (U)	Sex ratio (U)	Hospital	School
LoU	1	-0.035	0.102	-0.035	-0.181	.449(*)	.775(**)	.765(**)	.780(**)	0.175	-.716(**)	.705(**)	-.473(**)
GR (U)	-0.035	1	-0.078	0.01	-0.34	-0.314	-0.118	-0.096	-0.052	-0.301	-.368(*)	-0.147	-0.167
Ind. enterprise	0.102	-0.078	1	0.103	-0.012	-0.026	0.056	0.085	0.155	0.055	-0.325	-0.063	0.105
Agri. output	-0.035	0.01	0.103	1	0.027	0.275	0.023	0.035	0.046	-0.352	-0.056	-0.051	0.084
Road	-0.181	-0.34	-0.012	0.027	1	0.176	-0.263	-0.324	-0.316	-0.01	0.258	0.084	0.341
Railway	.449(*)	-0.314	-0.026	0.275	0.176	1	0.245	0.232	0.254	0.213	0.003	0.341	0.002
Telephone	.775(**)	-0.118	0.056	0.023	-0.263	0.245	1	.990(**)	.979(**)	0.247	-.551(**)	.720(**)	-0.323
Bank deposits	.765(**)	-0.096	0.085	0.035	-0.324	0.232	.990(**)	1	.989(**)	0.262	-.577(**)	.682(**)	-0.341
Ind. credit	.780(**)	-0.052	0.155	0.046	-0.316	0.254	.979(**)	.989(**)	1	0.265	-.623(**)	.684(**)	-0.312
Literacy (U)	0.175	-0.301	0.055	-0.352	-0.01	0.213	0.247	0.262	0.265	1	0.194	0.34	0.193
Sex ratio (U)	-.716(**)	-.368(*)	-0.325	-0.056	0.258	0.003	-.551(**)	-.577(**)	-.623(**)	0.194	1	-0.327	.436(*)
Hospital	.705(**)	-0.147	-0.063	-0.051	0.084	0.341	.720(**)	.682(**)	.684(**)	0.34	-0.327	1	-0.179
School	-.473(**)	-0.167	0.105	0.084	0.341	0.002	-0.323	-0.341	-0.312	0.193	.436(*)	-0.179	1

Notes: * Correlation is significant at the 0.05 level (2-tailed). ** Correlation is significant at the 0.01 level (2-tailed).

Source: Computed by Authors.

TABLE 6.5c

Interdependence among Indicators of Urbanization and Socio-economic Development at District Level in Maharashtra (2001)

	LoU	GR (U)	Ind. enterprise	Agri. output	Road	Railway	Telephone	Bank deposits	Ind. credit	Literacy (U)	Sex ratio (U)	Hospital	School
LoU	1.00	.380(*)	0.16	0.19	0.33	.742(**)	.712(**)	.702(**)	0.04	-0.02	-.743(**)	.559(**)	-.543(**)
GR (U)	.380(*)	1.00	.347(*)	0.21	0.14	0.06	0.03	0.01	-0.04	-0.18	-.563(**)	0.08	-0.015
Ind. enterprise	0.16	.347(*)	1.00	0.03	0.06	0.15	0.17	0.17	0.07	0.02	-.437(**)	0.03	-0.101
Agri. output	0.19	0.21	0.03	1.00	0.25	0.09	0.04	0.04	0.25	0.09	-0.19	0.28	-0.159
Road	0.33	0.14	0.06	0.25	1.00	0.09	0.05	0.04	0.28	0.21	-0.14	0.31	-0.201
Railway	.742(**)	0.06	0.15	0.09	0.09	1.00	.989(**)	.987(**)	-0.02	0.14	-.639(**)	.617(**)	-.362(*)
Telephone	.712(**)	0.03	0.17	0.04	0.05	.989(**)	1.00	.998(**)	0.01	0.17	-.598(**)	.607(**)	-0.309
Bank deposits	.702(**)	0.01	0.17	0.04	0.04	.987(**)	.998(**)	1.00	0.00	0.15	-.592(**)	.594(**)	-0.327
Ind. credit	0.04	-0.04	0.07	0.25	0.28	-0.02	0.01	0.00	1.00	.435(*)	0.18	0.27	0.07
Literacy (R)	-0.02	-0.18	0.02	0.09	0.21	0.14	0.17	0.15	.435(*)	1.00	0.10	.367(*)	0.044
Literacy (U)	-.743(**)	-.563(**)	-.437(**)	-0.19	-0.14	-.639(**)	-.598(**)	-.592(**)	0.18	0.10	1.00	-0.30	.382(*)
Sex ratio (U)	.559(**)	0.08	0.03	0.28	0.31	.617(**)	.607(**)	.594(**)	0.27	.367(*)	-0.30	1.00	-0.321
Hospital	-.543(**)	-0.015	-0.101	-0.159	-0.201	-.362(*)	-0.309	-0.327	0.07	0.044	.382(*)	-0.321	1

Notes: * Correlation is significant at the 0.05 level (2-tailed). ** Correlation is significant at the 0.01 level (2-tailed).

Source: Computed by Authors.

Maharashtra. In other words, increasing level of urbanization can be attributed to the development of industrial activity in the state.

Availability of physical infrastructure has played an important role in the process of urbanization in the state of Maharashtra. This may be inferred from the strong interdependencies between level of urbanization and the infrastructural indicators at all the time points. Particularly, the correlations of the former with railways per 100 sq. km. and telephone connections per 100 persons are very high at all the three points of time. The relationship of road network with level of urbanization is negative, that is −0.38 in 1981 and −0.18 in 1991, but the correlation has improved to 0.33 in 2001, suggesting increasing importance of roads as a factor in the urbanization process. Consequently, the districts having better infrastructural facilities are likely to have a higher share of urban population than those with poor infrastructure.

Similarly, all the indicators of financial infrastructure have reflected a positive and significant correlation with urbanization level. One can note this interdependency to exist generally between economic indicators and urbanization levels. The infrastructural facilities also seem to have accelerated the tempo of urbanization. One noticeable exception to this is the fact that the number of middle and higher schools (per thousand persons) has not increased with the level of urbanization. This is reflected in the negative correlation between the indicators during the 1980s as well as the 1990s. However, health facilities tend to go up with urbanization. The number of hospitals per thousand population exhibits a positive correlation with the level of urbanization.

The socio-demographic indicator, literacy in urban areas has a positive correlation with the level of urbanization, both in 1981 and 1991. The correlation coefficients, however, are not very high ranging between 0.17 and 0.33. Urban literacy tends to go down for higher levels of urbanization, at all the three points of time. This can be attributed to inflow of illiterate migrants to the cities and towns in the urbanized districts in search of livelihood.

Another interesting point is that the level of urbanization relates negatively with urban sex ratio over the past three decades. This implies that male population increases (relative to female population) as urbanization increases. This is possibly due to the migration of male population from rural to urban areas in search of jobs. This pushes up the sex ratio in large cities and urbanized districts in the state of Maharashtra.

PUNJAB

Punjab exhibits somewhat similar pattern of interdependence between urbanization and the developmental indicators (Tables 6.6a, 6.6b, and 6.6c), excepting the indicator on agricultural productivity. Unlike Maharashtra, the correlation between level of urbanization and value of agricultural output is positive and significant in the early 1980s, which became stronger during the early 1990s. Even the growth of urbanization has shown a stronger positive relationship with agricultural productivity in the latter period. In fact, the pattern of urbanization in Punjab is different from that of other states, as urbanization here is not restricted to a few industrialized towns. With the advent of the Green Revolution, agriculture became mechanized and improved infrastructure network led to the growth of agro-allied industries in the vicinity. Consequently, regions with high productivity in agriculture encouraged urban centres in a

TABLE 6.6a

Interdependence among Indicators of Urbanization and Socio-economic Development at District Level in Punjab (1981)

	LoU	GR (U)	Agri. output	Road	Bank deposits	Ind. credit	Literacy (U)	Sex ratio (U)	School
LoU	1.00	0.009	0.523	0.121	0.325	.826(**)	0.299	-0.525	-0.539
GR (U)	0.009	1.00	-0.345	0.126	-0.05	0.085	0.266	-.591(*)	-0.063
Agri. output	0.523	-0.345	1.00	-0.092	0.11	0.491	0.118	-0.077	-0.242
Road	0.121	0.126	-0.092	1.00	0.486	0.27	.795(**)	-0.199	0.261
Bank deposits	0.325	-0.05	0.11	0.486	1.00	0.484	.640(*)	-0.283	0.573
Ind. credit	.826(**)	0.085	0.491	0.27	0.484	1.00	0.572	-.654(*)	-0.152
Literacy (U)	0.299	0.266	0.118	.795(**)	.640(*)	0.572	1.00	-0.523	0.351
Sex ratio (U)	-0.525	-.591(*)	-0.077	-0.199	-0.283	-.654(*)	-0.523	1.00	0.072
School	-0.539	-0.063	-0.242	0.261	0.573	-0.152	0.351	0.072	1.00

Notes: * Correlation is significant at the 0.05 level (2-tailed).   ** Correlation is significant at the 0.01 level (2-tailed).

Source: Computed by Authors.

TABLE 6.6b

Interdependence among Indicators of Urbanization and Socio-economic Development at District Level in Punjab (1991)

	LoU	GR (U)	Agri. output	Bank deposits	Ind. credit	Literacy (U)	Sex ratio (U)	Hospital	School
LoU	1.00	0.434	.665(*)	0.551	.754(**)	0.123	-.693(*)	.707(*)	-0.485
GR (U)	0.434	1.00	0.435	-0.139	.629(*)	0.049	-0.439	-0.003	-0.229
Agri. output	.665(*)	0.435	1.00	0.089	0.519	-0.07	-0.54	0.396	-.839(**)
Bank deposits	0.551	-0.139	0.089	1.00	0.495	.604(*)	-0.325	0.397	-0.07
Ind. credit	.754(**)	.629(*)	0.519	0.495	1.00	0.51	-.775(**)	0.398	-0.319
Literacy (U)	0.123	0.049	-0.07	.604(*)	0.51	1.00	-0.015	0.192	0.081
Sex ratio (U)	-.693(*)	-0.439	-0.54	-0.325	-.775(**)	-0.015	1.00	-0.265	0.219
Hospital	.707(*)	-0.003	0.396	0.397	0.398	0.192	-0.265	1.00	-0.352
School	-0.485	-0.229	-.839(**)	-0.07	-0.319	0.081	0.219	-0.352	1.00

Notes: * Correlation is significant at the 0.05 level (2-tailed). ** Correlation is significant at the 0.01 level (2-tailed).

Source: Computed by Authors.

TABLE 6.6c

Interdependence among Indicators of Urbanization and Socio-economic Development at District Level in Punjab (2001)

	LoU	GR (U)	Ind. Enterprise	Road	Bank Deposits	Ind. Credit	Literacy (R)	Literacy (U)	Sex Ratio (U)	Hospital	School
LoU	1.00	0.069	-0.034	0.476	0.481	.670(**)	0.173	0.093	-.726(**)	.504(*)	-0.142
GR (U)	0.069	1.00	0.34	0.346	0.281	0.188	0.09	0.134	-0.13	0.152	-0.048
Ind. Enterprise	-0.034	0.34	1.00	.550(*)	0.112	0.199	0.336	0.379	0.087	-0.24	-0.252
Road	0.476	0.346	.550(*)	1.00	.515(*)	.791(**)	.552(*)	0.447	-0.42	0.071	-0.381
Bank Deposits	0.481	0.281	0.112	.515(*)	1.00	0.427	0.409	0.273	-0.251	0.415	0.038
Ind. Credit	.670(**)	0.188	0.199	.791(**)	0.427	1.00	0.308	0.146	-.707(**)	0.359	-0.394
Literacy (R)	0.173	0.09	0.336	.552(*)	0.409	0.308	1.00	.852(**)	-0.134	-0.152	-0.294
Literacy (U)	0.093	0.134	0.379	0.447	0.273	0.146	.852(**)	1.00	-0.043	-0.107	-0.169
Sex Ratio (U)	-.726(**)	-0.13	0.087	-0.42	-0.251	-.707(**)	-0.134	-0.043	1.00	-0.229	0.131
Hospital	.504(*)	0.152	-0.24	0.071	0.415	0.359	-0.152	-0.107	-0.229	1.00	-0.063
School	-0.142	-0.048	-0.252	-0.381	0.038	-0.394	-0.294	-0.169	0.131	-0.063	1.00

Notes: * Correlation is significant at the 0.05 level (2-tailed).   ** Correlation is significant at the 0.01 level (2-tailed).

Source: Computed by Authors.

more decentralized way. This has produced a positive correlation of urbanization with agricultural productivity.

Due to non-availability of information on physical infrastructure such as railways and telecom facilities, indicators pertaining to these aspects could not be built for all the three time points. The relationship of roads (for which information was available only for the last decade of 1991–2001) with the level of urbanization is positive though not statistically significant. Per capita credit to industry exhibits the strongest and the most significant relationship with the percentage of urban population in all the three points of time which underlines the importance of this factor. Correlations are also positive in case of per capita availability of bank credit, though the values are not significant. The values, however, have improved over the time. A pattern similar to Maharashtra is noticed with regard to urban sex ratio and middle and high school education. The correlation between growth of population and sex ratio in urban areas is –0.59 which is significant at 5 per cent level in 1981. It goes down to –0.44 and –0.13 in 1991 and 2001 respectively but still the correlation remains negative, suggesting male dominance in rapidly urbanizing districts. The negative relationship of urbanization with the indicator of middle and higher schools indicates that the facilities have not kept pace with the level and growth of urbanization in the state.

The other infrastructural indicator, hospitals per thousand population, relates positively and significantly with the level of urbanization in 1991 as well as 2001. The correlations are as high as 0.70 and 0.51 respectively. However, the decline in their values suggests that the medical facilities, too, have failed

to increase corresponding to the increase in urban population during the 1990s, as noted in case of schooling.

Socio-economic indicators like urban literacy exhibit positive but insignificant relationship with the level as well as growth of urban population across the districts. The difference between rural and urban literacy in Punjab is much less than the national average in 1981, 1991, and 2001. This, possibly, is due to lesser number of illiterate migrants in the urban areas. Reduction in the 0–6 age group of population would also enhance the crude literacy rate. Punjab, as a matter of fact, has reported a marked decrease in its 0–6 age group of population due to decline in birth rate between 1991–2001—much more than the national average.

BIHAR

The number of indicators available in case of Bihar is less as compared to the other two states discussed already. Temporal comparability of the interdependency between urbanization and other socio-economic indicators at the district level would, therefore, have certain additional limitations here. The agricultural productivity data for some of the districts of Bihar are not available and they are substituted by the mean value to keep the correlations unbiased. The correlations between the indicators of urbanization and agricultural productivity were insignificant in both the temporal periods under consideration. However, the correlation between level of urbanization and agricultural output was positive during the early 1980s as well as early 1990s. Importantly, the growth of urbanization has exhibited a negative relationship with agricultural productivity and it has become stronger over time. This is evident from the fact that districts which exhibited increase in urbanization have witnessed a declining trend in terms of agricultural productivity.

The indicator on roads per sq. km. does not show any positive relationship with the level or growth of urban population in 1981. Correlations of level of urbanization with per capita bank credit and credit to industry per capita, however, are positive and highly significant in 1981. The correlations, however, have weakened over the subsequent decades[12] (Tables 6.7a, 6.7b, and 6.7c). Further, interrelation of these indicators with the growth of urban population is neither significant nor gives a consistent story over the years.

Urban and rural literacy relate positively with the level of urbanization across the districts. A marked gap can be noticed between urban and rural literacy rates. The strong positive correlation between level of urbanization and urban literacy suggests that there is a concentration of educated persons in a few large cities and urbanized districts of the state.

It is evident that unlike Maharashtra and Punjab, Bihar has not been able to enjoy the benefits of urbanization. The numbers and percentage of urban population in the state have of course gone up due to natural growth and poverty-induced migration. Importantly, the level as well as growth in urban population have exhibited an inverse relation with the urban sex ratio in all the three decades. Poverty and lack of job opportunities in rural Bihar seem to be the main factors behind the RU migration which has been highly male selective. This has lowered the female–male ratio in the relatively urbanized districts of the state.

[12] Data for per capita bank credit and credit to industry per capita in 2001 is not available.

RAJASTHAN

The empirical investigations at the district level for the state of Rajasthan are also constrained by the non-availability of data on the selected indicators, as in the case of Bihar. An attempt has, however, been made to evaluate the nature of relationship of the level and growth of urbanization with the available developmental indicators (Tables 6.8a, 6.8b, and 6.8c). Urbanization in the state of Rajasthan has witnessed inverse relationship with agricultural productivity. This phenomenon was evident from the negative correlations in level as well as growth of urbanization in the early 1980s and in later years. This seems to be obvious, since agriculture is a component of village-oriented economy. Interestingly, its correlation with the growth of urbanization has become positive and significant in the early 1990s. This implies that much of the urban growth is occurring in the agriculturally developed areas.

The correlation matrix for 1981 shows positive and significant relationship of per capita bank credit and per capita credit available to industries with level of urbanization. This has been noticed throughout the 1980s and the 1990s. But, per capita bank credit does not show such high correlation with the growth of urban population. Of course, the correlation has improved over time but still remains statistically insignificant even in 2001. Similarly, credit to industry shows positive correlation with the growth of urban population since 1981 and the value has increased over the time. And yet, it is not significant even at the 5 per cent level.

The level of urbanization exhibits positive relation with urban literacy, though the values are insignificant at all the three points of time. In case of the growth rate, however, there exists no consistent pattern in the relationship.

TABLE 6.7a

Interdependence among Indicators of Urbanization and Socio-economic Development at District Level in Bihar (1981)

	LoU	GR (U)	Agri. output	Road	Bank deposits	Ind. credit	Literacy (U)	Sex ratio (U)	Hospital
LoU	1.00	0.028	0.105	-0.064	.889(**)	.763(**)	.431(*)	-.486(**)	0.209
GR (U)	0.028	1.00	-0.096	-0.053	0.105	0.208	-0.206	-0.05	0.042
Agri. output	0.105	-0.096	1.00	0.004	0.167	0.028	-0.122	0.086	-0.08
Road	-0.064	-0.053	0.004	1.00	-0.03	-0.118	0.025	0.149	0.02
Bank deposits	.889(**)	0.105	0.167	-0.03	1.00	.840(**)	0.34	-.506(**)	0.14
Ind. credit	.763(**)	0.208	0.028	-0.118	.840(**)	1.00	.366(*)	-.517(**)	.516(**)
Literacy (U)	.431(*)	-0.206	-0.122	0.025	0.34	.366(*)	1.00	-.361(*)	.528(**)
Sex Ratio (U)	-.486(**)	-0.05	0.086	0.149	-.506(**)	-.517(**)	-.361(*)	1.00	-0.121
Hospital	0.209	0.042	-0.08	0.02	0.14	.516(**)	.528(**)	-0.121	1.00

Notes: * Correlation is significant at the 0.05 level (2-tailed).   ** Correlation is significant at the 0.01 level (2-tailed).

Source: Computed by Authors.

TABLE 6.7b

Interdependence among Indicators of Urbanization and Socio-economic Development at District Level in Bihar (1991)

	LoU	GR (U)	Agri. output	Bank deposits	Ind. credit	Literacy (U)	Sex ratio (U)	Hospital
LoU	1.00	-0.302	0.178	0.163	0.27	.453(**)	-0.125	.533(**)
GR (U)	-0.302	1.00	-0.182	-0.11	-0.215	-0.262	-0.026	-0.124
Agri. output	0.178	-0.182	1.00	0.166	0.125	0.053	0.101	0.008
Bank deposits	0.163	-0.11	0.166	1.00	.914(**)	.358(*)	-.406(**)	0.192
Ind. credit	0.27	-0.215	0.125	.914(**)	1.00	.370(*)	-.404(**)	.383(*)
Literacy (U)	.453(**)	-0.262	0.053	.358(*)	.370(*)	1.00	-0.065	.331(*)
Sex ratio (U)	-0.125	-0.026	0.101	-.406(**)	-.404(**)	-0.065	1.00	-0.051
Hospital	.533(**)	-0.124	0.008	0.192	.383(*)	.331(*)	-0.051	1.00

Notes: * Correlation is significant at the 0.05 level (2-tailed).   ** Correlation is significant at the 0.01 level (2-tailed).

Source: Computed by Authors.

TABLE 6.7c

Interdependence among Indicators of Urbanization and Socio-economic Development at District Level in Bihar (2001)

	LoU	GR (U)	Literacy (R)	Literacy (U)	Sex ratio (U)
LoU	1.00	-0.16	.473(**)	.400(**)	-0.191
GR (U)	-0.16	1.00	-.284(*)	0.061	-0.045
Literacy (R)	.473(**)	-.284(*)	1.00	.445(**)	0.204
Literacy (U)	.400(**)	0.061	.445(**)	1.00	0.053
Sex ratio (U)	-0.191	-0.045	0.204	0.053	1.00

Notes: * Correlation is significant at the 0.05 level (2-tailed).   ** Correlation is significant at the 0.01 level (2-tailed).

Source: Computed by Authors.

TABLE 6.8a

Interdependence among Indicators of Urbanization and Socio-economic Development at District Level in Rajasthan (1981)

	LoU	GR (U)	Agri. output	Bank deposits	Ind. credit	Literacy (U)	Sex ratio (U)
LoU	1.00	-0.204	-0.134	.864(**)	.588(**)	0.066	0.162
GR (U)	-0.204	1.00	-0.363	-0.124	0.104	-0.174	-0.127
Agri. output	-0.134	-0.363	1.00	-0.091	-0.241	0.061	-.443
Bank deposits	.864(**)	-0.124	-0.091	1.00	.684(**)	0.337	-0.04
Ind. credit	.588(**)	0.104	-0.241	.684(**)	1.00	0.357	-0.053
Literacy (U)	0.066	-0.174	0.061	0.337	0.357	1.00	-0.264
Sex ratio (U)	0.162	-0.127	-.443(*)	-0.04	-0.053	-0.264	1.00

Notes: ** Correlation is significant at the 0.01 level (2-tailed).

Source: Computed by Authors.

TABLE 6.8b

Interdependence among Indicators of Urbanization and Socio-economic
Development at District Level in Rajasthan (1991)

	LoU	GR (U)	Agri. output	Bank deposits	Ind. credit	Literacy (U)	Sex ratio (U)
LoU	1.00	-0.181	-0.096	.819(**)	.467(*)	0.152	0.066
GR (U)	-0.181	1.00	.439(*)	-0.134	0.153	0.156	-0.214
Agri. output	-0.096	.439(*)	1.00	-0.05	-0.042	0.162	-.725(**)
Bank deposits	.819(**)	-0.134	-0.05	1.00	.589(**)	.434(*)	-0.06
Ind. credit	.467(*)	0.153	-0.042	.589(**)	1.00	.410(*)	-0.137
Literacy (U)	0.152	0.156	0.162	.434(*)	.410(*)	1.00	-0.089
Sex ratio (U)	0.066	-0.214	-.725(**)	-0.06	-0.137	-0.089	1.00

Notes: * Correlation is significant at the 0.05 level (2-tailed).   ** Correlation is significant at the 0.01 level (2-tailed).

Source: Computed by Authors.

TABLE 6.8c

Interdependence among Indicators of Urbanization and Socio-economic Development at District Level in Rajasthan (2001)

	LoU	GR (U)	Bank deposits	Ind. credit	Literacy (R)	Literacy (U)	Sex Ratio (U)	Hospital	School
LoU	1.00	0.259	.727(**)	.418(*)	0.316	0.155	−0.049	−.361(*)	0.004
GR (U)	0.259	1.00	0.23	0.303	0.086	−0.26	−0.259	−0.009	0.138
Bank deposits	.727(**)	0.23	1.00	.605(**)	0.125	.408(*)	−0.074	−0.305	−0.041
Ind. credit	.418(*)	0.303	.605(**)	1.00	−0.02	.354(*)	−0.157	−0.284	0.01
Literacy (R)	0.316	0.086	0.125	−0.02	1.00	−0.117	−0.01	−0.234	0.151
Literacy (U)	0.155	−0.26	.408(*)	.354(*)	−0.117	1.00	0.046	−0.26	0.101
Sex ratio (U)	−0.049	−0.259	−0.074	−0.157	−0.01	0.046	1.00	−.413(*)	−0.289
Hospital	−.361(*)	−0.009	−0.305	−0.284	−0.234	−0.26	−.413(*)	1.00	−0.16
School	0.004	0.138	−0.041	0.01	0.151	0.101	−0.289	−0.16	1.00

Notes: * Correlation is significant at the 0.05 level (2-tailed). ** Correlation is significant at the 0.01 level (2-tailed).

Source: Computed by Authors.

High growth of urban population seems to be having a negative impact on urban literacy at the district level in Rajasthan, as is the case in many other states. The reason lies in the fact that most of the rural migrants to urban areas, who come to cities and towns in search of jobs, are illiterate. Corroborating evidence is also the fact that there exists a marked differential in urban and rural literacy in the state.

Level of urbanization exhibits insignificant positive relation with urban sex ratio both in 1981 and 1991 whereas in 2001 the value is still less. In case of growth of urban population, however, the correlation with the sex ratio is negative and significant. As elsewhere high urban growth is associated with male selective migration leading to low female–male ratio.

Among the other infrastructure indicators like hospitals and middle and higher schools per thousand population, the data are available only for the year 2001. Level of urbanization has a strong inverse relation with the availability of medical facilities. The indicator pertaining to middle and higher schools however shows a negligible positive correlation with both the level and growth of urban population. It may be concluded that with the increase in the levels and growth in urban population, infrastructure facilities come under stress, reflected in low per capita values in the urbanized districts.

VII
The Policy Perspectives

The Indian census is an internationally well-acknowledged and established operation. Though the census has been carried out five times since independence, we are still confronted with definitional issues and significant problems in temporal comparability of data. These aspects have been discussed in Chapter II. There appears to be a real need to revisit the criteria for census towns which is restrictive in content and rigorous in application.

The 74th Amendment to the Constitution mentions in Article 243 (R) several factors such as population, density, economic importance, and non-agricultural employment, to be taken into account for constituting a municipality or a nagarpalika which is a generic term for urban local bodies. However, the responsibility for according legal status to an urban settlement rests with the state governments. This study has revealed that several state governments have not applied their mind adequately in conferring this legal status. Most of the statutory towns appear to have been so classified more because they were called 'towns' prior to the 74th Amendment and it seemed convenient to continue with that. The study indicates that out of the total number of 5161 urban places, 102 are called corporations, 1653 municipalities, and 1842 nagar panchayats, and the rest are non-statutory or other towns. The criteria for setting up these civic entities vary considerably between the states. The need for some uniformity is an important aspect of urban governance.

Apart from definitional problems and issues of statistical comparability, for purposes of governance, there is no merit in having so many statutory towns and categorizing them as municipal as has happened, for example in Tamil Nadu or Uttar Pradesh. Many of the statutory towns do not fulfil the criteria for being a census town in the first place. For example, in Uttar Pradesh as well as the newly created state of Uttaranchal, there are several nagar panchayats which have less than 5000 people. These settlements may not also fulfil the economic criteria such as 75 per cent of the male working force in non-agricultural occupations. Most of these settlements do not have the tax base to perform any worthwhile municipal function. The position holds good for several settlements in Tamil Nadu as well. The inclusion of such settlements as statutory towns or conferring on them municipal status is of no more than statistical value. As the present study indicates even that statistical value is complicated and limited.

For purposes of urban governance, it will be much more practical and useful to have a tighter definition of urban areas. It is better to have a lesser number of municipalities which can fulfil minimum municipal functions rather than having a large number of sub-critical, non-performing entities classified as municipal only in name. It will be preferable to regard these as panchayats and deal with them as provided for in the 73rd Amendment. This may also be more practical since under the present financial dispensation, panchayats receive much more financial assistance through several central and state-sponsored programmes.

URBANIZATION AND MIGRATION TRENDS AT THE MACRO LEVEL

It is necessary to make a distinction between the level of urbanization and the pace or tempo of urban growth. So far as the level is concerned, for a country of India's large size, an arithmetical figure like 27.78 per cent as urban does not convey the full sense. The variations in the different states as also their absolute numbers have been brought out in Chapter II. As regards growth, excepting the period 1971 to 1981 when the annual growth rate was as high as 3.83 per cent, there has been a steady decline. During 1981–91, it came down to 3.09 and for 1991–2001 it was 2.73 per cent. However, it has to be noted that this rate is still higher than that of rural growth which is 1.68 per cent.

In popular perception urbanization in India is largely because of migration induced by rural distress. However, the present study has brought out the reality that migration has been on the decline. Relating the migration phenomenon to employment, the study has also emphasized that due to capital intensity and other factors, job increases have not been significant. At the same time, the growth of agriculture and agro-industries has not been able to absorb the increase in labour force.

While the motivation for RU migration continues to be pressing, the flow of migration is limited which is only an indication of a stagnant rural economy and limited urban economic growth.

The study has re-established the position well known by now that natural increase accounts for the principal share of urban growth of about 60 per cent. The share of new towns within the context of the census is less than 10 per cent. Territorial expansion of urban areas provides another 13 per cent whereas net RU migration is only about 21 per cent.

The study further brings out that class I cities and towns have grown at a faster rate. The bulk of India's urban population of about 69 per cent live in such cities. The number of metropolitan cities has also gone up to thirty-five from twenty-three with 38 per cent of the urban population living in such cities. Large city growth has therefore to be accepted as a reality. The policy implication is that there is not much merit in pursuing a programme for small and medium towns. While the case for improving urban services is common across the board, a programme like the Integrated Development of Small and Medium Towns (IDSMT) has not succeeded in reducing or deflecting large city growth. Whether in comparatively developed states like Maharashtra or Punjab or in other states like Bihar or Rajasthan, it is seen that the growth rates of IDSMT towns continue to be below the average growth rates for the small and medium towns in the state and well below the rate of class I cities.

Significantly, the bulk of increase in population share of large cities has come because of the size-class jumping phenomenon and not due to high population growth of large cities. The growth rate needs to be worked out by holding the number of towns and cities in each

TABLE 7.1
Growth Rates of Selected IDSMT Towns

Maharashtra Towns A.	Expend. (lakhs) under IDSMT (6th & 7th Plan)	Anl. expn. gr. rate 1981–91	Maharashtra Towns B.	Expend. (lakhs) under IDSMT (8th & 9th Plan)	Anl. expn. gr. rate 1991–2001	Bihar Towns A.	Expend. (lakhs) under IDSMT (6th & 7th Plan)	Anl. expn. gr. rate 1981–91	Bihar Towns B.	Expend. (lakhs) under IDSMT (8th & 9th Plan)	Anl. expn. gr. rate 1991–2001
Ratnagiri	148.93	1.84	Ichalkaranji	389.54	1.81	Katihar	135.58	2.56	Munger	35.94	2.22
Satara	118.06	1.32	Bhusawal	341.31	1.72	Hajipur	89.25	3.38	Muzaffarpur	15.61	2.37
Jalna	116.09	3.58	Sangli	304.38	2.16	Begusarai	89.03	2.31	Gaya	12.71	2.73
Ambejogai	77.02	2.98	Ambad	37.18	3.71	Bihar Sharif	26.24	2.84	Rajgir	10.82	3.51
Selu	72.74	2.65	Dondaicha	25.90	2.31	Bodh Gaya	21.17	3.22	Supaul	0	2.86
Morshi	67.92	3.31	Mukhed	7.09	2.78	Sitamarhi	21.00	3.51	Sheohar	0	4.27
State (S & M)		2.50	State (S & M)		2.36	State (S & M)		2.43	State (S & M)		2.62
State (Class I)		3.28	State (Class I)		2.91	State (Class I)		2.14	State (Class I)		3.23
State (Urban)		3.27	State (Urban)		2.95	State (Urban)		2.65	State (Urban)		2.57

(contd.)

TABLE 7.1: contd.

Punjab Towns	Expend. (lakhs) under IDSMT	Anl. expn. gr. rate	Punjab Towns	Expend. (lakhs) under IDSMT	Anl. expn. gr. rate	Rajasthan Towns	Expend. (lakhs) under IDSMT	Anl. expn. gr. rate	Rajasthan Towns	Expend. (lakhs) under IDSMT	Anl. expn. gr. rate
A.	(6th & 7th Plan)	1981–91	B.	(8th & 9th Plan)	1991–20001	A.	(6th & 7th Plan)	1981–91	B.	(8th & 9th Plan)	1991–2001
Batala	217.93	0.20	Rajpura	162.77	1.51	Bhilwara	295.73	4.05	Nimbahera	161.06	2.41
Kapurthala	186.36	2.26	Faridkot	65.77	2.12	Bharatpur	245.45	3.99	Rajasamand	122.83	3.60
Hoshiarpur	182.01	3.58	Anandpur Sahib	53.43	2.63	Ganganagar	199.97	2.66	Jhunjhunu	89.24	3.31
Moga	95.70	2.99	Mukheria	30.88.	1.82	Jalor	87.51	3.34	Fatehnagar	41.00	1.74
Sangrur	84.17	2.21	Fatehgarh Sahib	21.97	3.59	Sirohi	80.03	1.62	Sadarshahar	36.65	1.81
Gobindgarh	54.67	4.10	Patti	11.75	2.15	Barmer	72.50	2.22	Beawar	8.51	1.60
State (S & M)		2.43	State (S & M)		2.34	State (S & M)		2.89	State (S & M)		2.50
State (Class I)		3.04	State (Class I)		2.99	State (Class I)		3.28	State (Class I)		3.24
State (Urban)		2.55	State (Urban)		3.19	State (Urban)		3.31	State (Urban)		2.71

Notes: (a) Sixth and Seventh plan together coincide with the 1981–91 census period; (b) Eighth and Ninth plan together coincide with the 1991–2001 census period; (c) S & M denotes small and medium towns; (d) 1991–2001 growth rate is shown for bifurcated Bihar; (e) Supaul and Sheohar (Bihar) did not report any expenditure though received Central assistance. Expenditure as reported in the IDSMT Status Report.

Sources: Census of India 1991, Paper-2, Rural–Urban Distribution; Census 2001, IDSMT Status Report, 2000–1, TCPO, Ministry of Urban Development & Poverty Alleviation.

size-class category same as in the base year. At the same time the number of urban centres at the lower levels through transformation of rural settlements has not increased correspondingly. The absence of the process of graduation of large-sized villages into towns, particularly through growth of industrial and tertiary activities, remains a major problem in India's urbanization. At present the census depends on the last census urban frame for the next census operations. This problem can be addressed if there is a mechanism of revising the urban frame of the last census continuously before the operation of the next census.

An important conclusion of this study is that large city growth in many cases is also the growth of large agglomerations. However, within these agglomerations, there are significant differentials in the growth of the core and the periphery. The mega cities of Mumbai, Kolkata, Delhi, Chennai, and Hyderabad are witnessing higher growth in the periphery and a decline in the core. Bangalore is the only exception. In other metropolitan cities we are seeing both the phenomenon of growing core and growing periphery as well as declining core and declining periphery. The policy implication of this is that a disaggregated view of UAs is necessary to understand better the problems and the objectives of remedial strategy. The study also indicates an emerging pattern of agglomerations which coalesce with each other to form urban corridors. This is a highly significant spatial phenomenon of India's urbanization which is already being witnessed in several other countries. The planning, development, and management of these agglomerations cannot be merely a collection of individual city programmes. Multi-municipal UAs require a metropolitan-wide perspective not constrained by narrow municipal definitions. Here again the constitutionally mandated Metropolitan Planning Committee (MPC) provides a platform for a metropolitan-wide perspective and development strategy. Excepting Kolkata, an MPC has not been set up anywhere. Since these metropolitan cities account for over 38 per cent of India's urban population, the absence of MPC signals a major planning and institutional failure.

In the era of economic reforms, liberalization, and globalization, cities and towns are emerging as the centres of domestic and international investment. In fact, estimates reveal that urban India at present contributes more than 50 per cent of country's gross domestic product although it contains less that one-third of its population. In this background, urban development policy calls for an approach that aims at optimizing the productive advantages of cities and towns.

Out of 593 districts in the country, in 165 the level of urbanization is above the national average of 27.78 per cent. The districts with a level of 10 per cent or less are 146. These predominantly or even overwhelmingly rural districts are mainly in eastern UP, Bihar, Orissa, and Assam; the remaining districts are in a flux and moving towards urbanization. The district thus becomes an important entity to monitor and manage urbanization.

SOCIO-ECONOMIC ASPECTS OF URBANIZATION: STATE-LEVEL ANALYSIS

While urbanization has been generally regarded as a manifestation of economic change, the 2001 Census has revealed the interrelationship strikingly. During the 1990s, the country has witnessed a steady dismantling of locational regulations and preferences in investments. By and large, the marketplace and investor preference have emerged as the principal factors.

The correlations between urbanization and economic indicators have come out more prominently in the case of the so-called developed states. It is seen that apart from industry, agricultural growth and the increase in employment opportunities as a result have also helped a better spread of urbanization as in Punjab and Haryana. In either case, economic development emerges both as a determinant and characteristic of urbanization. This in turn has to be recognized as an ingredient of urban development policy.

The outcome of the study in regard to the relationships between urbanization and socio-demographic indicators is somewhat mixed. While physical and social infrastructure have been perceived to be generally better in urban areas, the level of disparities within them appear to be serious. Intra-urban inequities are, therefore, an important policy and programme concern.

The data on slum population presented for the first time in the Census of 2001 also reveal that in socio-demographic terms, the slum population is not that different from what is obtaining in the rest of the city. Sex ratio, literacy, and percentage of children indicate that slums are not transient settlements but an almost established part of the city in the socio-economic sense. The important policy implications arising from this picture are the following.

(a) While urban poverty can be calculated in economic and percentage terms, its spatial location is not always easy to establish.

(b) All slums cannot be regarded as a surrogate for poverty.

(c) The infrastructure deficiencies may also be city-wide. In such a situation, it may not be possible to insulate parts and pockets of a city.

(d) Programmes for employment and income increase alone may not be sufficient to address non-food poverty especially in regard to physical and social infrastructure.

SOCIO-ECONOMIC ASPECTS OF URBANIZATION: DISTRICT-LEVEL ANALYSIS IN FOUR SELECT STATES

If it is unwise to rely on national averages of urban growth and levels, it may be equally unwise to rely on them at the state level as well. Even in a state like Maharashtra, the coefficient of variation in the level of urbanization is nearly 68 per cent. While some districts like Nagpur, Pune, and Thane, apart from Mumbai, have experienced high urban growth, several others like Beed, Kolhapur, or Satara have had low urban growth. In the case of Punjab, urbanization appears to be more balanced. In the case of undivided Bihar, the coefficient of variation between districts is nearly 96 per cent. It is higher than what it was in 1991. The dichotomy between class I cities and others is also sharp. The position in Rajasthan is similar. Thus even at the state level a broad generalized development strategy may not help in managing urbanization. A more conscious assessment of growth at the district level and its spatial configuration are essential.

This makes district planning crucial. The 74th Amendment has specifically mandated district planning committees (DPCs) to address issues of common interest to panchayats and municipalities including spatial planning, integrated development of infrastructure, and environmental conservation. These committees are required to integrate urban and rural planning, facilitate the development of regional infrastructure, and promote environmental conservation. Sharing of physical resources and coordinating the development of the rural and urban parts will be a very critical function of the DPCs. Most of the states have provided for DPCs in the conformity laws. So far seventeen states/union territories have taken steps to constitute them. Where they have been set up, the focus is on schemes and financial allocations rather than strategy and planning. The locus of the DPC itself, as a stand-alone body, distinct from the district level panchayat or the zilla parishad has been one of the defects in the 74th Constitutional Amendment. By leaving the chairmanship of the DPC to be decided by the state government, an opportunity for integrating DPC with the zilla parishad and thereby strengthening the process of development strategy for the district as a whole has been missed. The zilla parishad itself has been envisaged as a zilla rural parishad rather than as a representative, self-governing local body for the district as a whole. This is yet another deficiency in the constitutional amendment which ignores the realities of economic and spatial transformation in the country. An opportunity for correcting this and moving towards RU integration has been missed and the institutional failure has remained.

VIII

Migration Update and Current Urban Agenda

Scholars have generally regarded the Indian population as highly immobile. It can be argued whether this is because of caste factors, family systems and traditional values acting as deterrents or economic factors like disparity in employment opportunities across the regions, and the costs associated with migration. But the fact remains that except 1951–61 period, when life time migrants accounted for about 30.60 per cent of the total population, the figure has been less than 30 per cent in other census years. The growth of migration did pick up marginally during 1971–81 and again during 1991–2001 but declined during the intervening decade of the eighties. Table 8.1 provides information on the volume of migration since 1961.

TABLE 8.1
Volume of Migration Since 1961

(in Millions)

	1961–71	1971–81	1981–91	1991–2001
Rural-Rural	42.49	46.26	46.25	53.35
Rural-Urban	10.98	15.33	16.76	20.59
Urban-Rural	5.33	6.45	6.08	6.27
Urban-Urban	9.00	12.39	11.58	14.39
Sub total	67.80	80.43	80.67	94.60
Place of origin not identified				3.00
Total				97.60

Source: Census of India.

AN UPDATED OVERVIEW

The 2001 Census indicates that out of 1.02 billion people in the country 307 million are migrants, enumerated in places other than their places of birth. This works to about 30 per cent which is slightly more than the 27.3 per cent reported in 1991. While in absolute terms, there has been an increase in the life time migrants from 222.6 million in 1991 to 307 million, *the commonly held perception is that much of this migration is from rural to urban areas. This simply is not true.* According to the Census data for the 1991–2001 period, the total number of migrants during the period was 97.6 million. Out of this 53.5 million was rural to rural migration. Rural to urban migration was only 20.59 million. About 14.39 million accounted for migration from one urban area to another. Urban to Rural migration was also not insignificant and amounted to 6.27 million. According to the Census Authorities exact nature of the place of origin, whether rural or urban, could not be determined in the case of 3 million. While this is the break-up of the total of 97.6 million, Urban to Rural migration will have to be deducted to arrive at net Rural to Urban migration which now works out to 14.32. This is very close to the figure of 14.20 which we had mentioned as the lower estimate in the earlier edition of this book and which may be seen in Table 3.4.

We may now consider what proportions of this migration are from within and across the states. Here again contrary to popular perceptions, the bulk of the Rural to Urban migration is intrastate or within the state amounting to 14.22 million. Interstate migrants account for only about 6.3 million. This phenomenon is not exclusive to urban destined migration, but is in keeping with the overall pattern of migration observed in the past. Out of the total of 98.3 million migrants, for the duration of 0 to 9 years covered by 2001 Census, 80.73 were 'intrastate' and only 16.82 million were 'interstate'. *This confirms the view that bulk of the migratory movements in India are not over long distances.* This is understandable because much of the RR migration within the state comprise women who move to other villages after marriage or for joining their husbands. This is not directly linked to economic factors. In contrast, migration into urban agglomerations, considered later on in this chapter, is determined largely by economic factors. The break-up of intrastate and interstate Rural to Rural. Rural to Urban, Urban to Rural and Urban to Urban migration for the decade 1991–2001 is given in table 8.2.

TABLE 8.2
Migration Streams 1991–2001

Migrant Stream	Persons	Males	Females
Total migrants	98,301,342	32,896,986	65,404,356
Intrastate migrants			
Total	80,733,441	23,998,283	56,735,158
	100	*100*	*100*
Rural to Rural	48,880,074	9,985,581	38,894,493
	60.5	*41.6*	*68.6*
Rural to Urban	14,222,276	6,503,461	7,718,815
	17.6	*27.1*	*13.6*
Urban to Rural	5,213,151	2,057,789	3,155,362
	6.5	*8.6*	*5.6*
Urban to Urban	9,898,294	4,387,563	5,510,731
	12.3	*18.3*	*9.7*
Unclassified	2,519,646	1,063,889	1,455,757
	3.1	*4.4*	*2.6*
Interstate migrants			
Total	16,826,879	8,512,161	8,314,718
	100	*100*	*100*
Rural to Rural	4,474,302	1,759,523	2,714,779
	26.6	*20.7*	*32.7*
Rural to Urban	6,372,955	3,803,737	2,569,218
	37.9	*44.7*	*30.9*
Urban to Rural	1,053,352	522,916	530,436
	6.3	*6.1*	*6.4*
Urban to Urban	4,490,480	2,201,882	2,288,598
	26.7	*25.9*	*27.5*

(contd.)

TABLE 8.2: contd.

Migrant Stream	Persons	Males	Females
Unclassified	435,790	224,103	211,687
	2.6	2.6	2/5
International migrants			
Total	740,867	386,461	354,406
	100	100	100
To rural areas	392,807	188,518	204,289
	5.3	48.8	57.6
To urban areas	348,060	197,943	150,117
	47	51.2	42.4

Source: Census of India 2001.
D Series

The Census 2001 has identified 10 states where intrastate migration relating to each stream such as rural to rural, rural to urban, urban to rural and urban to urban is high. Regarding Rural to Rural, Bihar tops the list with 79.9 per cent. In regard to rural to urban, it may be mentioned that in the case of Mizoram, Meghalaya, Nagaland, and Arunachal, internal security has also been a significant factor. As for the other states, migration into urban areas can be considered the effect of economic changes in Gujarat, Tamil Nadu, Haryana, Maharashtra, and Karnataka. Urban to Urban movement has also been significant in Tamil Nadu, Mizoram, Goa, and Nagaland. Table 8.3 contains relevant information.

TABLE 8.3
Intrastate Migration Streams for Top 10 States

Rank	Rural to Rural	Rural to Urban	Urban to Rural	Urban to Urban
1	Bihar (3.799,368; 79.9%)	Mizoram (32,555; 39.1%)	Goa (48,288; 26.7%)	Tamil Nadu (1,001,633; 27.4%)
2	Jharkhand (1,215,941; 75.8%)	Meghalaya (10,823; 27.4%)	Kerala (412,772; 13.3%)	Mizoram (21,271; 25.5%)
3	Assam (1,127,168; 73.0%)	Nagaland (13,782; 26.8%)	Nagaland (6,757; 13.2%)	Goa (39,519; 21.9%)
4	Himachal Pradesh (439,222; 71.8%)	Arunachal Pradesh (31,984; 26.1%)	Sikkim (5,818; 11.8%)	Nagaland (10,447; 20.3%)
5	Sikkim (35,039; 70.8%)	Gujarat (1,420,541; 25.9%)	Tamil Nadu (420,815; 11.5%)	Maharashtra (2,401,703; 19.2%)
6	Uttar Pradesh (6,261,203; 69.8%)	Tamil Nadu (852,824; 23.3%)	Meghalaya (4,343; 11.0%)	Punjab (264,685; 15.5%)
7	Rajasthan (3,285,585; 69.7%)	Haryana (339,483; 21.9%)	Mizoram (7,108; 8.5%)	Karnataka (745,235; 15.3%)
8	Chhattisgarh (1,360,501; 69.2%)	Maharashtra (2,653,862; 21.2%)	Andhra Pradesh (606,004; 8.4%)	Gujarat (801,593; 14.6%)
9	Orissa (2,067,885; 67.5%)	Karnataka (1,033,723; 21.2%)	Maharashtra (1,020,045; 8.2%)	Arunachal Pradesh (15,779; 12.9%)
10	West Bengal (3,982,608; 66.5%)	Jammu & Kashmir (79,163; 21.1%)	Karnataka (363,542; 7.4%)	Manipur (8,024; 12.5%)

Source: Table D-2, Census of India 2001.

Declining opportunities for agricultural employment due to modernization of agriculture and increased productivity and other factors is a manifestation of the economic change applicable not only to India but to other countries. However, such situations are not uniformly present within a state or across states. It is well known that states like Punjab, Haryana, Maharashtra, and western Uttar Pradesh, which have maintained their front line status in agricultural production, have offered significant scope for seasonal as well as year-long agricultural employment which attracts migration. However, the situation varies between and within the states which has been discussed in some detail in the earlier chapters. It has also been mentioned that though the motivating factors for rural-urban migration continue to be pressing, *the limited quantum of migration is only an indication of a stagnant rural economy* and labour saving technologies underlying urban economic growth. Whether this will continue to be so in the future remains to be seen.

SOME MYTHS ABOUT MIGRATION

Myths about migration are many. Most are the results of ignorance and non availability of data rather than misinterpretation. While the main results of the census such as provisional and final population totals are available soon after the completion of every census, data on migration take anywhere between 3 to 5 years to be published. Though the census authorities highlight some important aspects of migration data, these do not receive necessary attention. The migration data pertaining to the Census 2001 was made available only in 2005. Some details about migration in some of the major states have been provided. In the case of Maharashtra, Punjab, Delhi, and UP where the migration volumes are significant as well as the states of West Bengal, Haryana, Gujarat, Jharkhand, and Chattisgarh where migration from other states has been important, profiles have been provided. A summary of interstate, intrastate, and international migration in respect of nine states is contained in Table 8.4.

TABLE 8.4
Migration Break-up for Some States 1991–2001

State	Total migrants	Intra-state		Inter-state		International	
Maharashtra	41,715,711	34,225,081	82%	7,313,139	18%	177,478	–
Punjab	9,189,438	7,121,921	78%	1,749,122	19%	318,391	3%
Delhi	6,104,458	411,552	7%	5,324,052	89%	278,854	4%
UP	41,217,266	38,242,846	93%	2,824,746	7%	149,667	–
West Bengal	25,097,629	20,055,625	80%	2,457,162	10%	2,584,806	10%
Haryana	7,574,493	4,694,478	62%	2,675,920	35%	204,093	3%
Gujarat	19,221,602	16,980,117	88%	2,182,741	11%	58,744	–
Jharkhand	7,428,159	5,682,016	76%	1,730,938	23%	15,130	–
Chattisgarh	6,907,199	5,941,915	86%	936,415	14%	28,861	–

Note: Percentages rounded off
percentages less than 1, not indicated.
Source: Census of India.
D Series

Regarding Maharashtra, total migration movements for the duration of 0 to 9 years till the Census of 2001 is a little over 15.7 million. The bulk of the migrants moved within the state of Maharashtra. Total inmigration from outside was only 3.28 million which is less than a quarter of the total migratory movement in the state for the relevant period. While it is true that Greater Mumbai alone received an inflow of 2.48 million migrants during the same period, it should be noted that only about 63 per cent of this number came from other states while about 36 per cent was from within the State of Maharashtra itself. *The commonly held belief that most of the migrants moving to Maharashtra come from Bihar is not true.* During the period covered by the Census of 2001, the bulk of the inmigration into Maharashtra was from UP amounting to 0.92 million followed by Karnataka (0.47 million), Madhya Pradesh (0.27 million) Gujarat (0.24 million), Bihar (0.22 million) and Andhra Pradesh (0.1 million). Inmigration from the rest of the country was about 0.89 million. Nearly an equal number of 0.89 million also moved out of Maharashtra. If this number is adjusted then the net migration from outside the State is 2.38 million [see Table 8.5(a)].

If we consider the case of Punjab the total immigrants from outside the state is 0.83 million, while out migrants numbered 0.50 million which leaves 0.33 million as the net inmigration total. In the case of Punjab, the principal states from which migrant come are Uttar Pradesh, Bihar, and Haryana. Ludhiana, and Amritsar are important destinations for the out of state migrants. Similarly in the case of Delhi the inflow of migrants from outside is 2.22 million. Significantly out migration amounted to 0.45 million, leaving the total of net migrants as 1.76 million. Here again Uttar Pradesh, Bihar, Haryana, and Uttaranchal fol-lowed by Rajasthan and West Bengal are the principal sources of inmigration. Other details about the migration profile of Punjab and Delhi are contained in the Tables 8.5(b) and 8.5(c).

It is also interesting to consider the migration profile of Uttar Pradesh. For the 2001 Census period migratory movement within the State was about 8.9 million. Migrants from out side the State amounted to 1.1 million. As can be expected, out migration significantly exceeded this number amounting to 3.8 million. Uttar Pradesh having the largest population in the country emerges as the principal source of migration to other states. Regarding the inflow itself, Bihar, Delhi, Madhya Pradesh and Uttaranchal constituted important sources. The principal urban centres in Uttar Pradesh such as Lucknow, Kanpur and Allahabad did not receive much inflow from other states. It is only about 25 per cent in the case of Lucknow and about 17 per cent in the case of Kanpur and Allahabad [see Table 8.5(d)].

Where Do the Migrants Go?

We may now consider the important destinations of Rural-Urban migration. In regard to major agglomerations numbering 35 according to the 2001 Census which have a population of one million or more, the total number of immigrants and migration as a component of decennial growth is indicated in table 8.6. It will be seen in the case of Kochi, this component is the highest while in the case of Asansol, it is the lowest. In absolute numbers, Greater Mumbai and Bangalore have received well over 2 million immigrants.

The origin of these migrants is indicated in table 8.7. It will be seen that immigrants from within the state is highest in the case of Vijayawada and lowest in the case of Delhi.

TABLE 8.5(a)
Migration Profile of Maharashtra 2001

Migrants	Total			Rural			Urban		
	Persons	Males	Females	Persons	Males	Females	Persons	Males	Females
(a) Total population	96,878,627	50,400,596	46,478,031	55,777,647	28,458,677	27,318,970	41,100,980	21,941,919	19,159,061
(b) From within the States	12,505,916	5,029,328	7,476,588	7,339,414	2,585,091	4,754,323	5,166,502	2,444,237	2,722,265
(c) Total in-migrants from outside	3,280,006	1,954,810	1,325,196	669,673	359,187	310,486	2,610,333	1,595,623	1,014,710
(d) From other States									
Total	3,231,612	1,922,629	1,308,983	662,721	354,121	308,600	2,568,891	1,568,508	1,000,383
Rural	2,143,586	1,331,571	812,015	537,548	284,385	253,163	1,606,038	1,047,186	558,852
Urban	1,021,520	553,516	468,004	113,543	63,584	49,959	907,977	489,932	418,045
Uttar Pradesh	921,142	639,007	282,135	64,078	47,378	16,700	857,064	591,629	265,435
Karnataka	473,979	225,316	248,663	178,264	79,052	99,212	295,715	146,264	149,451
Madhya Pradesh	275,990	132,572	143,418	131,452	59,938	71,514	144,538	72,634	71,904
Gujarat	245,968	113,930	132,038	40,217	17,570	22,647	205,751	96,360	109,391
Bihar	228,563	178,025	50,538	31,243	25,295	5,948	197,320	152,730	44,590
Andhra Pradesh	193,813	95,304	98,509	51,475	23,767	27,708	142,338	71,537	70,801
Rest	892,157	538,475	353,682	165,992	101,121	64,871	726,165	437,354	288,811
(e) From other countries	48,394	32,181	16,213	6,952	5,066	1,886	41,442	27,115	14,327
(f) Total out migrants	896,988	393,097	503,891	450,300	186,586	263,714	428,641	198,524	230,117
(g) Net migrants (+/- (Item (d) – (f))	2,383,018	1,561,713	821,305	219,373	172,601	46,772	2,181,692	1,397,099	784,593

Data Highlights—Table D1, D2 and D3.
Census of India 2001.

TABLE 8.5(b)
Migration Profile of Punjab 2001

Migrants	Total			Rural			Urban		
	Persons	Males	Females	Persons	Males	Females	Persons	Males	Females
(a) Total population	24,358,999	12,985,045	11,373,954	16,096,488	8,516,596	7,579,892	8,262,511	4,468,449	3,794,062
(b) From within the States	1,712,627	397,678	1,314,949	1,134,471	180,486	953,985	578,156	217,192	360,964
(c) Total in-migrants from outside	837,921	460,497	377,424	309,791	146,412	163,379	528,130	314,085	214,045
(d) From other States									
Total	811,060	442,664	368,396	300,208	140,002	160,206	510,852	302,662	208,190
Rural	571,036	331,376	239,660	247,152	116,775	130,377	323,884	214,601	109,283
Urban	221,768	101,328	120,440	46,647	19,967	26,680	175,121	81,361	93,760
Uttar Pradesh	241,987	155,103	86,884	72,777	43,607	29,170	169,210	111,496	57,714
Haryana	114,031	31,482	82,549	60,167	11,542	48,625	53,864	19,940	33,924
Bihar	149,375	115,102	34,273	46,317	36,039	10,278	103,058	79,063	23,995
Himachal Pradesh	55,795	22,808	32,987	24,756	7,248	17,508	31,039	15,560	15,479
Rajasthan	51,710	19,092	32,618	29,850	9,874	19,976	21,860	9,218	12,642
(e) From other countries	26,861	17,833	9,028	9,583	6,410	3,173	17,278	11,423	5,855
(f) Total out migrants	501,285	204,152	297,133	262,476	98,509	163,967	224,644	99,087	125,557
(g) Net migrants (+/−) (Item (d) − (f))	336,636	256,345	80,291	47,315	47,903	(588)	303,486	214,998	88,488

Data Highlights—Table D1, D2 and D3.
Census of India 2001.

TABLE 8.5(c)
Migration Profile of Delhi 2001

Migrants	Total			Rural			Urban		
	Persons	Males	Females	Persons	Males	Females	Persons	Males	Females
(a) Total population	13,850,507	7,607,234	6,243,273	944,727	522,087	422,640	12,905,780	7,085,147	5,820,633
(b) From within the States	131,895	64,553	67,342	54,110	25,656	28,454	77,785	38,897	38,888
(c) Total in-migrants from outside	2,222,041	1,253,996	968,045	183,239	98,715	84,524	2,038,802	1,155,281	883,521
(d) From other States									
Total	2,172,760	1,223,746	949,014	180,522	97,004	83,518	1,992,238	1,126,742	865,496
Rural	1,492,802	877,254	615,548	146,515	79,823	66,692	1,346,287	797,431	548,856
Urban	610,107	307,840	302,267	28,093	14,073	14,020	582,014	293,767	288,247
Uttar Pradesh	889,857	493,146	396,711	72,889	40,012	32,877	816,968	453,134	363,834
Bihar	424,093	293,563	130,530	41,564	27,329	14,235	382,529	266,234	116,295
Haryana	174,889	73,091	101,798	24,392	6,973	17,419	150,497	66,118	84,379
Uttaranchal	113,519	61,853	51,666	7,688	4,170	3,518	105,831	57,683	48,148
Rajasthan	90,317	46,321	43,996	6,678	3,485	3,193	83,639	42,836	40,803
West Bengal	86,249	49,912	36,337	4,291	2,432	1,859	81,958	47,480	34,478
Rest	393,836	205,860	187,976	23,020	12,603	10,417	370,816	193,257	177,559
(e) From other countries	49,281	30,250	19,031	2,717	1,711	1,006	46,564	28,539	18,025
(f) Total out migrants	457,918	199,397	258,522	54,914	17,681	37,233	393,658	177,156	215,502
(g) Net migrants (+/-(Item (d) − (f))	1,764,122	1,054,599	709,523	128,325	81,034	47,291	1,646,144	978,125	668,019

Data Highlights – Table D1, D2 and D3
Census of India 2001

TABLE 8.5(d)
Migration Profile of Uttar Pradesh 2001

Migrants	Total			Rural			Urban		
	Persons	Males	Females	Persons	Males	Females	Persons	Males	Females
(a) Total population	166,197,921	87,565,369	78,632,552	131,658,339	69,157,470	62,500,869	34,539,582	18,407,899	16,131,683
(b) From within the States	8,969,367	1,536,888	7,432,479	6,919,590	697,416	6,222,174	2,049,777	839,472	1,210,305
(c) Total in-migrants from outside	1,111,165	408,595	702,570	567,458	154,446	413,012	543,707	254,149	289,558
(d) From other States									
Total	1,079,055	398,230	680,825	548,716	151,308	397,408	530,339	246,922	283,417
Rural	658,330	223,042	435,288	445,795	114,263	331,532	212,535	108,779	103,756
Urban	386,167	159,440	226,727	85,524	30,033	55,491	300,643	129,407	171,236
Bihar	224,949	95,956	128,993	124,188	37,175	87,013	100,761	58,781	41,980
Delhi	149,361	62,238	87,123	32,841	11,299	21,542	116,520	50,939	65,581
Madhya Pradesh	141,836	26,070	115,766	93,939	9,966	83,973	47,897	16,104	31,793
Uttaranchal	103,375	35,099	68,276	44,123	8,972	35,151	59,252	26,127	33,125
Rest	459,534	178,867	280,667	253,625	83,896	169,729	205,909	94,971	110,938
(e) From other countries	32,110	10,365	21,745	18,742	3,138	15,604	13,368	7,227	6,141
(f) Total out migrants	3,810,701	2,156,885	1,653,816	2,813,949	1,631,720	1,182,229	897,156	469,932	427,224
(g) Net migrants (+/-) (Item (d) – (f))	(2,699,536)	(1,748,290)	(951,246)	(2,246,491)	(1,477,274)	(769,217)	(353,449)	(215,783)	(137,666)

Data Highlights – Table D1, D2 and D3.
Census of India 2001.

TABLE 8.6
Migration as a Component of Growth in Major Urban Agglomerations (1991 and 2001)

City/UA	1991 pop.	2001 pop.	Decennial growth	Total in-migrants (1991–2001)	In-migrants as % of decennial growth
Kochi	1,140,605	1,355,406	214,801	166,794	77.7%
Ludhiana*	1,042,740	1,395,053	352,313	265,003	75.2%
Surat	1,518,950	2,811,466	1,292,516	869,860	67.3%
Nasik	725,341	1,152,048	426,707	287,017	67.3%
Greater Mumbai	12,596,243	16,368,084	3,771,841	2,489,552	66.0%
Pune	2,493,987	3,755,525	1,261,538	744,194	59.0%
Vijayawada	845,756	1,011,152	165,396	90,894	55.0%
Faridabad*	617,717	1,054,981	437,264	237,800	54.4%
Nagpur	1,664,006	2,122,965	458,959	241,078	52.5%
Visakhapatnam	1,057,118	1,329,472	272,354	139,003	51.0%
Bangalore	4,130,288	5,686,800	1,556,558	761,485	48.9%
Delhi	8,419,084	12,791,458	4,372,374	2,112,363	48.3%
Bhopal	1,062,771	1,454,830	392,059	186,597	47.6%
Chennai	5,421,985	6,424,624	1,002,639	435,620	43.4%
Hyderabad	4,344,437	5,533,640	1,189,203	498,483	41.9%
Rajkot	654,490	1,002,160	347,670	141,177	40.6%
Kolkata	11,021,918	13,216,546	2,194,628	822,389	37.5%
Ahmedabad	3,312,216	4,519,278	1,207,062	428,910	35.5%
Lucknow	1,669,204	2,266,933	597,729	208,915	35.0%
Dhanbad	815,005	1,064,357	249,352	86,238	34.6%
Jaipur*	1,518,235	2,324,319	806,084	250,208	31.0%
Madurai	1,085,914	1,994,665	108,751	33,540	30.8%
Jabalpur	888,916	1,117,200	228,284	68,961	30.2%
Indore	1,109,056	1,639,044	529,688	159,191	30.1%
Jamshedpur	829,171	1,101,804	272,633	80,971	29.7%
Patna	1,099,647	1,707,429	607,782	161,372	26.6%
Varanasi	1,030,863	1,211,749	180,856	46,989	26.0%
Meerut	849,799	1,167,399	317,600	71,213	22.4%
Kanpur	2,029,889	2,690,486	660,597	138,708	21.0%
Allahabad	844,546	1,049,579	205,033	41,699	20.3%
Coimbatore	1,100,746	1,446,034	345,288	68,888	20.0%
Amritsar	708,835	1,011,327	302,492	56,024	18.5%
Asansol	763,939	1,090,171	326,332	59,501	18.2%
Agra	948,063	1,321,410	373,347	34,227	9.2%
	79,361,480	106,389,438	27,027,698	12,485,364	46.2%

Source: Census of India.

TABLE 8.7
Migration as a Component of Growth in Major Urban Agglomerations (1991 and 2001)

City/UA	Migrants	From within state	From other state	From other countries
Greater Mumbai	2,489,552	35.9%	63.1%	1.0%
Kolkata	822,389	57.2%	36.1%	6.6%
Delhi	2,112,363	3.7%	94.1%	2.2%
Chennai	435,620	76.9%	21.8%	1.3%
Bangalore	761,485	52.8%	46.4%	0.8%
Hyderabad	498,483	81.8%	17.7%	0.5%
Ahmedabad	428,910	68.7%	30.8%	0.5%
Pune	744,194	65.9%	33.2%	0.9%
Surat	869,860	49.7%	50.0%	0.3%
Kanpur	138,708	82.2%	17.0%	0.8%
Jaipur	250,208	63.8%	35.2%	1.0%
Lucknow	208,915	73.8%	25.4%	0.8%
Nagpur	241,078	53.9%	45.7%	0.4%
Patna	161,372	83.2%	16.5%	0.3%
Indore	159,691	62.2%	36.9%	0.9%
Bhopal	186,598	59.4%	39.6%	1.0%
Coimbatore	68,888	82.1%	17.4%	0.5%
Ludhiana	265,003	29.1%	68.7%	2.2%
Kochi	166,794	79.9%	18.3%	1.7%
Visakhapatnam	139,003	74.5%	25.2%	0.3%
Agra	34,227	68.8%	30.4%	0.8%
Varanasi	46,989	69.8%	28.2%	2.0%
Madurai	33,540	95.3%	4.0%	0.7%
Meerut	71,213	66.6%	32.6%	0.9%
Nasik	287,017	79.2%	20.3%	0.5%
Jabalpur	68,961	59.0%	40.5%	0.5%
Jamshedpur	80,971	28.0%	71.4%	0.5%
Asansol	59,501	51.9%	47.5%	0.6%
Dhanbad	86,238	35.6%	64.2%	0.2%
Faridabad	237,800	14.6%	83.6%	1.8%
Allahabad	41,699	82.8%	16.8%	0.5%
Amritsar	56,024	47.2%	50.5%	2.2%
Vijayawada	90,894	95.4%	4.5%	0.1%
Rajkot	141,177	89.6%	9.6%	0.8%
Total	12,485,365	47.0%	51.5%	1.5%

Source: Census of India.

But ignoring Delhi, which in essence is a city and a state only by name, Faridabad is the next agglomeration where intrastate migration is the lowest. Per contra, migration from other states is highest in the case of Delhi amounting to 94.1 per cent followed by Faridabad 83.6 per cent. Intrastate migration has been over 80 per cent in the case of Hyderabad, Patna, Coimbatore, Madurai, Allahabad, Vijayawada and Rajkot. These tables indicate that barring a few cases, metropolitan cities are not flooded by migration from other states.

Work is the most important reason for migration into major urban agglomerations followed by shifting of the household itself and marriage. Data in this regard arranged in the order of percentages accounting for work related migration is presented in the table 8.8. While in the case of Ludhiana 47.4 per cent of the migration has been on account of work, shifting of household has been the more important reason for migration into Faridabad. Marriage is cited as a prominent reason for 44.8 per cent of migration into Asansol. People of Allahabad will be happy to know that their city is still a major attraction for migrants in search of education accounting for 37.6 per cent. Varanasi, Patna, and Madurai are three other urban agglomerations citing education as a significant reason for migration.

Is migration into large cities an unremitting flow? Facts indicate otherwise. For six metropolitan cities for which data is available since the 1961–71 period, the volume of intrastate as well as from outside is presented in table 8.9. It will be seen that during 1961–71, Greater Mumbai, Kolkata and Delhi received considerable inflow apparently in the wake of the country's partition. During the two succeeding decades inflow of migration significantly declined in the case of all these three cities. But this has picked up again during 1991–2001

decade. In the case of other cities the increase in the flow of inmigration has been rather modest. It is also worth noting that the bulk of this inmigration has been from within the state.

How Large is Migration?

The main policy concern emerging from the migration data from the 2001 Census is, not that the volume of migration in the country is high but that it is quite low. International experience clearly shows that with economic change population shifts from the Urban to the Rural will be massive. In China, the volume of migration is very much more (see Table 8.10). In India, the globalization of the economy, increasing investments in various economic sectors and the significant stepping up of manufacturing activity will undoubtedly result out expansion of urban areas. This in turn may well stimulate migration. However, this should not be a cause for apprehension but should be viewed as a logical and positive means of finding employment to a labour force held captive for long by the limits of rural economy in many parts of the country.

The Urban Renewal Mission

Mention has been made at the beginning of this book about the role of governance in shaping urban perspectives and responses. It has been pointed out that viewing urbanization within the limited confines of a single municipality or corporation has serious consequences, as the pattern of urbanization has become increasingly that of urban agglomerations. The Jawaharlal Nehru National Urban Renewal Mission marks a significant beginning to address some of these issues. Launched in December 2005, the JNNURM is claimed to be the largest initiative in the country's

TABLE 8.8
Reasons for Total Migration into Major Urban Agglomerations (1991 and 2001)

City/UA	Migrants	Reason for Migration						
		Work	Business	Education	Marriage	After birth	Household	Other
Ludhiana	265,003	47.4%	0.9%	1.4%	13.5%	2.8%	25.4%	8.6%
Greater Mumbai	2,489,552	39.6%	0.7%	1.9%	16.3%	9.0%	21.6%	10.9%
Bangalore	761,485	38.7%	2.2%	6.1%	17.2%	4.4%	22.6%	8.8%
Delhi	2,112,363	36.9%	0.6%	2.7%	13.5%	2.5%	36.9%	7.0%
Hyderabad	498,483	35.2%	3.3%	5.9%	12.9%	3.5%	28.8%	10.4%
Coimbatore	68,888	33.6%	1.7%	6.5%	16.2%	5.1%	25.4%	11.6%
Surat	869,860	33.1%	8.3%	0.8%	11.9%	8.3%	31.6%	6.0%
Amritsar	56,024	32.3%	1.0%	5.1%	24.7%	1.4%	22.9%	12.7%
Faridabad	237,800	31.6%	0.6%	0.7%	14.3%	2.0%	42.9%	7.8%
Chennai	435,620	30.7%	1.9%	5.0%	16.4%	5.1%	29.1%	11.9%
Kanpur	138,708	30.4%	1.3%	5.4%	15.9%	1.2%	29.0%	16.9%
Pune	744,194	29.5%	0.7%	5.9%	16.0%	10.5%	29.4%	7.9%
Jaipur	250,208	29.3%	1.0%	5.0%	15.8%	2.5%	38.5%	7.9%
Visakhapatnam	139,003	29.1%	3.1%	4.1%	13.3%	5.0%	34.9%	10.5%
Indore	159,691	28.4%	1.2%	7.4%	21.1%	4.1%	28.8%	8.9%
Lucknow	208,915	27.7%	1.1%	7.6%	12.4%	1.5%	39.4%	10.3%
Nagpur	241,078	27.1%	0.6%	6.7%	21.8%	6.5%	29.1%	8.1%
Bhopal	186,598	26.9%	0.7%	6.7%	20.0%	3.4%	34.0%	8.3%
Vijayawada	90,894	26.5%	2.4%	8.7%	16.9%	5.5%	31.6%	8.5%
Nasik	287,017	26.2%	0.6%	3.0%	16.0%	13.9%	32.5%	7.9%
Jamshedpur	80,971	26.0%	1.0%	4.1%	26.3%	3.3%	28.4%	10.8%
Kolkata	822,389	24.8%	2.5%	3.7%	21.1%	3.8%	27.5%	16.6%
Jabalpur	68,961	22.3%	0.8%	7.7%	22.8%	1.8%	34.0%	10.5%
Madurai	33,540	22.1%	1.8%	12.0%	18.3%	5.1%	25.2%	15.6%
Ahmedabad	428,910	21.2%	7.0%	2.0%	19.4%	8.3%	33.9%	8.3%
Meerut	71,213	20.7%	0.6%	3.2%	24.8%	0.4%	38.1%	12.1%
Patna	161,372	20.4%	1.0%	12.9%	18.2%	1.6%	34.4%	11.6%
Dhanbad	86,238	19.9%	1.2%	4.0%	30.7%	2.5%	30.0%	11.6%
Kochi	166,794	19.3%	1.2%	3.2%	25.0%	8.6%	31.6%	11.7%
Varanasi	46,989	18.1%	1.0%	18.7%	18.5%	0.7%	24.8%	18.3%
Allahabad	46,699	16.3%	1.6%	34.6%	9.4%	0.7%	17.8%	19.7%
Asansol	59,501	13.7%	2.3%	1.3%	44.8%	3.5%	21.6%	12.9%
Agra	34,227	13.0%	1.0%	2.2%	21.4%	0.6%	37.3%	24.4%
Rajkot	141,177	11.3%	14.0%	4.1%	19.5%	7.7%	37.0%	6.5%
Total	12,485,365	32.6%	2.0%	3.8%	16.5%	5.7%	29.7%	9.7%
National level		14.7%	1.2%	3.0%	43.8%	6.7%	21.0%	9.7%

Source: Census of India.

TABLE 8.9
Migration flows into six Metropolitan Cities since 1961

City/UA	1961–71			1971–81		
	Migrants	Within State	Other States	Migrants	Within State	Other States
Greater Mumbai	3,395,095	41.94%	54.50%	1,814,304	54.70%	45.30%
Kolkata	2,276,985	22.75%	44.45%	607,921	63.51%	36.49%
Delhi	1,886,285	4.76%	74.78%	1,363,411	1.08%	98.92%
Chennai	786,545	70.13%	26.11%	569,046	77.74%	22.26%
Bangalore	624,215	56.38%	42.76%	509,930	56.50%	43.50%
Hyderabad	409,980	64.81%	34.16%	548,121	81.87%	18.13%
City/UA	1981–91			1991–2001		
	Migrants	Within State	Other States	Migrants	Within State	Other States
Greater Mumbai	1,557,042	42.82%	57.18%	2,489,552	35.90%	63.10%
Kolkata	692,009	55.37%	44.63%	822,389	57.20%	36.10%
Delhi	1,160,391	1.82%	98.18%	2,112,363	3.70%	94.10%
Chennai	677,204	78.88%	21.12%	435,620	76.90%	21.80%
Bangalore	504,657	58.61%	41.39%	761,485	52.80%	46.40%
Hyderabad	245,206	75.29%	24.71%	498,483	81.80%	17.70%

TABLE 8.10
Internal Migration in China

Figures on Migration in China are difficult to compare because of different sources and also the permit and control systems (Hukou).

Rural to Urban Migration
According to one estimate, the figures on Rural to Urban Migration are as follows

Year	No. of migrants
As of 1980	2 million
As of 1990	70 million
As of 2002	94 million

According to another estimate, Rural to Urban Migration totalled the following

Year	No. of migrants
1997	45 million
1998	55 million
1999	67 million
2000	77 million

Rural to Rural Migration
According to the National Statistics Bureau and Ministry of Labour and Social Security (2000), People's Republic of China, an estimated *20 million migrants moved from Rural to Rural areas.*

Source: National Statistics Bureau and Ministry of Labour and Social Security (2000).
National Statistical Bureau.

urban history committing Central Government support of Rs 50,000 crores to 63 cities across the country over a seven year period.

The creation of 'sustainable, equitable and economically vibrant cities' is the proclaimed objective of JNNURM. Of the 63 cities and towns being covered under this programme, 35 are million plus cities including the 7 mega cities of Mumbai, Bangalore, Chennai, Hyderabad, Kolkata, Ahmedabad, and Delhi.

TABLE 8.11
List of JNNURM Cities

1. Hyderabad	Andhra Pradesh	33 Nanded	Maharashtra
2 Vijayawada	Andhra Pradesh	34 Nashik	Maharashtra
3 Vishakhapatnam	Andhra Pradesh	35 Pune	Maharashtra
4. Itanagar	Arunachal Pradesh	36 Imphal	Manipur
5 Guwahati	Assam	37 Shillong	Meghalaya
6 Bodhgaya	Bihar	38 Aizwal	Mizoram
7 Patna	Bihar	39 Kohima	Nagaland
8 Chandigarh	Chandigarh (UT)	40 Bhubaneshwar	Orissa
9 Raipur	Chattisgarh	41 Puri	Orissa
10 Delhi	Delhi (NCT)	42 Pondicherry	Pondicherry (UT)
11 Panaji	Goa	43 Amritsar	Punjab
12 Ahmedabad	Gujarat	44 Ludhiana	Punjab
13 Rajkot	Gujarat	45 Ajmer-Pushkar	Rajasthan
14 Surat	Gujarat	46 Jaipur	Rajasthan
15 Vadodara	Gujarat	47 Gangtok	Sikkim
16 Faridabad	Haryana	48 Chennai	Tamil Nadu
17 Shimla	Himachal Pradesh	49 Coimbatore	Tamil Nadu
18 Jammu	Jammu and Kashmir	50 Madurai	Tamil Nadu
19 Srinagar	Jammu and Kashmir	51 Agartala	Tripura
20 Dhanbad	Jharkhand	52 Agra	Uttar Pradesh
21 Jamshedpur	Jharkhand	53 Allahabad	Uttar Pradesh
22 Ranchi	Jharkhand	54 Kanpur	Uttar Pradesh
23 Bangalore	Karnataka	55 Lucknow	Uttar Pradesh
24 Mysore	Karnataka	56 Mathura	Uttar Pradesh
25 Cochin	Kerala	57 Meerut	Uttar Pradesh
26 Thiruvananthapuram	Kerala	58 Varanasi	Uttar Pradesh
27 Bhopal	Madhya Pradesh	59 Dehradun	Uttaranchal
28 Indore	Madhya Pradesh	60 Haridwar	Uttaranchal
29 Jabalpur	Madhya Pradesh	61 Nainital	Uttaranchal
30 Ujjain	Madhya Pradesh	62 Asansol	West Bengal
31 Greater Mumbai	Maharashtra	63 Kolkata	West Bengal
32 Nagpur	Maharashtra		

Source: JNNURM.
Ministry of Urban Development, Government of India.

The Mission consists of two sub-missions. One is titled as 'Urban Infrastructure and Governance' and the other as 'Basic Services for the Urban Poor'. Integrated development of slums and provision of basic services for the urban poor are the prominent components of one sub-mission but several items like water supply, sewerage and sanitation, solid waste management etc., are common components. The Government of India has committed itself to provide grants totaling Rs 50,000 crores on the expectation that the cities and the respective state governments will mobilize an equal amount. The Mission is also anchored on a reform agenda, which includes effective decentralization as per the 74th Constitution Amendment, entrustment of city planning and other municipal functions to urban local bodies, property tax and other budgeting and financial reforms, enactment of public disclosure, and community participation laws etc.

The list of 63 towns and their state-wise distribution is contained in Table 8.10. It will be seen that in addition to the 35 million plus cities, all state capitals and several other towns of tourist and religious importance have been covered. The Mission envisages that for each of these cities a City Development Plan will be prepared with the active involvement and endorsement of the urban local body concerned. Detailed project reports for various components will be prepared in keeping with the CDPs. A Memorandum of Understanding will be concluded between the Government of India on the one hand and the State/City governments on the other committing to implement the mandatory and other reforms. In the process it is hoped, cities will be enabled to move from the present fragmented project based approach to one of comprehensive and integrated vision.

Given the highly ambitious objectives of the Mission as well as the past and recent history of local self-government in the country, it is too early to pronounce any judgement about the Mission. But it is to be acknowledged that the Mission does mark a major initiative in the urban sector after the enactment of the 74th Constitution Amendment in 1992. For most of the towns City Development Plans have been prepared already, appraised and endorsed. To say the least, the scope, substance, and quality of the CDPs are uneven. Several of them have been prepared by Consultants to whom urban local bodies have given a formal stamp of endorsement in the hope of not being left out of the race for Central government funds. Nevertheless the beginnings of a serious debate are seen about the nature and scope of a city development plan including its territorial coverage. In many cases there is a recognition that urbanisation has crossed traditional municipal boundaries and a view of the agglomeration is essential. The process of preparing CDPs has also prompted the compilation and analysis of socio-economic and spatial data as well as information on the status and needs of infrastructure. This by itself will help a better understanding of urbanisation in the present and the future.

The mandatory reforms have also prompted a revival of the impetus processes for implementing the 74th Amendment, in particular, the establishment and functioning of District Planning and Metropolitan Planning Committees which are envisaged by the Constitution as participatory platforms for aggregating and addressing issues common to rural and urban areas and also in multi municipal metropolitan agglomerations. The issue of decentralization within a large city is also receiving some attention. The long delayed process in establishment of Ward Committees and taking decentralization further down to local neighbourhoods to enable community and citizen participation are receiving some attention.

Some major problems do persist. One is the rather artificial division of the Mission into two sub-missions, one for urban infrastructure and governance and another for basic services for the urban poor. This is an inevitable but unfortunate outcome of the fact that there are two ministries at the Government of India level dealing with these subjects. To what extent cities can prevail over this artificial and bureaucratic division of turf remains to be seen. Another factor for concern is the disconnect between the City Development Plans and detailed project reports as well as the disconnect between these projects and implementation of the reform agenda. This is not the place for any elaborate discussion about the JNNURM. However, the Mission does represent an effort to recognize the interstate and massive urbanization of the country in the hope that eventually city governments may be able to take charge of cities and their destiny.

Appendix

APPENDIX–I
Socio-economic Indicators for Seventeen Major States in India (1981)

States	LoU	Urban growth rate	Per capita income (Rs crore)	Agri. prod. (Rs Hec.)	Avrg. size of land-holding (Ha)	Ind. prod. as % of NSDP	Rural poverty (%)	Urban poverty (%)	Average MPCE (rural)	Average MPCE (urban)	Road (per 100 sq km)	Railway (per 100 sq km)	Telephone (per 100 popn)	Village electrified (%)	Per capita bank deposit	Per capita credit to industry
(1)	(2)	(3)	(4)	(5)	(6)	(7)	(8)	(9)	(10)	(11)	(12)	(13)	(14)	(15)	(16)	(17)
Andhra Pradesh	23.30	4.00	1380	6276.23	1.94	16.61	26.53	36.30	115.40	153.50	36.42	1.75	0.41	60.38	304	86
Assam	11.08	3.30	1284	6906.69	1.36	3.62	42.60	21.73	113.00	154.00	73.54	2.66	0.12	19.21	157	38
Bihar	12.50	4.40	917	4048.56	1.00	15.03	64.37	47.33	93.80	138.50	46.44	3.06	0.09	28.78	189	54
Delhi	92.84	4.60	4030		1.94	8.33	7.66	28.32	217.10	228.80	888.81	11.33	0.05	100.00	5228	919
Gujarat	31.10	3.50	1940	5693.43	3.45	24.35	29.80	39.14	122.70	163.60	28.07	2.89	0.77	59.46	660	244
Haryana	22.00	4.70	2370	6229.13	3.52	7.86	20.56	24.15	151.80	186.90	48.89	3.28		100.00	418	234
Himachal Pradesh	7.60	3.00	1704	3917.69	1.54	1.85	17.00	9.25	150.80	258.60	33.71	0.46		52.74	403	39
Karnataka	28.90	4.10	1520	4989.92	2.73	15.84	36.22	42.82	116.80	166.30	9.79	1.57	5.1	60.64	439	170
Kerala	18.70	3.20	1508	12333.85	0.43	12.72	39.03	45.68	145.20	176.40	242.25	2.36	0.51	100.00	482	114
Madhya Pradesh	20.30	4.50	1358	3069.65	3.42	17.58	48.90	53.06	100.50	144.90	22.99	1.29	0.17	31.11	190	43
Maharashtra	35.00	3.40	2435	3794.68	3.11	72.65	45.23	40.26	110.40	184.40	55.90	1.70	0.68	71.15	987	398
Orissa	11.30	5.20	1314	4374.84	1.59	7.26	67.53	49.15	98.80	151.40	75.83	1.25	0.07	36.67	125	30
Punjab	27.70	3.70	2674	9707.65	3.82	11.22	13.20	23.79	170.50	185.20	90.33	4.25	N A	99.49	969	N A
Rajasthan	20.90	4.60	1222	2334.77	4.44	10.16	33.50	37.94	127.00	159.90	19.63	1.64	N A	41.53	206	62
Tamil Nadu	33.00	2.50	1498	8756.47	1.07	33.01	53.99	46.96	112.20	163.70	87.44	2.94	0.4	98.82	454	205
Uttar Pradesh	18.00	4.70	1278	5805.13	1.01	29.32	46.45	49.82	104.50	135.50	64.36	2.99	0.16	34.27	265	59
West Bengal	26.50	2.80	1773	5943.81	0.95	38.36	63.05	32.32	104.60	170.00	18.95	4.19	0.45	33.78	670	250
All India	23.73	3.80	1630.1	5090.42	4.45	89.46	45.65	40.79	112.40	164.00	45.38	1.85	0.3	43.36	466	250
CV	73.40	20.55	42.21	44.09	55.81	89.46	46.80	32.75	25.01	18.34	191.82	82.38	194.84	48.47	166.85	121.08

(contd.)

APPENDIX-I: contd.

States	URGD (1981–91)	Sex ratio (rural)	Sex ratio (urban)	Literacy (rural)	Literacy (urban)	Hospital (per '000 popn)	School (per '000 popn)	Access to safe drink. water (% U HH)	Sanitation facilities (% U HH)	Electricity use (%U HH)
(1)	(18)	(19)	(20)	(21)	(22)	(23)	(24)	(25)	(26)	(27)
Andhra Pradesh	2.39	983	948	23.24	51.13	0.470	0.084	63.27	44.07	52.22
Assam	1.27	963	833	22.50	51.88	0.349	0.213	75.03	57.31	65.10
Bihar	2.49	810	808	47.56	62.35	0.409	0.165	65.36	52.95	50.09
Delhi	3.81	959	905	36.20	60.25	2.077	0.055	94.91	68.02	74.94
Gujarat	1.46	876	850	30.33	56.78	1.047	0.415	86.78	60.11	74.40
Haryana	2.67	989	799	40.42	67.34	0.714	0.070	90.72	58.09	82.22
Himachal Pradesh	0.92	977	926	31.05	56.44	1.190	0.246	89.56	55.12	89.36
Karnataka	2.35	1034	1022	69.11	74.98	0.423	0.334	74.40	53.28	61.98
Kerala	1.73	955	883	21.22	53.98	1.991	0.110	39.72	59.14	54.57
Madhya Pradesh	2.69	987	851	38.15	63.82	0.393	0.197	66.65	52.73	56.42
Maharashtra	1.74	998	859	31.49	54.67	1.400	0.253	85.56	59.37	70.53
Orissa	3.76	883	861	35.21	55.77	0.469	0.271	51.33	41.88	51.74
Punjab	2.07	930	884	17.99	47.92	1.249	0.086	91.13	64.75	85.44
Rajasthan	2.19	987	957	38.56	62.24	0.629	0.156	78.65	56.48	63.67
Tamil Nadu	1.25	893	846	23.06	45.91	0.986	0.119	69.44	51.27	61.59
Uttar Pradesh	2.94	946	820	33.12	62.81	0.489	0.124	73.23	62.06	54.61
West Bengal	0.91	951	880	29.65	57.19	1.086	0.059	79.78	77.74	57.86
All India	2.05					0.848	0.177	75.08	58.20	62.51
CV	40.53	6.02	6.88	36.88	12.92	0.604	0.595	19.83	14.71	19.01

Note: Crude literacy rate is calculated.

Source: 1. Data on per capita income are obtained from Indian Public Finance Statistics, 2000–01, Ministry of Finance, Dept. of Economic Affairs. The latest figure pertains to 1998–9.

2. Data on industrial production are obtained from CSO estimates of state-wise and industry-wise figures for the respective years. The latest figure pertains to 1998–9.

3. Data on Agricultural production are obtained from the study of Bhalla and Singh (2000), 'Recent Developments in Indian Agriculture—A State-Level Analysis'.

4. Data on indicators on Poverty and Consumption Expenditure are obtained from 45th, 50th, and 55th rounds of NSSO.

5. Data on indicators such as size of landholding, road, railway, telephone, villages electrified, bank credit, credit to industry are obtained from CMIE Report 2000.

6. Socio-demographic and urban basic amenities indicators are obtained from Population Census for the respective years.

APPENDIX–II

Socio-economic Indicators for Seventeen Major States in India (1991)

States	LoU	Growth rate (U)	Per capita income (Rs crore)	Agri. productivity (Rs Hec.)	Avrg. size of land-holding (Ha)	Ind. prod as % of NSDP	WPR (P+S) in 15+ age by usual status (%) (R)	WPR (P+S) in 15+ age by usual status (%) (U)	% of reg. wor. to total wor. (R)	% of reg. wor. to total wor. (U)	Usual status (adjusted) unemp. rate (%) in 15+ age (R)	Usual status (adjusted) unemp. rate (%) in 15+ age (U)	Rural poverty (%)	Urban poverty (%)	Average MPCE (rural)	Average MPCE (urban)
(1)	(2)	(3)	(4)	(5)	(6)	(7)	(8)	(9)	(10)	(11)	(12)	(13)	(14)	(15)	(16)	(17)
Andhra Pradesh	26.84	3.60	2060	9390.64	1.56	18.50	81.00	53.80	5.20	34.10	5.30	8.20	15.92	38.33	288.70	408.60
Assam	11.08	3.30	1544	8196.82	1.31	3.28	54.50	44.00	14.40	43.10	24.70	16.00	45.01	7.73	258.11	458.57
Bihar	13.17	2.70	1197	5678.08	0.93	20.17	56.60	42.80	4.00	35.60	8.30	13.00	58.21	34.50	218.30	353.03
Delhi	89.93	3.80	5447		1.17	12.49	64.60	49.70	64.30	46.80		2.40	1.29	16.91	605.22	794.95
Gujarat	34.40	2.90	2641	7460.09	2.93	32.01	73.20	50.90	6.80	40.90	4.40	3.90	22.18	27.89	303.32	454.18
Haryana	24.79	3.60	3509	10,128.73	2.43	11.45	62.20	54.50	9.40	40.40	6.20	5.10	28.02	16.38	385.01	473.92
Himachal Pradesh	8.70	3.20	2241	5195.63	1.20	2.24	79.90	51.10	7.10	52.50	2.80	3.80	16.28	6.18	350.63	746.93
Karnataka	30.91	2.50	2039	6969.70	2.13	18.50	74.90	52.80	4.80	36.90	6.20	6.60	29.88	40.14	269.38	423.14
Kerala	26.44	4.80	1815	15,625.96	0.33	10.74	53.40	50.30	11.50	26.80	21.30	19.00	25.76	24.55	390.41	493.83
Madhya Pradesh	23.21	3.70	1696	4773.12	2.63	19.77	76.50	49.90	4.00	38.50	5.50	8.90	40.64	48.38	252.01	408.06
Maharashtra	38.73	3.30	3483	5176.94	2.21	81.13	77.70	51.10	7.60	49.60	4.70	6.30	37.93	35.15	272.66	529.80
Orissa	13.43	3.10	1383	5979.16	1.34	7.08	65.30	48.70	4.50	44.30	14.80	13.40	49.72	41.64	219.80	402.54
Punjab	29.72	2.50	3730	13,597.22	3.61	14.43	58.70	49.80	10.50	40.00	4.60	6.30	11.95	11.35	433.00	510.73
Rajasthan	22.88	3.30	1942	3715.22	3.95	13.34	77.60	51.60	4.60	37.90	4.10	2.10	26.46	30.49	322.39	424.73
Tamil Nadu	34.20	1.80	2237	14,073.94	0.93	35.08	74.80	55.60	9.30	37.30	9.70	9.00	32.48	39.77	293.62	438.29
Uttar Pradesh	19.89	3.30	1652	8656.20	0.89	38.46	61.90	48.40	4.50	29.50	3.10	5.20	42.28	35.39	273.83	388.97
West Bengal	27.39	2.60	2145	9958.45	0.90	33.69	58.90	49.70	9.50	47.00	9.40	13.20	40.80	22.41	278.78	474.19
All India	25.72	3.10	2222.2	7388.05	1.57		67.80	50.90	6.60	39.50	7.50	7.80	37.27	32.36	281.40	458.04
CV	64.80	21.08	45.09	42.30	57.54	85.65	14.16	6.50	132.08	16.91	76.48	58.96	47.76	45.53	29.74	24.57

(contd.)

180

APPENDIX-II: contd.

States	Road (per 100 sq km)	Rail-ways (per 100 sq km)	Tele-phone (per 100 popn)	Village electri-fied (%)	Per capita bank deposits	Per capita credit to indus-try	URGD (1981–91)	Sex ratio (rural)	Sex ratio (urban)	Lite-racy (rural)	Lite-racy (urban)	Hos-pital (per '000 popn)	School (Per '000 popn)	Access to safe drink. water (% U HH)	Sani-tation facil-ities (% U HH)	Electri-city use (% U HH)
(1)	(18)	(19)	(20)	(21)	(22)	(23)	(24)	(25)	(26)	(27)	(28)	(29)	(30)	(31)	(32)	(33)
Andhra Pradesh	48.68	1.83	0.48	99.92	1440	468	1.88	977	957	30.53	56.81	0.494	0.096	73.82	54.60	73.31
Assam	38.36	3.15	0.17	95.40	858	293	1.29	933	839	39.96	69.19	0.722	0.296	64.07	86.06	63.21
Bihar	48.97	3.06	0.11	68.39	983	145	0.62	921	846	27.17	57.05	0.449	0.157	73.39	56.54	58.77
Delhi	1408.99	11.35	5.08	100.00	18,831	4161	−3.56	807	831	53.42	64.62	2.324	0.054	96.24	66.64	81.38
Gujarat	50.50	2.70	1.05	98.77	2525	1017	1.51	949	909	44.79	64.81	1.629	0.433	87.23	65.71	82.96
Haryana	59.35	3.39	0.57	100.00	2136	787	1.73	863	868	40.25	61.62	0.685	0.085	93.18	64.25	89.13
Himachal Pradesh	44.19	0.46	0.57	99.73	2384	341	1.46	990	828	51.36	73.71	1.577	0.216	91.93	59.98	96.24
Karnataka	65.14	1.60	0.68	97.98	1902	677	0.97	973	930	39.63	63.63	1.043	0.385	81.38	62.52	76.27
Kerala	342.90	2.53	0.80	100.00	2283	511	4.44	1037	1033	77.00	81.13	2.786	0.102	38.62	72.66	67.65
Madhya Pradesh	31.08	1.32	0.26	84.13	1026	283	1.71	943	893	28.48	58.82	0.433	0.249	79.45	53.00	72.52
Maharashtra	70.45	1.77	1.26	99.37	4253	1570	2.92	972	876	45.94	68.12	1.957	0.236	90.50	64.45	86.07
Orissa	125.73	1.29	0.19	64.63	761	215	1.49	988	866	37.77	61.62	0.515	0.294	62.83	49.27	62.11
Punjab	107.78	4.27	0.95	100.00	4355	924	1.00	887	870	44.07	61.65	1.215	0.139	94.24	73.23	94.60
Rajasthan	35.25	1.69	0.32	74.86	1083	249	1.07	918	881	24.20	54.07	0.792	0.222	86.51	62.27	76.67
Tamil Nadu	149.86	3.08	0.78	99.89	2059	983	0.56	980	951	47.59	68.11	1.108	0.101	74.17	57.47	76.80
Uttar Pradesh	65.79	3.02	0.21	71.39	1314	234	1.27	883	862	29.70	50.51	0.537	0.107	85.78	66.54	67.76
West Bengal	19.99	4.29	0.46	69.41	2329	758	0.47	940	856	41.20	66.49	0.991	0.058	86.23	78.75	70.19
All India	60.35	1.89	0.55	81.30	2075	614	1.29	938	893	36.70	61.78	0.973	0.183	81.38	63.90	75.78
CV	207.24	80.35	139.92	15.51	142	118.14	127.02	5.95	6.04	30.40	11.64	0.620	0.601	18.33	14.67	14.49

Note: Crude literacy rate is calculated.

Sources: Same as Appendix I.

APPENDIX–III

Socio-economic Indicators for Seventeen Major States in India (2001)

States	LoU	Growth rate (U)	Per capita income (Rs crore)*	Per capita FDI (Rs)	Avrg. size of land-holding (Ha)	Indus. prod as % of NSDP	W E ratio (rural)	W E ratio (urban)	WPR (P+S) in 15+ age by usual status (%) (rural)	WPR (P+S) in 15+ age by usual status (%) (urban)	% of reg. wor. to total wor. (rural)	% of reg. wor. to total wor. (urban)	Usual status (adj.) unemp. rate (%) in 15+ age (R)	Usual status (adj.) unemp. rate (%) in 15+ age (U)	Rural poverty (%)	Urban Poverty (%)
(1)	(2)	(3)	(4)	(5)	(6)	(7)	(8)	(9)	(10)	(11)	(12)	(13)	(14)	(15)	(16)	(17)
Andhra Pradesh	27.08	1.40	9118	1597.98	1.56	20.91	3.43	3.96	76.70	50.10	5.90	38.70	6.80	6.90	11.05	26.63
Assam	12.72	3.10	5942	0.56	1.31	3.10	9.46	4.17	53.90	45.40	16.60	42.90	15.20	14.10	40.04	7.47
Bihar	13.00	2.60	4397	85.41	0.93	12.30	2.55	4.16	57.20	42.40	3.50	30.20	6.50	13.20	44.30	32.91
Delhi	93.01	4.10	19,091	23,387.20	1.17	5.49	5.31	11.59	47.20	46.80	45.40	54.80	6.50	4.60	0.40	9.42
Gujarat	37.35	2.80	13,709	2209.50	2.93	30.90	4.59	6.89	73.90	48.30	6.30	34.10	1.10	2.80	13.17	15.59
Haryana	29.00	4.10	13,084	1418.89	2.43	9.19	4.94	7.04	55.40	46.90	12.40	42.80	1.10	3.90	8.27	9.99
Himachal Pradesh	9.79	2.80	8864	595.10	1.20	2.39	2.41	6.26	73.70	45.20	10.10	51.60	3.70	9.60	7.94	4.63
Karnataka	33.98	2.50	11,153	3777.71	2.13	23.18	3.15	3.91	71.60	50.30	5.30	39.60	4.50	5.50	17.38	25.25
Kerala	25.97	0.70	9807	405.88	0.33	9.76	3.61	3.78	52.50	49.40	13.70	29.10	19.80	17.50	9.38	20.27
Madhya Pradesh	25.00	2.80	7350	1513.63	2.63	19.48	2.38	3.89	74.30	48.60	3.50	33.00	3.90	5.50	37.06	38.44
Maharashtra	42.40	2.90	15,805	4315.16	2.21	67.25	3.69	6.58	72.90	49.10	7.30	51.50	6.10	6.90	23.72	26.81
Orissa	14.97	2.60	5648	2175.83	1.34	4.44	2.13	5.49	63.20	46.60	4.20	35.80	15.70	15.30	48.01	42.83
Punjab	33.95	3.20	14,457	803.61	3.61	11.38	4.41	6.07	61.40	49.90	13.00	40.90	4.90	4.40	6.35	5.75
Rajasthan	23.38	2.70	7694	458.82	3.95	12.45	2.59	3.91	72.10	49.00	4.90	36.50	2.00	3.50	13.74	19.85
Tamil Nadu	43.86	3.60	12,287	3049.53	0.93	28.93	3.94	4.28	69.90	53.40	11.80	44.10	10.60	6.60	20.55	22.11
Uttar Pradesh	21.00	2.80	5890	241.86	0.89	29.25	3.59	4.11	58.60	47.70	5.60	32.30	2.80	7.30	31.22	30.89
West Bengal	28.03	1.80	8622	1045.73	0.90	21.36	2.94	6.22	54.30	46.40	7.00	40.00	11.10	11.20	31.85	14.86
All India	27.78	2.70	9660.3	2402.13	1.57		3.29	5.39	64.70	48.60	6.80	40.00	6.70	7.40	27.09	23.62
CV	62.92	31.34	40.05	197.30	57.74	85.60	45.12	36.81	14.94	5.22	95.05	18.90	76.19	55.30	68.52	55.22

(contd.)

182

APPENDIX-III: contd.

States	Average MPCE (rural)	Average MPCE (urban)	Road (per 100 sq km)	Railways (per 100 sq km)	Telephone (per 100 popn)	Village Electrified (%)	Per capita bank deposites	Per capita credit to industry	URGD (1981–91)	Sex ratio (rural)	Sex ratio (urban)	Slum pop as % of urban popn	Literacy (rural)	Literacy (urban)	Hospital (per '000 popn)	School (per '000 popn)
(1)	(18)	(19)	(20)	(21)	(22)	(23)	(24)	(25)	(26)	(27)	(28)	(29)	(30)	(31)	(32)	(33)
Andhra Pradesh	453.61	773.52	58.27	1.84	1.99	99.92	4857	1401	0.12	982	965	25.11	48.01	67.55	0.436	0.105
Assam	426.12	814.12	87.22	3.10	0.86	76.97	2868	386	1.60	940	878	2.50	50.48	76.44	0.523	0.304
Bihar	384.72	601.88	50.81	3.02	0.49	70.85	3027	304	0.17	934	869	5.85	35.93	64.53	1.070	0.134
Delhi	917.21		1796.08	11.55	12.50	100.00	57,048	16,790	4.08	806	821	15.80	65.86	70.74	1.764	0.047
Gujarat	551.33	891.68	46.37	2.72	3.21	99.44	8515	2921	1.31	945	879	7.13	49.96	69.92	1.971	0.424
Haryana	714.37	912.07	63.71	3.42	2.63	96.72	7132	2144	2.21	866	847	23.25	53.46	69.06	0.623	0.088
Himachal Pradesh	684.50	1242.93	54.24	0.48	3.74	97.87	8752	822	1.32	990	797	–	64.77	80.37	1.657	0.183
Karnataka	499.78	910.99	75.09	1.59	2.79	98.51	7305	2009	1.43	975	939	7.07	51.60	71.49	1.128	0.373
Kerala	765.70	932.61	374.95	2.70	4.18	100.00	10,239	1195	-0.25	1058	1057	0.55	79.53	83.20	1.343	0.096
Madhya Pradesh	401.50	693.56	45.13	1.33	1.18	94.37	3288	769	0.99	947	905	14.83	48.04	68.68	0.440	0.263
Maharashtra	496.77	973.32	117.61	1.80	4.10	100.00	14,035	5708	1.56	959	874	25.95	60.51	75.19	2.312	0.248
Orissa	373.17	618.48	168.71	1.41	0.91	69.86	2827	373	1.29	986	894	11.56	51.63	71.68	0.489	0.342
Punjab	742.43	898.82	127.78	4.25	4.59	100.00	13,912	2493	1.99	887	848	13.97	56.64	69.94	1.097	0.112
Rajasthan	548.88	795.81	37.89	1.72	1.72	88.56	3811	717	0.29	932	890	9.13	45.00	65.24	0.755	0.291
Tamil Nadu	513.97	971.61	158.78	3.07	3.43	100.00	7321	3375	4.14	991	979	9.29	58.99	73.62	1.175	0.090
Uttar Pradesh	466.68	690.67	86.77	3.02	1.01	77.20	4218	501	0.71	908	877	12.04	43.96	60.90	0.501	0.128
West Bengal	454.50	866.59	19.63	4.25	1.56	77.21	6345	1625	0.32	950	892	17.00	54.14	73.67	0.902	0.033
All India	486.07	854.96	75.01	1.91	2.15	85.95	6967	1876	1.05	945	900	14.12	49.44	70.10	0.945	0.197
CV	28.30	18.70	211.93	80.65	92.84	12.70	130.38	153.19	90.58	6.02	6.95	62.85	18.52	7.82	0.541	0.636

Note: Crude literacy rate is calculated.

Sources: Same as Appendix I. Data on FDI are obtained from Economic Times 21 March 2001.

183

References

CENSUS

Census of India 1981, Provisional Population Totals, Workers and Non-Workers, Paper 3 of 1981, India, Series I.

Census of India 1991, Provisional Population Totals, Paper 2 of 1991: Rural–Urban Distribution.

Census of India 1991, Provisional Population Totals, Paper 3 of 1991: Workers and Their Distribution, India, Series 1.

Census of India 1991, Housing and Basic Amenities.

Census of India: Migration Tables, 1981 and 1991.

Census of India 1991, Population Projections for India and States, 1996–2016.

Census of India 2001, Provisional Population Totals, Paper 1 of 2001, India.

Census of India 2001, Provisional Population Totals, Paper 1 of 2001, Supplement District Totals, India.

Census of India 2001, Provisional Population Totals, Paper 2 of 2001: Rural–Urban Distribution of Population, Andhra Pradesh, Series 29.

Census of India 2001, Provisional Population Totals, Paper 2 of 2001: Rural–Urban Distribution of Population, Bihar, Series 11.

Census of India 2001, Provisional Population Totals, Paper 2 of 2001: Rural–Urban Distribution of Population, Chandigarh, Series 5.

Census of India 2001, Provisional Population Totals, Paper 2 of 2001, Goa, Series 31.

Census of India 2001, Provisional Population Totals, Paper 2 of 2001: Rural–Urban Distribution of Population, Gujarat, Series 25.

Census of India 2001, Provisional Population Totals, Paper 2 of 2001, Haryana, Series 7.

Census of India 2001, Provisional Population Totals, Paper 2 of 2001: Rural–Urban Distribution of Population, Himachal Pradesh, Series 3.

Census of India 2001, Provisional Population Totals, Paper 2 of 2001: Rural–Urban Distribution of Population, Jammu & Kashmir, Series 2.

Census of India 2001, Provisional Population Totals, Paper 2 of 2001: Rural–Urban Distribution of Population, Jharkhand, Series 21.

Census of India 2001, Provisional Population Totals, Paper 2 of 2001: Rural–Urban Distribution of Population, Karnataka, Series 30.

Census of India 2001, Provisional Population Totals, Paper 2 of 2001: Rural–Urban Distribution of Population, Kerala, Series 33.

Census of India 2001, Provisional Population Totals, Paper 2 of 2001: Rural–Urban Distribution of Population, Madhya Pradesh, Series 24.

Census of India 2001, Provisional Population Totals, Paper 2 of 2001: Rural–Urban Distribution of Population, Maharashtra, Series 29.

Census of India 2001, Provisional Population Totals, Paper 2 of 2001: Rural–Urban Distribution, Nagaland, Series 13.

Census of India 2001, Provisional Population Totals, Paper 2 of 2001: Rural–Urban Distribution of Population Orissa, Series 22.

Census of India 2001, Provisional Population Totals, Paper 2 of 2001: Rural–Urban Distribution of Population, Punjab, Series 4.

Census of India 2001, Provisional Population Totals, Paper 2 of 2001: Rural–Urban Distribution of Population Rajasthan, Series 9.

Census of India 2001, Provisional Population Totals, Paper 2 of 2001: Rural–Urban Distribution of Population, Tamil Nadu, Series 34.

ECONOMIC CENSUS

Economic Census 1980, District-wise Aggregates of Principal Characteristics of Enterprises.

Economic Census 1980, All India Report.

Economic Census 1990, State/District-wise Aggregates of Principal Characteristics of Enterprises.

Economic Census 1990, State/District-wise Aggregates of Principal Characteristics of Enterprises.

Economic Census 1990, Provisional Results.

Economic Census 1990, Number of Non-agricultural Enterprises and Employment Therein in States/Union Territories According to Major Activity Groups.

Economic Census 1998, All India Report.

Report on the Fourth Economic Census 1998, Andhra Pradesh.

Report on the Fourth Economic Census 1998, Arunachal Pradesh.

Report on the Fourth Economic Census 1998, Chandigarh.

Report on the Fourth Economic Census 1998, Dadra and Nagar Haveli.

Report on the Fourth Economic Census 1998, Delhi.

Report on the Fourth Economic Census 1998, Goa.

Report on the Fourth Economic Census 1998, Gujarat.

Report on the Fourth Economic Census 1998, Haryana.

Report on the Fourth Economic Census 1998, Karnataka.

Report on the Fourth Economic Census 1998, Madhya Pradesh.

Report on the Fourth Economic Census 1998, Meghalaya.

Report on the Fourth Economic Census 1998, Mizoram.

Report on the Fourth Economic Census 1998, Nagaland.

Report on the Fourth Economic Census 1998, Orissa.

Report on the Fourth Economic Census 1998, Pondicherry.

Report on the Fourth Economic Census 1998, Punjab.

Report on the Fourth Economic Census 1998, Rajasthan.

Report on the Fourth Economic Census 1998, Tamil Nadu.

Report on the Fourth Economic Census 1998, Uttar Pradesh.

Report on the Fourth Economic Census 1998, West Bengal.

NSS REPORTS

NSS Organization, Employment–Unemployment Situation in Cities and Towns during Early Eighties, 1983–4, 38th Round.

NSS Organization, Employment and Unemployment in India, 1993–4, 50th Round.

NSS Organization, Employment and Unemployment Situation in India, 1999–2000, Part I & II, 55th Round.

OTHERS

Bhalla, G. S. and A. Kundu (1984), 'Small and Medium Towns in a Regional Perspective—The Case of Batala and Moga in Punjab State (India), in O.P. Mathur (ed.), *The Role of Small Cities in Regional Development*, UNCRD, Nagoya.

Bhalla, G. S. and G. Singh (2001), *Indian Agriculture: Four Decades of Development*, Sage Publications, New Delhi.

Centre for Policy Research (2001), Future of Urbanization—Spread and Shape in Selected States, June.

CMIE (2000), Economic Intelligence Service—Profiles of Districts.

Dyson T. and P. Visaria (2004), 'Migration and Urbanisation: Retrospect and Prospects in 21st Century India' in T. Dyson, R. Cassen, and L. Visaria (eds), *Population Economy, Human Development and the Environment*, Oxford University Press.

Economic Survey (1998–9), Government of India.

Expert Group of Commercialization of Infrastructure (1996), *The Indian Infrastructure Report: Policy Imperatives for Growth and Welfare*, Ministry of Finance, Government of India, New Delhi.

Government of India (2001), *IDSMT Status Report 2000–2001*, Ministry of Urban Development and Poverty Alleviation, Town and Country Planning Organization, New Delhi.

Krishan, Gopal (1998), 'Demographic Change' in J. S. Grewal and Indu Banga (eds), *Punjab in Prosperity and Violence: Administration, Politics and Social Change, 1947–1997*, K.K. Publishers, Chandigarh.

Kundu, A. (1983), 'Theories of City Size Distribution and the Indian Urban Structure; A Reappraisal', *Economic and Political Weekly*, July.

——— (1989), 'Housing and Basic Services: Role of Urban Local Government', *Yojna*, Vol. 33, No. 2.

——— (1992), *Urban Development and Urban Research in India*, New Delhi: Khama Publications, New Delhi, 1992.

——— (1997), 'Trends and Structure of Employment in the Nineties—Implications for Urban Growth', *Economic and Political Weekly*, Vol. 32, No. 24, June.

Kundu, A. and S. Basu (1995) 'Informal Manufacturing Sector in Urban Areas: An Analysis of Recent Trends', *Manpower Journal*, Vol. 34, No. 1, New Delhi, 1998.

Kundu, A. and S. Bhatia (2000), Industrial Growth in Small and Medium Towns and Their Vertical Integration: The Case of Gobindgarh, Punjab, India, MOST Discussion Paper no. 58, UNESCO, Paris.

Premi, M. K. (1961) 'Reclassification of the 1951 Census Population into Rural and Urban Areas on the Basis of the 1961 Census Definition of Urban Areas', *Indian Population Bulletin*, No. II.

——— (1984) , 'Internal Migration in India 1961–81', *Social Action*, July–September.

Premi, M. K., D. B. Gupta, and A. Kundu (1977), 'The Concept of Urban Areas in 1961–71 Census' in A. Bose et al. (eds), *Population Statistics in India*, Vikas Publishing House, New Delhi.

Survey of Indian Industry, Chennai: The Hindu, 2001.

United Nations, World Urbanization Prospects—The 1999 Revision, New York: United Nations, 2001.

Index

agriculture(al), development, as indicators of
    development 84, 85
    and correlation with level of urbanization
        98–100
    growth, and correlation with urbanization 124,
        136, 140, 144, 145
    modernization of, in Punjab 120, 121
    workforce in 53, 104
agro-based industries, in Punjab 124
Andaman and Nicobar Islands, share of population
    in towns in 64
Andhra Pradesh, agricultural productivity and
    urbanization in 98, 124
    census towns in 19
    concentration of population in cities 64
    declassified of towns in 21, 23, 24
    groundnut production and level of urbanization
        in 102
    growth of class I cities in 69
    non-agricultural workforce in 23
    slum population in 107, 109
    urban growth in 2
    urban population in 19
    urban poverty in 105
    urbanization of Krishna district in 98
Assam, foreign direct investments inflows into 97
    growth of class I cities in 69
    slum population in 109
    poverty in 105
    urbanization in 4, 59

backward states, correlation with urbanization
    106–7
    and less urban growth 62
    pattern and trend of urbanization in 82
Bangalore, growth in core area of 157
    migration to, and growth of 112

bank credit, availability, and correlation with
    urbanization 144
Basu, S. 46
Bhalla, G.S. 69, 86, 121, 136n
Bihar 3, 126–31
    foreign direct investments in 97
    growth of class I cities in 69
    growth rates in class I cities in 83
    growth of small towns in 69
    industrial development in 126
    level of urbanization in 126–30
    per capita income in 86
    population in class I cities of 131
    poverty and rural urban migration in 145
    sex-ratio in 145
    size class wise distribution in 131
    slum population in 109
    socio-economic indicators and urbanization in
        144–8
    trends of district-wise urbanization in 113, 126–31
    urban growth in 82, 126, 131
    urban population in 97, 126
Bombay (Mumbai) 62
Brihan Mumbai, rehabilitation of slum/hutment
    dwellers in 54n

Calcutta (Kolkata) 5
    high urban population in 82
cantonment 8
Census of 1951 2, 7, 27
Census of 1961 7, 8, 27
Census of 1971 18
Census of 1981 27, 121
Census of 1991 17, 18, 21, 23, 27
Census of 2001 1, 2, 4, 17, 20, 24, 28, 35, 54, 59, 107,
    109, 113, 118, 121, 125, 133, 136n, 157, 160–4
census data 160

census towns 2, 8–10, 17, 24, 27
  decline in 18
  identification of 19, 20–1, 23
Centre for Monitoring Indian Economy (CMIE)
  3, 106
Centre for Policy Research 43
Chandigarh, urban population in 5, 64
Chennai, growth in periphery of 157
  high urban population in 82
Chhattisgarh, share of population in cities in 64
Chhotanagpur, urban industrial growth in 126
cities, capital, growth rates of 3, 83
    class I, demographic growth rates in 39–40
      growth rates of 69, 82, 83, 131
      high share of population in 64, 120, 135
      population in Maharashtra 120
      population in Punjab in 124, 125
    million-plus 3, 57
      growth rates of 82–3
      population in 6–7
      slum population in 110
    -oriented growth 24
    size class of 1
    slum population in 109
City Development Plan 175–6
civic amenities, as indicators of development 8, 53,
  58, 84, 86
  government investments in 54
common towns, growth rates of 64, 69
  population of 39
Constitution of India, 73rd Amendment to 20, 154
  74th Amendment to, 2, 19, 20, 53, 153
    on district planning committees 158, 159
corporations 8, 153

Davis, Kingsley 28
'degenerated peripheries', jobs in 52
decentralization/decentralized 62
  urban management 53
declassified towns 11–14, 18
Delhi, foreign direct investments flows to 97
  growth in periphery of 157
  high growth of urban population in 97
  per capita income in 86
  slum population in 107
  urban population in 5, 64
  as urbanized state 59
demographic criteria, to identify census towns 19
  for urban centres 17
  versus discretionary criteria 18

demographic growth, in large urban centres 69
developed states, and urban growth 62
Dhanbad, population in urban areas of 126
displaced population, absorption of, in class I cities
  37
district headquarters 3
District Planning 175
district planning committees 158–9
drinking water, access to safe 84, 106
drought, and affect on employment 46
Dyson, T. 56

Economic Census 1
  of 1998 100n
economic development, correlation with
  urbanization 3, 82, 105, 158
  indicators of 84, 85, 136
economic and social disparities 31, 58
economic indicators, and urbanization 86, 97,
  100
economic reforms, and urban growth 26
  and urbanization and migration 57
economy, India's 1
  opening up of 2
electricity, use of 84, 106
employment, and change in urbanization scenario
  45–51
  decline in, in rural areas 51
  increase in casual 50, 51
  indicators of development 84–6
  programmes 158
  rate, decline in 51
  in urban areas 46
  urban growth and impact on 2
Expert Committee for Population Projections 28
Expert Group on the Commercialization of
  Infrastructure Projects of India, Reports 28
exponential growth rate, of urbanization 63

fertility, data on 28
foreign direct investments 97–8
  data on per capita 84, 86
  infrastructure indicators, and inflow of 98
  relation to urban population 98

'global centres of growth' 54
globalization 26
Goa, share of population in towns in 64
  urban population in 5
  as urbanized state 59

government, control on land use and by-laws in
    urban areas 53
    interventions 1
    investments in infrastructure and basic
        amenities 54
Green Revolution 31, 121, 140
gross domestic product, urban India's contribution
    to 157
groundnut production, and level of urbanization
    100, 102–3
Gujarat, agricultural productivity and urbanization
    in 98
    concentration of urban population in cities
        64
    declassification of census towns in 19, 21, 24
    foreign direct investment flows to 97
    groundnut production and level of urbanization
        in 100, 102
    growth of class I cities in 69
    level of urbanization in 2, 4, 82
    per capita income in 86
    poverty level in 105
    urban growth in 62, 97
    urban population in 5, 23
    as urbanized state 59
Gupta, D.B. 19

Haryana, agricultural growth and urbanization in
    98, 124
    growth of class I cities in 69
    high growth of urban population in 97
    high level of urbanization in 82, 158
    per capita income in 86
    slum population in 107
    urban growth in 62
    wheat production, and growth of urban
        population in 100
        and level of urbanization 101
head count ratio 106
    of poor 105
health facilities, correlation with urbanization 140,
    144, 152
    see also hospitals
Himachal Pradesh, growth of class I cities in 69,
    82
    per capita income in 86
    share of population in towns in 64
    urbanization in 59
hospitals/dispensaries 84, 86
Hyderabad, growth in periphery of 157

illiterate migrants, to cities 140
immigration, partition and 7
    rate of 55, 82
income, impact of urban growth on 2
    per capita 2, 62, 84, 86, 97, 98
India Infrastructure Report 27
industries/industrial, development, in urban areas
    54
    employment in 46, 52
    indicators of development 84, 85
    growth, and migration 45
        restrictions on, in urban areas 53
    production, and correlation with urbanization
        100
industrialization 62
    and growth of urban population 100
    and slum settlements 107
informal sector, in urban areas and poverty
    reduction 104
infrastructure (facilities), development of, as
    indicators of development 84, 85, 136
    and growth of urban population 106
    investments in 52, 54, 62
    correlation with urbanization 3, 106, 158
in-migrants/in-migration, in rural areas 31
    of poor 54, 161, 163, 176
in-migrants, population 160, 163–4, 171
Integrated Development of Small and Medium
    Towns (IDSMT) 154, 155–6
intrastate 161–3, 171
intra-urban agglomeration, of large metropolis 40
intra-urban inequities 158

Jaipur, urban population 131, 132, 135
    urbanization of 133
Jawaharlal Nehru National Urban Renewal Mission
    171
Jharkhand 126
    share of population in cities in 64
    urban growth in 131
JNNURM 171, 174, 176
job opportunities, in urban centres and slum
    settlements 107
    see also employment
Jodhpur, urban population in 131, 132, 135

Karnataka 25
    concentration of urban population in cities in 64
    declassification of census towns in 19, 23
    foreign direct investments flows into 97

growth of class I cities in 69
high growth of urban population in 97
level of urbanization in 2
per capita income in 86
towns merged in 24
urban population in 5
urban poverty in 105
as urbanized state 59
Kerala 18
    census towns in 19, 21, 23
    concentration of urban population in cities in 64
    growth rate of class I cities in 83
    growth rate of urban population in 19
    growth of smaller towns in 69
    per capita income of 97
    urban centres in 4
    urban growth in 2
    urbanization in 97
    working population in 19
Kolkata, growth in periphery around 157
    see also Calcutta
Kota, urban population in 131, 132, 135
    urbanization in 133
Krishan, Gopal 121n, 124
Kundu, A. 46, 52, 69, 121

labour, market, change in 50
    mobility of 31
land, -holding size 84
    scarcity of, in cities 53
    -use, government control on, in urban areas 53
liberalization, industrial activity in post- 136
    and shift of population to urban centres 97
    and urbanization 26
literacy 2, 84, 86
    correlation with level of urbanization 140, 144, 145, 152

Madhya Pradesh 25
    growth of class I cities in 83
    growth of smaller towns in 69
    high urban growth in 82
    urban population in cities in 64, 97
    urban poverty in 105
Madras (Chennai), 62
Maharashtra 3
    addition of towns in 24
    agricultural productivity and urbanization in 98
    declassification of towns in 20, 23, 120
    as developed state 113

developmental indicators and urbanization of 136–40
district-wise urbanization in 113–20
foreign direct investment flows to 97
groundnut production, and level of urbanization in 103
growth of class I cities in 69
    and population in 125
industries, and level of urbanization in 136, 140
infrastructure in 140
level of urbanization in 2, 82, 113–18, 158
per capita income in 86
poverty level in 105
size class-wise distribution of towns in 120
slum population in 107, 109
urban growth in 62, 97, 118–20
urban population in 5, 62, 64, 113, 120
    in backward districts of 118
as urbanized state 59
manufacturing work, employment in 51, 62
market forces, urbanization and 1
marriage, and migration by women 28, 31, 56
mega cities, growth tendencies of 43
Meghalaya, urban population in 64
    share of population in towns in 64
merged towns 11–14
metropolitan cities, core and periphery of 40, 42
    growth of 40, 41, 154
    relocation of slum dwellers from 54
Metropolitan Planning 175
Metropolitan Planning Committee (MPC) 157
migrants 160, 164
migration 2, 3, 29–30, 55, 106
    data on 57
    deterrents to 28
    distress, from rural areas 62
    impact of structural reforms on urbanization and 51–3
    intercensal 31–2, 55, 57
    interstate 32, 56
    international 56
    lifetime 31, 56
    male 31, 57, 140, 145, 152
    marriage and 28, 31, 56
    rural-urban, and urban growth 27, 33, 36, 52, 53, 57, 62, 107, 154
    urban-rural, rural to rural 160–2
    share of, in urban growth 111
    trends and projections 28–32
    and urban growth 109, 111–12

and urbanization, at macro level 26–58, 154, 157
  by women 28, 31, 32, 56
migrant population 31
million-plus cities, demographic growth rate of 40
Ministry of Health and Family Planning 18n
Mizoram, as urbanized state 59
mobility, of population 29, 32
  decline in 56
mortality 28
Mumbai, growth in periphery around 157
  high urban population in 82
municipal boundaries, of class I cities, expansion of 40
municipalities 8, 153

Nagaland, share of population in towns in 64
nagarpalika (urban local bodies) 153
nagar panchayats 153
National Building Organization 109
National Sample Survey (NSS) 1, 3, 32, 57, 105
  data, 55th round of 17
National Sample Survey Organization (NSSO) 46, 86, 109
'new' towns 27
non-agricultural activity/enterprises 3, 19, 23
  employment in rural areas in 17, 51
non-resident Indians (NRIs), investments by 120–1
notified area committees (NACs) 8, 18

occupation, shift in, and urbanization 136
organized sector, employment in 46
  work opportunities in 58
Orissa, agricultural productivity and urbanization in 98
  foreign direct investments inflow into 97
  groundnut production and level of urbanization in 103
  growth of class I cities in 69
  high growth of urban population in 97
Orissa,...
  high urban growth in 82
  per capita income in 86
  poverty in 105
  Sambalpur district in, urbanization of 100
  urban population in cities in 64
own account enterprises, growth rate of 51

panchayats 154
  rural town 20
  town 24

town and village, in Tamil Nadu 21
  urban town 20
per capita expenditure, and poverty 105
per capita income 62, 84
  and agricultural productivity 98
  correlation with urbanization 86, 97
Planning Commission 28, 56, 105
  reports of 3
Plans, Five-Year, Eighth, Approach Paper to 28
  Ninth 27
policy, government 11
  perspectives 153–9
Pondicherry, urban population in 5, 64
population, growth rate of, in common towns/urban agglomerations 70–3
  growth in rural and urban areas 31
  of India 5–6
  living in different size categories to total urban population 65–8
  total increase in 36
population census data 1
The Population of India and Pakistan 28
population shift 171
Port Blair, as class I city 64n
poverty, casual employment, and decline in 51
  impact of urban growth on 2
  incidence of 105, 106
  indicators of development 84, 85
  per capita income and 86
  rural 51–2
  rural and urban 84
  and urbanization 104–6
poverty line, population below 105
  in urban areas 52
Premi, M.K. 19, 54
Punjab 3
  agricultural growth and growth of urbanization in 98, 124, 140, 144
  agro-based industries in 124
  backward districts of, decline in growth in 125
  deceleration of population growth in small towns in 124
  decline in birth rate in 144
  growth of class I cities in 69
  growth of industries in 124
  growth and urbanization in 124
  industrial growth in 124, 144
  level of urbanization in 121–3, 158
  Ludhiana district in, urbanization of 98
  population in class I cities in 124, 125

trends of district wise urbanization in 120–6
urban growth in 62, 97, 123–6
urban population in 5, 121
urban poverty in 105
urbanization and developmental indicators of
    140–4, 158
as urbanized state 59
wheat production, and growth of urban
    population in 100
    and level of urbanization in 101

Rajputana 135
Rajasthan 3, 131–5
    foreign direct investment inflow into 97
    growth of class I cities in 69, 83
    growth of smaller towns in 69
    growth of urban population in 97, 135
    level of urbanization in 131–5, 158
    per capita income in 86
Rajasthan,...
    population in class I cities of 135
    rural-urban migration in 152
    size class distribution of towns in 135
    socio-economic development and urbanization of
        145, 149–52
    trends of district-wise urbanization in 113,
        131–5
    urban growth in 82, 145, 152
    urban population in cities in 64
    urban poverty in 105
    wheat production in, and level of urbanization 101
regional balance 1
Registrar General of India 2, 17, 21, 24
rice production, and level of urbanization 98–9
roads, correlation with urbanization 140, 145
rural economy 106
rural migrants, in peripheries of cities 52
rural poverty, and urbanization 105
rural urban migration 27, 33, 36, 52, 53, 55, 57, 62,
    107, 154, 163–4
Rural-Urban Relationship Committee 18n
rural workforce, casualization of 51

Sample Registration System (SRS) 28, 33
sanitation facilities 84, 106
schools/schooling, and correlation with
    urbanization 152
    facilities 84, 86
    urban population and correlation to 107
    and urbanization 140, 144

settlement structure, changing 37
sex ratio 2, 84, 85, 145
    negative correlation with urbanization 106
    in urban areas 140, 144
    and urban growth 106
Sikkim, share of population in towns in 64
Siliguri, growth in 82
Singh, G. 86, 136n
Sirohi, growth rates in 135
slum(s), population across states 3, 107, 109, 110, 158
    eviction of 54
    settlements, in urban centres 107–9
social development 62
socio-economic development, interdependence
    among indicators of urbanization 87–96
    and slum population 107
    urbanization and indicators of 135–52
socio-economic indicators, of development 84–6,
    136, 160–5
socio-demographic development 84
    and urbanization 106–7, 109–12
state(s), capital cities, growth of 43–5
    socio-economic indicators of 160–5
statutory towns 2, 8–10, 20, 21
    criteria for 18–19
    new 24–5
structural reform, and development strategy 57
    impact of, on urbanization and migration 51–3
subsidiary employment, share of 50, 51
sub-Mission 175

Tamil Nadu, agricultural growth and urbanization
    in 98, 124
    Chengalpattu district in, urbanization of 98
    declassified towns in 21
    foreign direct investment flows into 97
    groundnut production, and level of urbanization
        in 100, 103
    growth of cities in 69, 82
    level of urbanization in 2, 4, 82
    per capita income in 86
    poverty level in 105
    slum population in 109
    statutory towns in 153
    town and village panchayats in 20, 21, 24–5
    towns in 18, 19
        declassified towns in 23
        merged 24
        statutory towns in 20, 24
    urban growth in 18, 62, 97

urban population in 5, 21, 23, 62, 64, 113
   as urbanized state 59
Taskforce on Urban Development (Planning
   Commission) 28
Town and Country Planning Organization
   (TCPO) 109
towns/cities, causes of reduction of 17–18
   class II and III, urban population in 64
   class V and VI, growth rates in 39
   committees 8
   declassified, and adjusted population in India
      21–3, 24
   emergence of new 1, 11–14, 57
   growth rates of, as per size class distribution of
      1, 8, 74–81, 82
   identification of 17
   population in class I 6
   population growth rates in urban agglomerations
      and 70–3
   and urban agglomerations 15–16
   urbanization of 62, 64
town area committees (TACs) 18
Tripura, share of population in towns in 64

unemployment 46–50, 57–8, 84, 104
   increase in 51
United Nations 55, 56, 58
   reports of 3, 55
unorganized sector, employment in 46
urban agglomerations 15–16, 20–1, 24
   decline in 8, 17–18
   growth of 3, 8, 40, 57, 64, 69, 157
   population growth rates of 36, 70–3
   towns within and outside 15–16
urban areas, development and management of 1
   natural growth rates in 55
   territorial expansion of 154
urban centres 4, 6–8, 23, 36, 59, 157
   definition of 2
   disparity in growth 69, 82
   in-migration of poor to 54
urban civic status 20
urban corridor, development of 43
'urban explosion' 27
urban growth 1, 7, 8, 20, 28, 33–6, 56, 57
   components of 32–6
   concentration of 36
   deceleration in 18
   decline in 28
   impact of open economy on 2

   rural urban migration and 33–6
   and urbanization 82
urban local bodies 175
urban management, and urban growth 53–4
urban population, agricultural production and
   growth of 98–100
   correlation with hospitals 106
   definitional problems on 19–20
   in India 5–6, 37, 38
   growth of 1, 2, 26, 27, 54–5, 97
   projected 28
urban poor, government programmes for 105
urban poverty 58, 105–6, 158
   and rural poverty 105
urban renewal mission 171
urban rural growth differentials (URGD), and
   foreign direct investments 98
   rise in 56, 84
urbanization, cause and effect of 3
   dynamics of 2–3
   and employment scenario 45–51, 104
   impact of structural reforms on migration and
      51–3
   and infrastructure 106
   level of, across states 60–1
   level and growth rates of 23
   and migration at macro level 26–58
   objective of 1
   pattern across size class of urban centres 37,
      39–40
   poverty and 104–6
   regional pattern of 59
   socio-economic aspects of 13–52, 84–112, 113–52,
      157–9
   trend and pattern of 1, 26–8, 59–83
Uttar Pradesh, agricultural productivity and
   urbanization in 98
   foreign direct investment flow into 97
   growth rates in class I cities in 83
   growth of small towns in 69
   high urban growth in 82
   nagar panchayats in 153
   per capita income in 86
   slum population in 109
   towns in 18
   urban population in cities in 64, 97
   urban poverty in 105
   wheat production and level of urbanization 100,
      101
Uttaranchal, nagar panchayats in 153

share of population in cities in 64
as urbanized state 59

Visaria, P. 56

wages, of casual workers in urban and rural areas 51
West Bengal 59
    addition of towns in 24
    agricultural productivity and urbanization in 98
    declassification of towns in 19, 23
    growth of cities in 82
    class I cities in 69
    per capita income in 86

population in class I cities in 125
population in urban areas of 62
slum population in 107, 109
urban growth rates in 62
urban population in 64
wheat production, correlation to urbanization 100, 101
women, migration by 28, 31, 32, 56
workforce participation rate (WPR), decline in 45, 46, 57, 84
    and infrastructural indicators 104

Zilla parishads 159